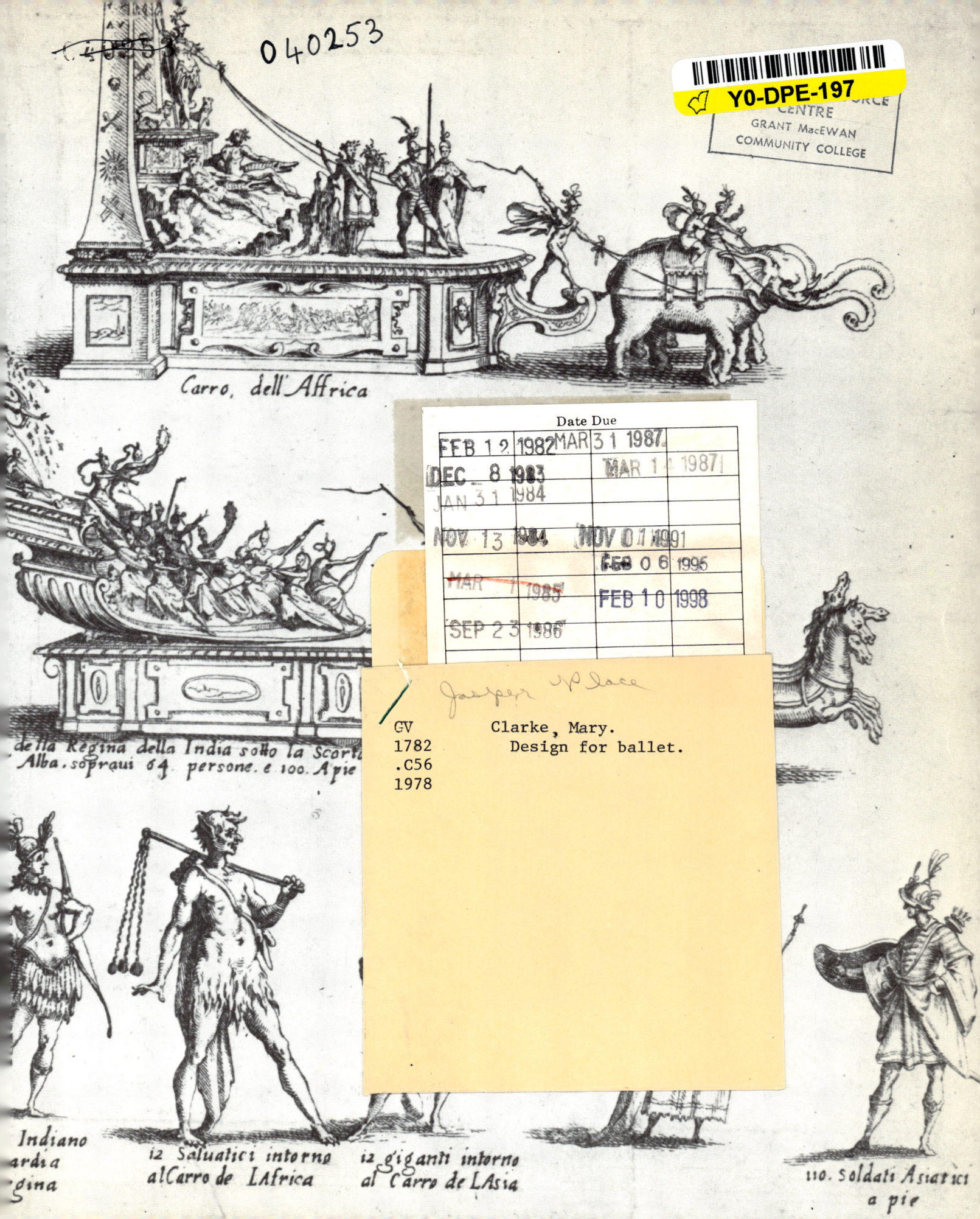

DESIGN FOR BALLET

DESIGN FOR BALLET

Mary Clarke and Clement Crisp

HAWTHORN BOOKS, INC.
PUBLISHERS
NEW YORK

For Dame Ninette de Valois
with affection and admiration

Copyright © 1978 by Mary Clarke and Clement Crisp. Copyright under International and Pan-American Copyright Conventions.

All rights reserved, including the right to reproduce this book or portions thereof in any form, except for the inclusion of brief quotations in a review. All inquiries should be addressed to Hawthorn Books, Inc., 260 Madison Avenue, New York, New York 10016. This book was published simultaneously in Canada by Prentice-Hall of Canada, Limited, 1870 Birchmount Road, Scarborough, Ontario.

First published in the UK by Studio Vista, a division of Cassell and Co Ltd.

Library of Congress Catalog Card Number: 77-93100

ISBN: 0-8015-2020-7

1 2 3 4 5 6 7 8 9 10

Printed in Great Britain by Sackville Press Billericay Limited

CONTENTS

Acknowledgements 6

Preface 7

RENAISSANCE SPECTACLE 9

FROM COURT TO THEATRE 26

ROCOCO, NEOCLASSICAL, ROMANTIC 53

THE DIAGHILEV ERA 108

AFTER DIAGHILEV 165

In Russia 191

DESIGN FOR TODAY 204

Traditional Design 205

French Style 260

Modern Ballet and Modern Dance 267

Bibliography 285

Picture credits 285

Index 286

Acknowledgements

We are indebted to a great many people for kindness and help in finding and lending material for this book. Roland Petit has not only decorated his ballets with the work of the finest artists but was kind enough to have material from his private collection photographed for us. Marian Eames gave us the benefit of her extensive knowledge at the start of the enterprise and Freda Pitt went to enormous pains to provide material from Italy. In Sweden, Anna Grete Ståhle, Bengt Häger (director of the Dansmuseet) and Erik Näslund were most helpful. In Denmark the staff of the Teaterhistorisk Museum were more than gerous with time and advice. In Paris the staff of the Musée de l'Opéra gave invaluable help, as always. For Polish material we are indebted to Dr Janina Pudelek, the distinguished dance historian. In Vienna, Professor Dr Rikki Raab answered many queries. In New York, the staff of the Dance Collection in the Museum of the Performing Arts gave every assistance and we must also gratefully acknowledge the help of Charles Engell France of American Ballet Theater, Virginia Donaldson of the New York City Ballet, the Alwin Nikolais Foundation, James Klosty, David Vaughan and the Cunningham Foundation, Parmenia Migel Ekstrom and Fred Fehl; from Chicago Ruth Page gave us the benefit of using some of her collection of the superlative designs commissioned by her. Lincoln Kirstein's encouragement kept up our spirits and Edwin Binney, 3rd lent us one of his many treasures. We must record our gratitude to the late Natalia Roslavleva for material from Russia and also to the generous help of the Novosti Press Agency and the Anglo-Soviet Friendship Society. In pursuit of Graham Sutherland's designs for *The Wanderer* (believed at one time to have been 'eaten by rats') we owe everything to the artist himself, to Lord Clark and to the Hon. Colette Clark. Liliana Archibald lent us her hitherto unreproduced Benois design. Raymond Haworth visited galleries in New York for us; Kenneth Rowell was generous with time and advice; Nicholas Georgiadis was extremely helpful; and Richard Ralph sought out reference material for us with great kindness. Leslie Hurry and Desmond Heeley also gave us much assistance and we are happy to thank Ivor Guest, Rachel Caldin, Carole Berman of Sotheby's, Sara Scott, Janet Laming, and Christina Gascoigne, who furnished photographs from her collection. Our work would have been much more difficult without the generous help of the Press officers of various ballet companies; Ton Leenhouts of Nederlands Dans Theater went to great trouble for us, and the Press departments of the Royal Ballet, London Festival Ballet, the Ballet-Théâtre Contemporain, the National Ballet of Canada, Les Grands Ballets Canadiens were exemplary in help. Noel Pelly of the Australian Ballet and David Palmer gave invaluable help in providing a transparency of Leslie Hurry's design for Helpmann's *Hamlet* and we must also record our deep gratitude to Sir Robert for his kindness in allowing us to reproduce this magnificent design as our cover.

Jeffrey Phillips of the Royal Opera House, Covent Garden, gave much assistance and we are also indebted to the staff of the British Council. Among libraries we have been much helped by the staff of the Victoria and Albert Museum, and the Royal Academy of Dancing. We cannot praise too highly the assistance given by all the staff at the Theatre Museum and the Print Room in the Victoria and Albert Museum, in the British Museum Print Room, the Department of Prints and Drawings in the National Gallery of Scotland, the Mansell Collection, the Radio Times Hulton Picture Library, the Courtauld Institute, the Warburg Institute, the Wadsworth Atheneum in Hartford, Connecticut, and the National Theatre Museum in Prague. For the Inigo Jones material we are much indebted to the Trustees of the Chatsworth Settlement and for permission to quote from their writings we are most grateful to Stella Mary Newton for her *Renaissance Theatre Costume* and to Richard N. Coe for his translation of Stendhal's *Life of Rossini*, and to all other authors quoted within.

We stand in enormous debt to the photographers whose work is represented in this book and we would make a special note of thanks to Anthony Crickmay, Serge Lido and Pierre Petitjean, and to Group Three of London and Godfrey New.

The help offered by three people in particular has made this book possible. Josephine Hickey has nursed the book from the very first and has been an exemplary editor; Tristram Holland has supported and sustained our endeavours; as always, the secretarial work of Carol Venn has been beyond praise. We give them most grateful thanks.

Preface

In selecting the examples of design for the ballet which are included in this book we have been guided by a desire to give as representative a selection as lay within our power. But it would be entirely unrealistic to suppose that we could do more than skim the surface of the vast treasury of material which is to be found in many collections both public and private. Some reflection of the vagaries of stage design as an art form will be found in the representative weighting of different periods, and this in itself we hope may be found significant. Certain eras in the past are more generally known than others as far as ballet design is concerned: we have endeavoured to do justice to these without stressing material already overfamiliar to the public. In the case of the Diaghilev years – that golden age for the decoration of ballet – we have eschewed much of what may be found in the several admirable books about the Diaghilev enterprise. For more recent periods and for the ballet of our day we must note that serious problems exist for anyone researching design.

Certain companies, and indeed certain nations, have been unable to furnish the kind of material that was requested or that would reproduce – and we must here stress a most important point: choice of illustrations has been inevitably guided by the suitability of the design for reproduction on the printed page. Furthermore, there is an evanescence in much contemporary design. Many modern dance companies, in particular, decorate works in an impromptu fashion, or are impelled by financial stringency into arbitrary or severely restricted decorative ways. A few important designers are not represented properly either because their work is so delicate that it has not been caught by the camera – Sophie Fedorovitch a case in point – or because it relies upon particular qualities of fabric and light which exist only in the theatre. Occasionally the work of a major designer is not adequately preserved and we must note the rather curious fact that we have been unable to discover a truly representative photograph of Noguchi's superlative setting for *Seraphic Dialogue*.

RENAISSANCE SPECTACLE

Design for Ballet

BECAUSE the origins of ballet lie in the court spectacles of the Renaissance, and because the attitudes towards design formulated then govern so much of the subsequent activity in the dance theatre, it is necessary to begin this survey with Renaissance spectacle itself.

As early as the fifteenth century there is testimony to the elaboration and complexity of court entertainments. These were devised as celebrations of some important event – a dynastic marriage, a political alliance – and could take the form of either vast street spectacles mounted on decorative cars led in procession, or more static displays in palaces and open courtyards. These were a potent manifestation of Renaissance thought, both signifying the involvement of artists, writers and musicians in the political nature of their world, and providing signs and portents about the politics of the age that were to be easily comprehensible to observers. With the passage of time these spectacles were to become increasingly elaborate and wide-ranging in their manifestations: processions, masquerades, water tournaments, horse ballets, dinner ballets and *ballets de cour*, triumphal entries into cities, fleets of galleys sailing to greet an important personage, were all part of the paraphernalia of glory that surrounded the figure of the reigning monarch and his family.

The mixture of dance, declamation, machines, animals, music, cars and stage effects at court and royal fêtes was to be a constant of performances throughout the fifteen, sixteenth and seventeenth centuries. A prime example of a French court ballet is *Le Ballet des Polonais* of 1573 (plate 1). This was mounted at the Palace of the Tuileries in Paris on the occasion of the visit of the Polish ambassadors to the court of the Valois to elect Henri of Anjou (third son of Catherine de' Medici) as King of Poland. A temporary theatre had been built in one of the great halls of the palace and the spectators were placed on three sides: as was customary, the entire performance was directed towards the 'presence', that is towards the royal party and the ambassadors in whose honour the entertainment was staged. The climax, intended to convey the devotion of France to the newly elected monarch of Poland, was the appearance of sixteen court ladies who were placed on a huge lath and plaster rock coloured silver-gilt from which they in turn declaimed verses. Each represented one of the provinces of France and they eventually descended from their rock to perform a 'ballet' which had been devised by Catherine de' Medici's dancing master, Balthazar de Beaujoyeulx.

In this court spectacle and its later and more celebrated successor in 1581, *Le Ballet Comique de la Reine*, there can be sensed the importance of even temporary decoration when its elaboration was dictated by the symbolism which underlay most of such displays. The ephemeral nature of court ballets encouraged the production of paintings, books and engravings in which some permanent record could be made to fix the transient magnificence and thus *épater* the world. (The first full libretto we know of a court ballet, its themes and production, is the printed description of *Le Ballet Comique de la Reine* (plate 2) which was circulated throughout Europe to tell of the splendour at the court of the Valois.)

The revival of the classical drama during the fifteenth century, and the rediscovery of the structural theories of the theatre which came from the reading of the Roman architect and author Vitruvius, had by the beginning of the sixteenth century led to the building of the first theatres of modern times in Italy, and soon theatres were being constructed throughout Europe. However, the court ballet remained a vital dance form until 1670 in France, and up to that date the preponderance of noble amateurs as performers, and

On previous page
Engraving showing the court ballet staged in the Vladislav Hall of Prague Castle on 5 February 1617 to celebrate the presence of Maximilian I, Duke of Bavaria.

1 Scene from *Le Ballet des Polonais*, performed at the Palace of the Tuileries, Paris, on the visit of the Polish ambassadors to the court of the Valois to elect Henri Duc d'Anjou as King of Poland, 1573.

the special circumstances surrounding the performance, meant that the palace itself was often the location of danced events. Even when performances took place in the theatre the changed locale did not alter the underlying inspiration: the manifestation of the Prince's glory.

Great influence on stage design was exerted by the processional festivities, as, too, by *intermezzi*, masquerades, *trionfi* and the later carrousels. The Florentine *intermezzi* (interludes) were performances of dancing, singing and mechanical effects given between the scenes of a play or used as divertissements in a court display. Masquerades involved decorated cars or floats carrying a kind of *tableau vivant* and their popularity was such that many of the greatest festivities of the Renaissance were cast in this form. *Trionfi* (triumphal entries), as their name indicates, were staged to celebrate an event of political importance. Carrousels were equestrian entertainments in which the knightly attributes of the monarch and his court were asserted in procession on horseback. They developed from the jousts of the Middle Ages and in the later sixteenth century were to become extremely complex horse ballets in which the choreography for the horse and rider followed the usual plan of choreography at this time, insisting upon complexity of pattern rather than complexity of step. Another development from the joust was the *combat à la barrière*, a mock tourney in which the participants fought across a barrier.

In the theatre itself stage design and architecture developed from the rediscovery of Vitruvius's theories. By the beginning of the sixteenth century Vitruvius's ideas of three kinds of stage set – *scena tragica*, *scena comica*, and *scena satyrica* – were given practical form: the first recognized 'set' in perspective was designed for the première of Ariosto's *Cassaria* at Ferrara in 1508. Sebastiano Serlio in his *Architettura* of 1551 declares that the tragic stage must show 'columns, statues, pedestals and all other objects suited to monarchs'; the comic stage will feature only the houses used by the general public; and the satyric stage must feature pastoral scenes. This provided a clear architectural background for the performers and initially it remained a background. It was in no sense the evocation of a place in which the action was situated, but it was to lead on to the grander and more specific settings of the seventeenth century with their insistence on perspective.

The fact that the designing of stage sets as well as the building of the theatres was entrusted to architects meant that the painted backdrop was very like a continuation of the forestage itself, albeit the reality of the physical building gave way to the inevitably more fanciful location suggested by the backdrop. In his *Secondo libro di prospettiva* of 1545 Serlio shows scenery as a background intended to lend dignity to the drama, but in court production, in *intermezzi*, it was important for stage effects to underline the symbolism of the production. The great majority of the various danced entertainments until the middle of the seventeenth century were considered not merely as entertainment but as metaphors. They contained very clear messages for their audience, and to ignore this fact is to ignore their essential nature. The Florentine *intermezzi* were among the grandest statements about spectacle. The dumbfounding of the audience by theatrical means was an acute political activity but more than that, it also reflected the Renaissance acceptance of the Aristotelian theory of amazement, the purging of the emotions, as a valid function of the theatre. The entire development of theatrical craft, through 'machines' (devices of ropes and built properties which enabled gods and heroes to make their appearance from the skies), through elaboration of costume and magnificence of presentation in the sixteenth century, illustrates how real was this double concern. It was to the inestimable benefit of the theatre that it should be so. The complexity of stage machinery in the seventeenth-century Italian theatre reflects the obsession in court fêtes with all forms of transformation, and while France still concerned itself with the *ballet de cour* under Henri IV and Louis XIII as a weaker extension of the great festivities during the time of Catherine de' Medici, the architects and engineers of the Italian theatre were producing prodigies of stage spectacle. This tradition, fostered in the Florentine performances, was to be responsible for the creation of the theatre of illusion that reached its most splendid form in the court displays and the theatre of the Baroque period.

The first recorded use of changeable scenery in the theatre is in 1543. It took the form of *periaktoi*. These were three-sided decorated prisms which could be turned on a swivel to present a different face to the audience: the sides of the triangle were of different lengths, so that turning of the prisms could alter the size of the acting area. They had been described by Vitruvius. But *periaktoi* were only a temporary solution to scene change. There followed the idea of a change of backdrop. Niccolo Sabbatini in his *Pratica di Fabricar Scene e Machine Ne' Teatri* (1637–8) indicated several ways of altering the backdrop. It could be split down the middle and removed at each side along a groove; it could be raised or lowered like a curtain or, indeed, it could open and shut like doors. This painted back-scene inevitably allowed a greater illusion of depth and width to the stage and there followed a further development when the raked stage (which already existed) was divided laterally so that a scene might be played on a front stage while behind a curtain another scene could be changed.

At this time the proscenium arch appeared as part of the theatrical structure. It was used as early as the mid-sixteenth century to frame temporary scenery in a court ballet, but the first known stage framed by a permanent proscenium arch was the Teatro Farnese in Parma, which was completed in 1618/19. In its early years the depths of the stage were used to contain the three traditional settings according to Serlio: tragic, comic or satyric. But these were soon to become dated and the proscenium was to have the effect of a masking frame behind which considerable scene change was to be possible. It was this type of theatre which was to influence the whole later development of theatre design, making it fluid, more dramatically apt and less stereotyped. By the beginning of the seventeenth century wings had also been invented and were to be most effectively used at the Teatro Farnese. These canvas-covered wooden frames were fixed to a wheeled undercarriage which ran on rails placed in the area below the stage. They were manipulated from below and were pushed backwards and forwards through slits in the stage floor. With suitable scenery painted upon them, they spelled the doom of the *periaktoi*. They were arranged symmetrically in threes or fours. In addition, certain effects traceable to the machinery that featured in the temporary theatres of the court ballet and in the processions and *intermezzi* naturally featured in the theatre. These were the trapdoors which allowed the appearance and disappearance of characters, and even more important the complicated network of ropes and pulleys which raised and lowered platforms and 'machines' on which gods, demons and heroes might fly. As the spectacle so much associated with the Baroque theatre became increasingly elaborate, machines and engineering were devised to produce effects with fire, water, smoke and steam. Eventually, a special engineer – *capo mestre delle teatri* – was appointed to provide machinery capable of dealing with the complex effects.

In the evolving theatrical traditions of the sixteenth century, the emergence

of stage setting was dominated by the development of perspective as an aid to illusion. This implied a single focal point to the staged event, in contrast to the dispersed and disparate decorative elements of the *ballet de cour* and the other spectacles of the time. It maintained, though, the ideal of a special and select viewing point which had already become a convention of these displays. The ballets were directed towards 'the presence' – that is, towards the monarch and his honoured guests – and often the illustrations of all forms of court spectacle indicate a central royal party to whom the entertainment is addressed, with a surrounding mass of courtiers whose view is progressively worse the further they sit from the monarch, a parallel with the underlying political nature of the court itself and a recurrent theme in court ballet. In *Le Ballet Royal de la Nuit* in which the young Louis XIV impersonated the sun – hence his subsequent title of *le roi soleil* – distance from the sun, from the monarch, was equated with disgrace and death. In the *Ballet des Polonais*, the libretto shows the entertainment directed towards the royal party and the Polish ambassadors on a raised dais, while the rest of the court watched from the tiered sides of the hall.

During the 1580s two royal fêtes in particular illustrate the magnificence of court spectacle: these were *Le Ballet Comique de la Reine*, performed in Paris in 1581, and the *intermezzi* staged in the Uffizi theatre in Florence in 1589. *Le Ballet Comique de la Reine* is one of the most significant examples of the French *ballet de cour*. Its theme was taken from the Circe legend and its allegorical purpose was to suggest that the recent religious strife that had so riven France might now be calmed by the triumph of good sense, harmony and reason. The occasion for the performance was the marriage of the Queen's sister, Margaret of Lorraine, to the Duc de Joyeuse, a favourite of the King (Henri III). Staged in a hall of the Louvre Palace, the entertainment lasted no less than five hours. Jacques Patin was responsible for the design of sets and costumes for the *Ballet Comique* and in his frontispiece for the published libretto (plate 2) we see the integration of the performance into the setting of the hall itself. Two large pieces of standing scenery on either side of the hall are a cave obscured by clouds – a machine in which the singers were placed – and on the right the small rustic grove in which Pan is seated. At the end of the hall there is a perspective of a garden with three alleys of carefully worked greenery which is the domain of Circe who is seated, surrounded by beasts, with on either side a fountain and the seated figures of a chorus. Patin's etching is a wonderfully vivid evocation of how this great entertainment must have seemed when it was staged by Beaujoyeulx, with courtiers pressing forward from their tiered seats on either side of the hall and the royal party as the focus of attention.

Le Ballet Comique was central to the tradition referred to by Louis de Cahusac in his treatise *La Danse ancienne et moderne* (Paris, 1754), when he observed that

> to keep up and to strengthen the dramatic illusion, they had recourse to the art of machines. The ballet was founded on the marvellous. The most extraordinary things, dazzling prodigies, the descents of the gods, the movement of the waves of the sea, all the marvels of fable furnished the subjects of these spectacles. To render them realistic and to give a new charm to their representation, art had to come to the aid of nature, and they found in machinery, in painting, in carpentry, in sculpture, etc., all the means to excite curiosity and to enrapture.

2 Jacques Patin: etching showing the Salle de Bourbon in the Palace of the Louvre, Paris, as it was at the beginning of *Le Ballet Comique de la Reine*, performed as part of the festivities for the marriage of Margaret of Lorraine to the Duc de Joyeuse, 1581. Henri III is the central crowned figure with his back to us; on his right in her traditional widow's weeds is the Queen Mother, Catherine de' Medici.

Design for Ballet

A particularly significant use of machines for the development of theatre design was seen in Florence in 1589 in the *intermezzi* introduced into the play *La Pellegrina*. In *intermezzi* there was little attempt at realism: décor was flat and the most astounding effects were produced by machines, already complex in their ability to cause the appearances of gods and mythological figures. In Florence they were brought to a remarkable peak of elaboration towards the end of the sixteenth century and those which were introduced into *La Pellegrina* are some of the most complicated on record. Clouds descended bearing allegorical figures, perspective views of the city of Pisa were shown: the entire apparatus of the Renaissance theatre was put to use to delight and inspire the audience. The occasion was the marriage of the Duke Ferdinand of Tuscany to Christina of Lorraine, a granddaughter of Catherine de' Medici, and the *intermezzi* offered allegories related to the idea of dynastic union. The designs were by Bernardo Buontalenti (1536–1608), nicknamed 'delle Girandole', 'of the fireworks', because among his many tasks was the design of fireworks for the Medici festivities.

Buontalenti supervised the production and design of spectacles for the Medici in Florence for nearly sixty years, and the tradition and manner he

3 Giulio Parigi: scene for an *intermezzo* introduced into the play *The Judgement of Paris*, performed in honour of the marriage of Cosimo de' Medici to Maria Maddelena of Austria, in Florence, 1608. Etching by Remigio Catagallina. Catagallina's letterings indicate the important actions. *B* shows the limping Vulcan with an attendant bearing the armour for Cosimo, while *A* shows the descent of a celestial chariot upon a cloud machine.

Above
4 Giulio Parigi: a float which took part in the celebrations for the arrival of the Prince of Urbino in Florence in 1616. Engraving by Callot. Thetis is seen perched on a shell surrounded by branches of coral and pendant seaweed while mermaids, nereids and tritons surround her. The car was part of a sequence featuring all the chief oceans of the world.

Below
5 Jacques Callot (1592–1635): engraving showing horsemen and performers for a triumphal entry.

established were continued after his death in 1608 by Giulio Parigi (1580–1635), who was in turn succeeded as designer in 1620 by his son Alfonso (d. 1656). Plate 3 illustrates a design for an *intermezzo* by Giulio Parigi, one of six performed in Florence in 1608 in honour of the marriage of Cosimo de' Medici to Maria Maddelena of Austria. The *intermezzi* were interpolated into the play *The Judgement of Paris*, and the fifth *intermezzo*, illustrated here, is set in Vulcan's workshop, where armour is being made for Cosimo. A recurrent theme in many of the *intermezzi* was a scene cast in the Underworld. The 'inferno' was considered an important dramatic contrast to the nobler and more laudatory passages with their insistence upon celestial beings. The tradition of the fiery hell scene is one which dates back both to the iconography of the Christian Church and the mystery plays of the Middle Ages and even

Design for Ballet

further back to the classical drama of the ancients. For the designers of the Renaissance the hell–mouth or scene in the Underworld was a continuing source of inspiration (compare the inferno scene for Lully's *Armide* by Berain, plate 24).

The illustrations which survive from this period demonstrate how theatrically vivid were the masks and costumes for the spectacles. A combination of naturalism and allegorical fantasy meant that the clothing was almost always theatrically effective. Stage dress was opulent in material and effects, but it seems to have been guided throughout by a recognition of its appositeness to the dramatic theme. For the male performer there emerged a conventional outfit based upon the contemporary idea of Roman dress, the *habit à la Romaine*. A tight-fitting doublet gave the impression of the cuirass and a short draped skirt fell below it; tightly laced boots and a tiara or helmet completed the ensemble. This costume permitted of different elaborations to suit dramatic necessity. It is important to realize that any decoration was not simply for its own sake but was guided by allegorical and metaphorical

Renaissance Spectacle

6 Giulio Parigi: scene from the third *intermezzo* from the *Liberazione di Tirrenio*, a *veglia* (a dramatic evening's entertainment) staged in the Teatro Ducale inside the Uffizi Palace in Florence on 6 February 1616 as part of the wedding festivities of Ferdinando Gonzaga, Duke of Mantua, and Caterina de' Medici, who was the sister of the Grand Duke Cosimo II. Etching by Jacques Callot. The *intermezzi* were performed by members of the court and the last scene, illustrated here, shows the appearance of Amor, who intervenes in the *combat à la barrière* and descends to the stage on a machine. Callot's remarkable print gives a very fine idea both of the use of perspective that was by now an essential part of stage decoration and of the way in which machines were employed to dramatic effect. The combination of music and spectacle can be seen in the placing of the court musicians on either side of the stage with the members of the court fighting in neat perspective which mirrors the symmetry of the scene.

considerations. As in Chinese opera, or in Kabuki and Indian dance drama, costuming and make-up had an almost ritual significance.

Plate 8 is a design for the costumes of two female dancers who appeared in the *intermezzi* of *La Pellegrina*. They are probably for the dancers who appeared in the first *intermezzo*, which showed the harmony of the spheres. The shape of the dress and its ornamentation indicate how 'theatricalized' costuming could be; the scalloped and embroidered tunics surmount a second tunic which is fringed and this in turn covers a light silk skirt, which enables the dancer to move with much greater freedom than in formal court dress. The hair style is perhaps theatrical too, but the wedged shoes are typical footwear of the period. Something of the identity of the character represented is shown by the figuration on breast and shoulders.

In her valuable *Renaissance Theatre Costume* (London, 1975) Stella Mary Newton provides a detailed description of the costuming of some earlier Muses, who took part in the wedding banquet of Eleanora of Toledo to

7 Stefano della Bella (1610–64): costume design for a *furie infernale*. It was deliberate policy to contrast these grotesque and evil beings with the beautiful representations of divinities and mythological characters who dominated the spectacle.

Design for Ballet

8 Bernardo Buontalenti: costume designs for two female dancers in an *intermezzo* introduced into *La Pellegrina*, performed in the Uffizi theatre 2 May 1589 as part of the festivities for the marriage of the Grand Duke Ferdinand of Tuscany to Christina of Lorraine.

9 Jacques Callot: engraving of a *combat à la barrière* which formed part of the festivities held in honour of the Duchesse de Chevreuse at the ducal palace in Nancy on 14 February 1627. Illustration from a book published by Humbert in Nancy, 1627.

Cosimo de' Medici in Florence in 1539. A contemporary account of the wedding provided Mrs Newton with the following information:

> The first Muse, for instance, in draperies of palest colour scattered with branches of olive wore on her head a helmet in the discarded antique style – *disusata foggia antica* – ornamented with crystals and beryls and, as a crest, a chameleon. Her flowing wavy hair was sprinkled with flowers of wild thyme among which could be seen bees. A Panther-skin was flung across her breast and her little classical boots were covered with cat-skin.
>
> The hair of the second Muse was scented with the flowers of marjoram with which it was sprinkled: her dress of greenish-yellow was partly hidden by a hyena-skin: a parrot was mounted on her helmet which, enriched with agates and topazes, was garlanded with pimpernels. Her boots, covered with the skins of monkeys, were ornamented with their heads, placed behind the knee.

Although these court entertainments insisted upon eye-catching splendour, the increasing need to facilitate transformation brought advances in the actual nature of the stage. By the early seventeenth century a device to divide the backdrop was developed which helped the scene changes. Moreover, the emergence of opera as an art form was also reflected in the demands it made on the design of the stage itself. The stage area became more fluid. It was possible now to create a setting for the stage action rather than a background against which it took place, and a new world of illusion was created in which the interaction of immortals and humans became increasingly magical.

Design for Ballet

10 Design for the fourth scene of *La Délivrance de Renaud*, staged in the Grande Salle of the Louvre Palace, Paris, 29 January 1617.

At the same time, the *ballets de cour* carried on a parallel tradition in their temporary settings. The continuing significance of these productions is well exemplified by two which took place in the same year, 1617, in different courts.

The political implications of *La Délivrance de Renaud* (plate 10) were clearly comprehensible to an audience already accustomed to the idea that *ballets de cour* were expressly designed to convey certain truths about the monarch's feelings and ambitions. At the time when *Renaud* was staged the young Louis XIII was still under the control of his mother, Marie de' Medici, and the adaptation of a theme from Tasso's *Gerusalemme Liberata* was to be read by its audience as an assertion of Louis's decision to rule. The young King was still only sixteen years old, but he was on the brink of manhood and preparing to assert himself as monarch, and against a background of political unrest this

Renaissance Spectacle

ballet was to indicate to the court the King's determination. In the last scene of the ballet the King himself appeared as Godefroy, the leader of the celestially inspired army who had freed Jerusalem. So, too, was Louis now to free France from everything but his own rule.

The political *raison d'être* for the court ballet staged in Prague Castle on 5 February 1617, officially to celebrate the presence of Maximilian I, Duke of Bavaria, was the necessity to reassert the dominance of the Catholic faith in Bohemia. At the entertainment the most important members of the aristocracy (keyed and named in a text accompanying the engraving of the scene which is illustrated on page 9) took part in a dance spectacle in honour of Maximilian. The stage setting itself, which included the appearance of Dionysus on a cloud machine below the royal crown and cypher, is strictly symmetrical, with the members of the aristocracy placed in straight lines on either side of the stage. The dancers have in fact descended from the stage to perform in the main body of the hall, as was usual at this time when the final 'grand ballet' brought the participants directly among the audience.

Equally concerned with the monarchy and the identity of the monarch as an absolute being, were the masques of the Stuart period in England. The masque as practised at the English court was the creation of two men: Inigo Jones and Ben Jonson. They were jointly responsible for supervising these entertainments of song, speech, dance, machines and theatrical devices for a quarter of a century from 1605 onwards: after they quarrelled and parted company, the remaining masques were largely entrusted to Jones as creator of their visual excitement. Inigo Jones (1573–1652) had received some of his education as a painter, and perhaps as an architect and man of the theatre, in

11 Alfonso Parigi the Younger: ballet scene from the opera *Le Nozze degli dei*, performed in honour of the marriage of Ferdinando II, Duke of Tuscany, to Vittoria of Urbino on 1 August 1634. This etching, by Stefano della Bella, offers an imaginatively worked perspective of a garden with, behind it, a view of Florence and the River Arno. It is an exceptional piece of designing, notably in the free treatment of the trees and the precise location suggested by the distant prospect of Florence itself. The costuming, with its complex draperies and elaborate head-dresses, is typical of the stage dress of the time. The use of two machines is indicated by the appearance of the flying figure of Mercury in the sky on the left and the cloud in the centre bearing the inevitable deities with cornucopia.

This designne I conceaue to bee fitt for the inuention and if it pleas hir Ma:^{tie}
to add or alter any thing I desire to recceaue his ma:^{ts} comaund and the
designne againe by this bearer. The collors allso are in her ma:^{ts}
choise; but my oppinion is that seuerall frost coulleurs mixt with gould and
siluer will bee most propper

24

Opposite
12 Inigo Jones: costume design for Queen Henrietta Maria in Ben Jonson's masque *Chloridia*, first produced on 22 February 1613. *Chloridia* featured the Queen as the central figure of the masque. Her costume is an adaptation of court dress and beneath the design Inigo Jones provided a note intended for Her Majesty in which he announced his willingness to change anything which the Queen did not find pleasing. 'The colours allso are in Her Majesty's choise; but my oppinion is that several fresh greenes mix with gould and silver will bee most propper.' *Chloridia* was also notable as the first time Inigo Jones made use of a rudimentary fly gallery.

Above
13 Inigo Jones: setting for the first scene, Night, in Sir William Davenant's *Luminilia*, first performed on 6 February 1638. Inigo Jones was to introduce the idea of perspective into design for the British theatre and this setting for *Luminilia* is a charming piece of naturalistic design.

Italy; his first masques were an extension of established court entertainments from the time of Elizabeth I. Their subsequent elaboration and splendour reflected the ideals of absolutism and their symbolism was meant to suggest to the court audiences important facts which it was their duty and pleasure to decipher. Jones's visual inspiration inevitably came from Italian models – from such artists as Giulio Parigi – but his development of it was highly personal, and can be studied in several collections, notably that of the Dukes of Devonshire at Chatsworth in Derbyshire.

It is significant that the masques of the great sequence given during the years 1631–40 were largely dedicated to propounding the pacifying and ennobling qualities of the monarchy, and the devastating effects of rebellion and opposition to a king. They represent a magnificent achievement in design, a reflection of the way the monarch and the court were meant to see themselves and their political roles in the elaborate rituals of the masque itself. That they should have ceased not long before the Civil War in 1642 is hardly accidental.

FROM COURT TO THEATRE

THE DEVELOPMENT of opera from earlier Renaissance entertainments owed everything at first to the impermanent stages in the princely courts of Italy. Its emergence into the theatre brought it into the domain of public performance, and the building of theatres to house opera, particularly in Venice, in the 1630s and 1640s, was to occasion an important advance in design for opera and its close companion, ballet. As machinist as well as designer, the most crucial figure for stage design in the first half of the seventeenth century is Giacomo Torelli, who was born in Fano, northern Italy, in 1608. Of noble family, he was celebrated both as an architect and as a constructor of machines, but it is his stagings when he moved to Venice in approximately 1640 that first insist on his importance.

Venice had become the leading operatic city of Europe and Torelli's designs for *La Finta Pazza* in 1641, *Bellerofonte* of 1642 and *Venere Gelosa* in 1643 were to be a sensational success at the newest theatre in Venice, the Teatro Novissimo. Torelli's designs were thought important enough to be included as engravings in the libretti of these operas (plates 14, 15) and they indicate his extraordinary skill in using stage machinery. The designs were clearly made for a framed, proscenium stage and Torelli initiated new systems involving tracks below the stage to move scenery swiftly and easily. The importance of this development can be understood in its power to free the librettist and composer so that a change of locale would be effected with maximum speed. In 1645 John Evelyn's diary records a visit to a Venetian theatre:

> This night, having with my Lord Bruce taken our places before, we went to the Opera, where comedies and other plays are represented in recitative music, by the most excellent musicians, vocal and instrumental, with variety of scenes painted and contrived with no less art of perspective, and machines for flying in the air, and other wonderful notions; taken together, it is one of the most magnificent and expensive diversions the wit of man can invent. The history was Hercules in Lydia; the scenes changed thirteen times. This held us by the eyes and ears till two in the morning.

Torelli's effects were achieved by his inventiveness as a machinist. By the use of counterweights he could have eight pairs of wings moved by a single stagehand where previously each wing had required the services of an individual. This system eventually spread throughout Europe and replaced the earlier, more cumbrous method.

In 1645 Anne of Austria, the mother of Louis XIV, was Regent of France and she requested the Duke of Parma to provide a choreographer, some players and a stage designer to supplement her Italian troupe in Paris. The Duke sent a choreographer and players but in preference to his own stage designer

Design for Ballet

On previous page
Vincenzo Rè (d. 1762): scene for a *serenata* held in the royal palace in Naples in 1747. Engraving by Giuseppe Vasi. The stage area is gently opened out with its diagonal perspective. It shows how the illusory world of the theatre and that well known to the court audience could be combined: there seems little conflict between reality and fantasy.

Left
14 **Giacomo Torelli**: setting for the first act of *Venere Gelosa*, first performed at the Teatro Novissimo, Venice, 1643. Later French engraving by Aveline. The design is remarkable not only for the use of perspective in the depiction of the cave containing the kings' tombs on the island of Naxos, but in the imaginative use of a machine, in the chariot borne on clouds in the left, and in the distant prospect of the world above ground.

Opposite
15 Giacomo Torelli: setting of the garden which formed the final design of *Venere Gelosa*. The engraver has in fact updated the costuming of the characters to the beginning of the eighteenth century, but the excellence of Torelli's triple perspective is truly represented.

Above
16 Giacomo Torelli: scene from *Les Noces de Pélée et de Thétis*, staged in the Salle du Petit Bourbon, Paris, 1654. Later French engraving by Aveline. The crucial point of the action of this scene was a sacrifice to Mars, and his statue stands focused by the design in the central spot beneath the hanging buttress.

suggested that Torelli should go, and in due course Torelli's first staging in France was seen at the Salle du Petit Bourbon in December 1645. This was *La Finta Pazza* with which he had triumphed in Italy, although it had become a combined display of song and dance rather than the opera which it had been in Venice.

The impact of Torelli's mechanical skill was immense and his years in France were to mark the real expansion of the theatre of machines. With a masterly use of perspective, and a talent in lighting quite as fine as his skill in the mechanics of scene change, Torelli brought to the French stage an increasing virtuosity of effects.

Until the middle of the seventeenth century, although court performances could take place either by day or by candlelight, theatrical performances were given only in daylight. But the invention of oil lamps and candelabra enabled far more elaborate lighting effects to be obtained on stage. Both Torelli and Alfonso Parigi created increasingly brilliant effects with reflectors (mirrors) so that colour and light might play one upon the other. The splendour of costuming, its jewels and gold and silver embroidery and tissues shone in the new artificial light. Moreover, in 1634 the Jesuit Athanasius Kirschner had produced a kind of magic lantern which could throw images of a city on a backdrop.

Les Noces de Pélée et de Thétis, staged in 1654, was one of the most important and elaborate of the court spectacles designed by Torelli. The ballet scenes were specifically designed to allow the young King and his courtiers to dance. Ladies of the court appeared for the first time (as Muses in the first scene), and

Design for Ballet

the sixteen-year-old Louis XIV took the role of Apollo in the Prologue, of a Fury in the third scene of Act I and of a Dryad in the second scene of Act II, and a Warrior in the final scene. Torelli's design for the third scene of Act II (plate 16) is one of his most outstanding. The stage was conceived as a continuation of the auditorium, a theatre in which the noble cast were to perform a *combat à la barrière*. The members of the court sat in three ranks on either side of the stage dressed in the by now usual *habit à la Romaine*, as were the participants in the mock combat, while the actual architecture of the setting was a combination of elements of classical, Renaissance and Baroque theatre architecture. Torelli deepens the effect of his stage through a splendid design concept. The back opening of the stage was made as a double archway with its central pillar missing – its capital only remaining as a hanging buttress – and the perspective was still further deepened by a triple view of streets, a device dating back to the *scena comica*. The effect, a dazzling feat of perspective, was of course only to be appreciated fully by those members of the audience seated in the middle of the auditorium. In court entertainments the presentation of a work to a specific and favoured group still obtained, a relic of the tradition of performing to the 'presence' which was the guiding principle of the sixteenth-century *ballet de cour*.

Torelli's career was to receive a setback in 1659. In that year the Duchess of Modena sent her architect, Gasparo Vigarani, then aged seventy-one but accompanied by his two sons Carlo and Lodovico, to build a theatre in the Palace of the Tuileries. This new theatre was intended to outdo any other in Europe and Vigarani was determined that Torelli should have no part in it. Torelli's career suffered a further decline two years later when he was employed by the all-powerful Minister for finance, Nicolas Fouquet, to provide the designs for the series of festivities Fouquet planned in order to welcome Louis XIV to his magnificent château at Vaux-le-Vicomte. The opulence of display infuriated the monarch and sealed Fouquet's fate. He was tried and banished and his estates confiscated. Torelli, as designer, naturally shared something of Fouquet's disgrace and in the following year he returned to Italy where he continued working until his death in 1678.

Thus Vigarani was alone responsible for the great Salle des Machines in the Tuileries, and it was his son Carlo who was to remain as chief decorator of spectacles in the succeeding years.

In May 1664 Louis XIV commanded a particularly elaborate court festival, in honour of no fewer than three of the women in his life: his mother, Anne of Austria, his wife, Maria Theresa, and his mistress, Louise de la Vallière, and the entertainment was to be spread over three days. *Les Plaisirs de l'Ile Enchantée* was conceived as a single event combining ballets, dinners, plays, mock combats and firework displays. The overall producer was the Duc de St Aignan, and Carlo Vigarani was called upon to design the ensembles. The main theme was taken from Ariosto's *Orlando Furioso*. On the first day the King led a group of knights who had been enslaved by the enchantress Alcina through the park in a quadrille. After the performance of an allegorical scene a candle-lit banqueting table rose through the floor on a trap door and the royal party took dinner while the rest of the court looked on. On the second day (illustrated in plate 17), the climax came with the first performance of Molière's comedy-ballet *La Princesse d'Elide*. Plays and concerts were also given throughout the park and on the third day an artificial lake was used to show Alcina's palace. Around it swam whales and sea monsters while dwarfs, giants and demons tried to prevent the knights escaping. Eventually Alcina's

17 Carlo Vigarani: setting for *La Princesse d'Elide*, staged at Versailles as part of *Les Plaisirs de l'Ile Enchantée*, May 1664.

Seconde Journée
tre fait dans la mesme allée, sur lequel la Comédye, et le Ballet de la Princesse d'Elide furent representéz.

spell was broken and her palace vanished amid a giant firework display. Vigarani's talent was called upon to produce a setting compatible with the open air surroundings and also to ensure that the magical effects were effective. The use he made of the carefully planted alleys in Le Nôtre's inspired garden planning is remarkable.

By the middle of the seventeenth century dress at court had become overtly opulent. Vast sums of money were spent on the most extravagant silks and satins and embroidered fabrics, and considerable use of real gold and precious stones as an integral part of their decoration. Contemporary records of the period speak of courtiers bankrupting themselves to provide suitably impressive clothing (and of tailors who could rarely expect to be paid). Professional performers in the plays of the period were expected to dress well; the noble amateurs and the professional dancers of the *ballet de cour* had to outshine them.

Henri Gissey (1621–73) held a court appointment as artist to the King from

Design for Ballet

18 Henri Gissey: costume design for Philippe, Duc d'Orléans, as the King of Persia in the carrousel held in Paris in 1662 to celebrate the birth of the Dauphin.

From Court to Theatre

1668–73 and during this time he was called upon to provide costumes and some scenery for royal fêtes and ballets. The nature of these entertainments insisted upon both elegance and wit in making the allegorical nature of the character clear. The various genres of costuming could range from the supremely stylish to the frankly grotesque.

Ingenuity and a lively sense of fantasy were considered prerequisites for these clothes. There was no demand for the kind of respectable reflection of reality that was to come with the nineteenth century: symbols, allegories, metaphors abounded in the designs. The world of court ballet was in itself so enclosed, so special in its appeal to a very limited audience and so intimately linked with the *persona* of the monarch, that it became as ritualistic as the ceremonial that grew up around the figure of the monarch himself. The costumes were laden with symbols – this in itself no novelty since it was a tradition already established by the Florentine *intermezzi* – but in its increasing stylization and also in its codification it presents us with a remarkable insight into the attitudes of both performers and audience. For men the *habit à la Romaine* had developed into a kind of uniform. Any sort of national difference would be suggested by some alteration in the accoutrements or the head-dress – a Turk or Persian was usually capped with a turban. For the female performer the height of fashion was *de rigueur*. Etiquette obliged them to appear before the monarch in court dress and this was to remain the standard costume for actresses and dancers for a considerable length of time. Local colour was suggested by detailed decoration and ornament. This formal nature of stage dress was entirely suited to the conventions of the theatre: the line between performers and public was so often crossed both in fact and in performance that the fantasy world of the stage must have seemed no more than a heightened reflection of court life itself. Because of the feebleness of the candle lighting and later of oil lamps, stage dress had to be easily read and its elaboration was a matter both of dramatic expediency and of taste. The costuming in the *ballet de cour* was also required to reflect etiquette as well as fashion. It was unthinkable that a humble character should appear in torn or dirty clothes; rather would a poor peasant girl be dressed decently in satin and velvet and the social distinction from her superiors be marked by dressing them in vastly richer gold tissues and fabrics. 'I would never dare to allow a maid to appear in a torn skirt. I would give her a good skirt, and heighten the elegance of her mistress,' was a comment of the time.

Plate 18 shows an engraving of a design by Gissey for Philippe, Duc d'Orléans, as the King of Persia in the great carrousel held in Paris in 1662 to celebrate the birth of the Dauphin, first son of Louis XIV. This carrousel comprised five entries by squadrons each led by members of the court: the King appeared leading the Roman quadrille, the Duc d'Enghien introduced the Indian quadrille, the Duc de Guise led the American, the Turkish quadrille was headed by the Prince de Condé, and the Duc d'Orléans led in the Persians. Monsieur, as the Duc d'Orléans was called, appeared dressed in silver brocade embroidered with silver and set with rubies; his rose brocade cloak and turban were decorated with gold, rubies and pearls and his horse was outfitted in the same colours. (Monsieur was a frivolous soul, with a marked affection for eye-catching outfits.) Yet the fantasy of costuming was controlled by sure taste: as in all these seventeenth-century court ballets and entertainments extravagance was not an end in itself but employed to make a significant political as well as an artistic point.

Costuming respected the lines of the body: male roles were allowed

19 Henri Gissey: costume design for a male grotesque dancer representing Music in the ballet of the *Fêtes de Bacchus*, first performed in 1651 at the Palais Royal, Paris.

complete freedom of the trunk and limbs; for the male dancer *en travesti*, taking a female role, a skirt would come to the knee; it was only the female performers whose skirts had to reach to the ground. Certain roles were required to wear a mask since it facilitated the stylization of the character. For demons, this was properly hideous; for nymphs it would be sweetly naïve; rivers wore venerable bearded masks, while dwarfs and juveniles might be encumbered with massive heads. Masks were also sometimes placed upon knees, elbows and the chest to indicate something more of the character – as in Berain's costume for Mystery in *Le Triomphe de l'Amour* (plate 23).

The French tradition of design which flowered so interestingly with the work of Gissey reached its full glory in the work of Jean Louis Berain (1637–1711). Berain started as an engraver and after an apprenticeship with le Brun – when he became a decorative jack of many trades – he succeeded Gissey as Graveur et Dessinateur de la Chambre et du Cabinet du Roi. Until his death he was overseer for all the decoration of court entertainments and was associated with the composer Lully and the choreographer Beauchamp in the presentation of opera-ballets at the Paris Opéra (Académie Royale de Musique). His work was soon preferred to that of Vigarani. The designs illustrated here give some idea of the quality of his work. The costume for the Prince (plate 21) represents a high point of the noble style of costuming for the court ballet. The costumes for an Indian Man and an Indian Woman in *Le Triomphe de l'Amour* (plate 22) are excellent examples of Berain's remarkable

20 Stefano della Bella: engraving of *Il Mondo festeggiante*, a horse ballet staged by Alessandro Carducci, who was referred to as 'the inventor of the ballet and the battle', with Ferdinando Tacha as 'engineer'. This pageant, held in Florence in 1661, celebrated the marriage of the Grand Duke Cosimo IV of Tuscany to Marguerite Louise d'Orléans.

From Court to Theatre

21 Jean Berain: costume design for a Prince in a court ballet.

On pages 36 and 37
22 a, b Jean Berain: costume designs for an Indian Man and an Indian Woman in *Le Triomphe de l'Amour*, performed at St Germain en Laye in 1681. *Le Triomphe de l'Amour* is celebrated in the annals of ballet as the first work in which professional female dancers appeared. However, the shortened over-tunic in the costume for the female Indian indicates that this was in fact a role taken by a male dancer.

J. Berin del.

J. Berin del.

Opposite
23 Jean Berain: costume for Mystery in *Le Triomphe de l'Amour*. Berain's use of masks, both on the chest and peeping mysteriously from the dancer's knees, and the plainly lightweight sleeves and train, suggest some of the qualities ascribed to the character.

24 Jean Berain (attributed to): design for an inferno scene. This drawing which has been attributed to Berain as a project for the last act of Lully's opera-ballet *Armide et Renaud* (1686) shows the remarkable continuity of the tradition of the hell scene (see plate 3).

sense of fantasy, and his use of masks in the costume for Mystery (plate 23) is a particularly evocative exploitation of a traditional device. That his talent extended equally to set design is evident from the superb inferno scene (plate 24). In Berain's work we see the apotheosis of the French style at the end of the seventeenth century before the lightening of the stage picture which was to come with the age of Rococo.

The political rivalry that existed between Paris and Vienna was mirrored in the theatre. Parallel with the work of Torelli in France came the great age of Baroque stage design in Vienna, with the arrival of Giovanni Burnacini in 1651. Invited by Ferdinand III and his wife Eleanora of Mantua, an enthusiast for the theatre, Burnacini had already known success as an architect and designer in Italy, both in Mantua and Venice. Giovanni had been a colleague of Torelli's and in Vienna he started to design operas for the court theatre which reflected the magnificent pretensions of the monarch. In his production of the opera *La Gara* in 1652 the spectacle spilled over from the stage into the body of the theatre but since the function of the performance was to astonish the audience and to reflect the glory of the monarch this was no bad thing. In his Vienna stagings – in the building of theatres as well as in the designing of sets and costumes – Burnacini used the most up-to-date techniques for ballets and triumphal processions, and for transformations.

Since it was not usual to lower a curtain between the scenes, the changing of scenery provided an opportunity to display the ingenuity of the designer. And in the almost magical transformations that Giovanni Burnacini achieved, his assistant and pupil was his son Lodovico Ottavio.

From the age of fourteen Lodovico Burnacini (1636–1707) worked with his father, and when in due time he succeeded Giovanni as designer to the court he was to create the settings, machines and costumes for no fewer than 115 operas and an even greater number of court spectacles between the years 1656 and 1705. Under Lodovico Burnacini stagings of operatic and dance performances at Vienna reached their most splendid form. They continued the tradition of performances specially conceived for festive occasions in order to arouse public enthusiasm and also to reflect upon the glorious nature of the monarch, and they called for a prodigal use of machinery and transformation to astound the audience. It was Burnacini's task as designer to the court to reflect the magnificent aspirations of the monarchy itself and to insist upon Vienna's political pre-eminence, despite the rival claims of Versailles.

Left
25 Engraving by Valk showing Mlle Subligny, one of the principal dancers at the Opéra at the turn of the eighteenth century. She is wearing a costume typical for noble roles in the opera-ballets that were being staged at that theatre.

Above and on pages 42, 43 and 44
26 a, b, c Lodovico Burnacini: scenes from *Il Pomo d'Oro*, staged in Vienna in 1667 as part of the celebrations of the marriage of the Emperor Leopold I and the Infanta Margareta Theresa. Engravings for the libretto by Matthaeus Kusel. (a) shows the imaginative skill of Burnacini's view of the traditional hell mouth. The volcanic monster's head is surrounded here by rocks which take the form of agonized skulls and tormented faces. Through the jaws we see a city in flames with a boat to provide a focal point for perspective. (b) depicts a stormy

sea involving both Neptune and his cohorts on the left and a goddess surrounded by mermaids on the right. The wings have been used to suggest a rocky promontory with trees. The wrecked ship and the storm itself are shown as the focal point of the perspective. In (c) the court ballet scene shown as an apotheosis reveals how close was the interrelation of the court's world with that of the stage. Here the architectural perspective suggests a complexity of styles but also conveys something of the real world of Vienna. The dancers wear the conventional *habit à la Romaine*; while at the back the distant prospect of the sea with tritons and nereids is given a stronger image by the celestial figures seen in the apotheosis. Among the clouds, gods, goddesses and cupids hail the figures of the royal couple whose marriage has been celebrated.

In 1667, as a climax to the celebrations of the marriage between the Emperor Leopold I and the Infanta Margareta Theresa, daughter of Philip IV of Spain, the opera by Antonio Cesti *Il Pomo d'Oro* (plate 26) was staged (it had to be postponed for a year in order to allow a proper theatre to be built in which it could be shown). *Il Pomo d'Oro*, which dealt with the legend of Paris and the golden apple, gave Burnacini the most extraordinary opportunities to transport his audience through time and space. The scenes included Hades and Olympus, the slopes of Mount Ida, Paris's palace, a fleet at sea, Mars's fortress, the temple of Athena, the sky and the Milky Way, and the swift movement from one magical setting to another suggested how freely Burnacini's imagination could range, and how his technical virtuosity could leave his imagination untrammelled by problems of locale.

In use of machines he could show Discord flying down on a dragon to Hades and then mounting on a cloud to the peak of Mount Olympus in order to throw the golden apple among the goddesses. These in their turn journeyed to see Paris, with Hera descending in a golden *galleria* while Athena appeared

Design for Ballet

on a triumphal arch and Aphrodite transformed Paris's courtyard into a garden. Battles, mythical animals, furies and goddesses, heroes and nymphs and the whole catalogue of mythology became involved in the dispute: to show it Burnacini divided his stage laterally so that a broad forestage and a narrower backstage could encompass all the fantasy.

Burnacini's staging, with its twenty-one miraculous scenes, could not be allowed to die after a single performance, although that had been the original intention. In the event it was performed more than a hundred times, and given a more permanent life still by being recorded in engravings.

Contemporary with the Burnacini family, and yet another example of Italian supremacy in design, are the most remarkable and influential figures in stage decoration in the late seventeenth century. These are the members of the Galli Bibiena family, four generations of whom were to dominate scene design for over a hundred years. The founding father was Giovanni Maria Galli Bibiena (1619–65). His sons Ferdinando (1657–1743) and Francesco (1659–1739) and his four talented grandsons Alessandro (1687–1769), Giuseppe (1696–1757), Antonio (1700–74) and Giovanni Carlo (d. 1760) and Giuseppe's son Carlo (1725–87) were to continue a tradition of excellence that might be said to have decided the development of European stage techniques. Their work was seen throughout Europe, from Vienna and Italy through to Prague, Barcelona and even Petersburg and London. Although they were extraordinarily prolific, of the surviving examples of their work none falls back on mere formula. Their creation of theatrical effects was

26 c (see page 41)

44

always lively, and it is this quality, as well as an inbred elegance, which distinguishes them from their many imitators.

In the work of the Bibiena family can be seen not only the grandest demonstration of Baroque design ideals but also the inter-relationship between the court and the entertainments it chose to watch. In this age when splendid palaces were being constructed in which the elaborate ballet of court ritual was played out, theatrical design and theatrical performance reflected this same grandiloquence and splendour of show. If court life was ritualistic so too was court entertainment. If everything might be read about a man's position at court by the bows he gave and received, so too could court audiences understand the symbolism of costuming and action in the court ballets. In the theatre the court audience could see made real the illusions of their day to day life. The monarch's power might not be total but it was flattered and lulled by the illusions fostered in stage performances. The glorification of the monarchy in the great court festivals of the seventeenth and eighteenth centuries was yet another aspect of the glorification implied in architecture, sculpture and painting. The apotheosis of the court ballet would show the ruler manifest as the Sun or Apollo, and thus he was to be considered within the narrow confines of his own court.

The magical nature of the court ballet and court spectacle was a necessary homage to the quasi-divine nature of the monarch, but it required a stage area capable of making such magic seem both easy and amazing. The stage design of the high Baroque period finds the theatre itself becoming an extraordinary

27 Lodovico Burnacini: a ballet scene from the open air spectacle *La Constanza d'Ulysse*.

Design for Ballet

From Court to Theatre

28 Ferdinando Galli Bibiena: architectural design for stage scenery. This design reveals with exceptional clarity the major development which is associated with Ferdinando Galli Bibiena at this time: the abandoning of straight perspective in favour of perspective at an angle. This breaking of the thrall of pure geometric drawing implies a freeing of stage convention as it also frees the eye and frees the stage by suggesting vast untapped areas of space from which the action may emerge.

On pages 48 and 49
29 Giuseppe Galli Bibiena: design, *c.* 1690. for the theatrical performance on the occasion of the marriage of the Prince Elector of Bavaria, Maximilian II Emanuel.

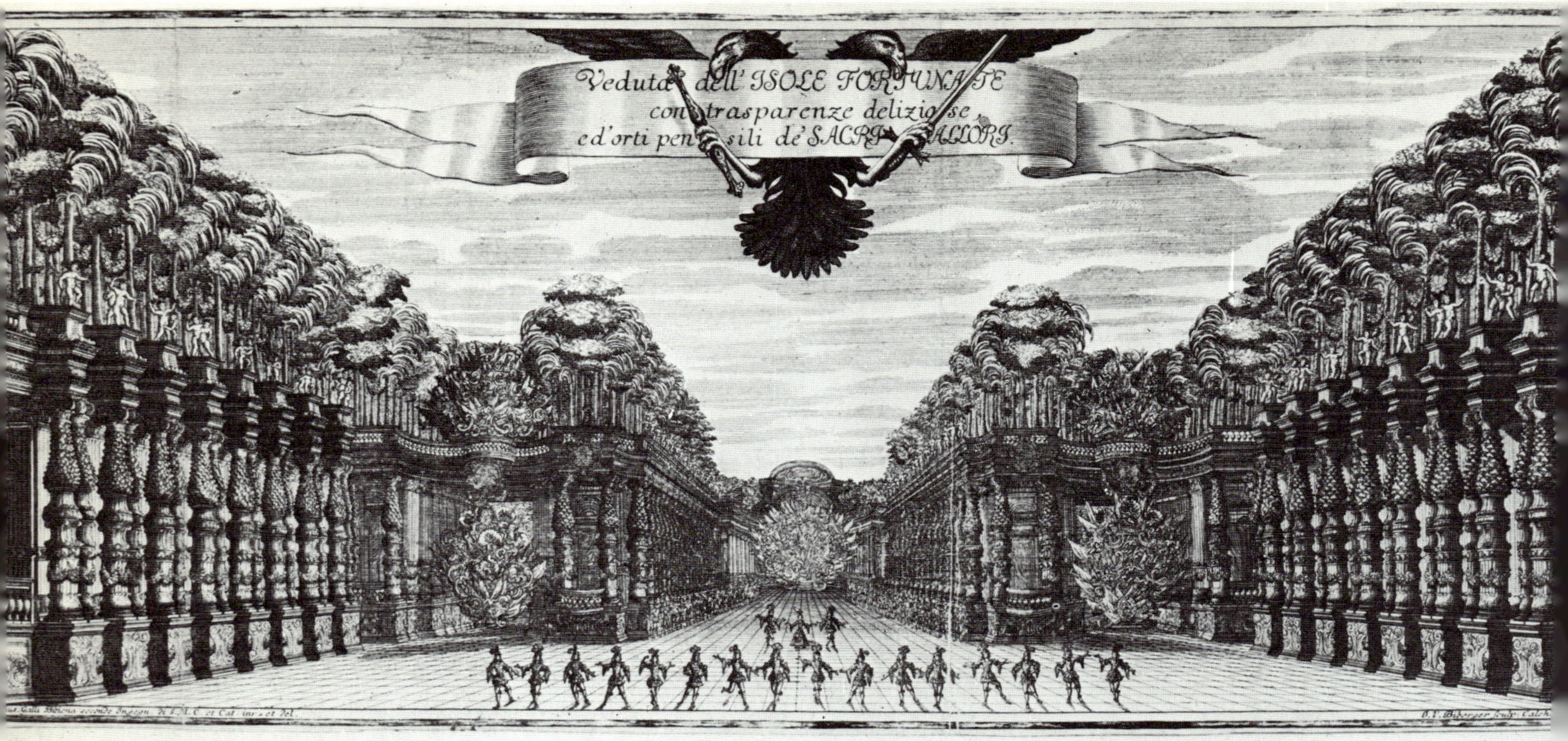
Veduta dell' ISOLE FORTUNATE
con trasparenze deliziose
ed'orti pensili de' SACRI ALLORI.

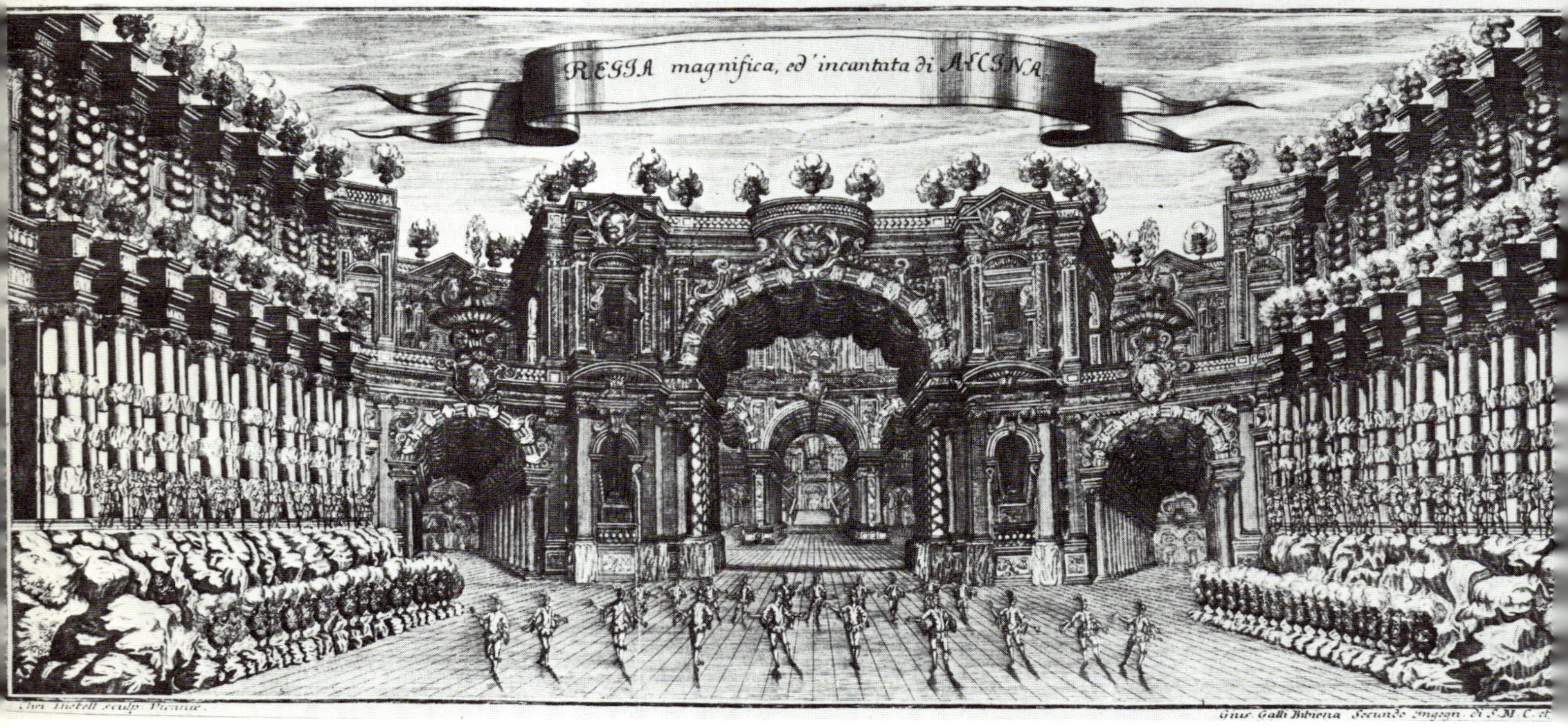
REGIA magnifica, ed'incantata di ALCINA

30 a, b, c Giuseppe Galli Bibiena: designs for the court spectacle *Angelica Vincitrice di Alcina*, which was composed by Johann Josef Fux and first performed in Vienna on 21 September 1716. (a) *opposite above* is a garden scene in which the two side perspectives have been blocked and the trees which decorate the tops of the architectural colonnades are as formalized as the columns themselves. (b) *opposite below* shows the domain of the enchantress Alcina, again making use of the diagonals of perspective which frame the central distant prospect. (c) *above* indicates Bibiena's skill in combining both grandeur and a feeling of space in his designs. Suggestions of perspective, both direct and axial, are enhanced by the drawing of the front wings of this open air setting.

and magical place. It could be opened out by the use of perspective; machines enabled the appearance and disappearance of every sort of being; and it is to one of the second generation of the Bibiena family, Ferdinando, that the Baroque stage owed the development of an important innovation: the *scena per angolo*. This was a departure from the customary central perspective by suggesting lines of perspective which moved at an angle away from the centre of the stage, thus leading the eye to hidden but imagined vistas. The effect was of much greater space lying on these divergent axes.

On his work in Vienna, where he and his brother Francesco had been in the service of the Archduke Charles, Ferdinando published a treatise which stated the ground rules of the new theatrical space at the beginning of the eighteenth century and this concept of an area for every form of theatrical entertainment, opera, ballet, drama, even the serenades (*serenate*), was to last until the end of the century.

It is in the work of Giuseppe, the second son of Ferdinando, that the Bibiena style reached its peak. Here we see the formalization of the ideas of perspective which had been so acutely developed by Ferdinando.

In September 1716 Lady Mary Wortley Montagu wrote from Vienna to Alexander Pope, describing the court spectacle *Angelica Vincitrice di Alcina* (plate 30), which was designed by Giuseppe Galli Bibiena:

> Don't fancy, however, that I am infected by the air of these popish Countrys, tho I have so far wander'd from the Discipline of the Church of England to have been last Sunday at the Opera, which was perform'd in the Garden of the Favorita, and I was so much pleas'd with it, I have not yet repented my seeing it. Nothing of that kind ever was more Magnificent, and I can easily believe what I am told, that the Decorations and habits cost the Emperour £30,000 Sterling. The stage was built over a very large Canal, and at the beginning of the 2nd Act divided into 2 parts, discovering the Water, on which there immediately came from different parts 2 fleets of little gilded vessels that gave the representation of a Naval fight. It is not easy to imagine the beauty of this Scene, which I took particular Notice of, but all the rest were perfectly fine in their kind. The story of the Opera is the *Enchantments of Alcina*, which gives Oppertunity for a great variety of Machines and changes of the Scenes, which are perform'd with a surprizing swiftnesse. The Theatre is so large that 'tis hard to carry the Eye to the End of it, and the Habits in the utmost magnificence to the number of 108. No house could hold such large Decorations, but the Ladys all sitting in the open air exposes them to great Inconveniencys, for there is but one canopy for the Imperial Family, and the first night it was represented, a shower of rain happening, the Opera was broke off and the company crouded away in such confusion, I was allmost squeez'd to Death.

The nobility and grandeur of Giuseppe Bibiena's designing can be studied in his extraordinary collection of theatrical and architectural designs *Architetture e Prospettive*, published in 1740 in Vienna. The excitement of this high Baroque design lies in the massive vistas, the grandiose aspirations that are implied by the soaring architecture and the sweep of line which helps to keep the observer's eye active as he contemplates the setting. The theatre has become a place of great dignity, and if it appears slightly oppressive, the succeeding Rococo theatre lightened and refined the nature of the stage space in which dancing was to take place.

This change is implicit also in the political nature of the time. In France the marmoreal and tragic splendour of the later years of Louis XIV was to give way to the different aesthetic of the periods of Louis XV and Louis XVI. In Vienna the days of the Baroque were also numbered; new movements were afoot and the court entertainments were no longer merely the toy of the Emperor. The Empress Maria Theresa, for instance, had a private corridor from her apartments to the Burgtheater, but she was no longer the sole owner and commander of the productions staged there.

ROCOCO, NEOCLASSICAL, ROMANTIC

Design for Ballet

WITH THE emergence of a strong influential dance tradition at the Paris Opéra (a fully professional theatre no longer dependent on court approval in any way) in the early decades of the eighteenth century, ballet itself seemed free to develop as an art form. Although Italian stage decoration was still to be a dominant force in European theatres – witness the influence of the later generations of the Bibiena family and the members of the Galliari family (Bernadino, 1707–94, who worked in Italy and Vienna and his brother Fabrizio, 1709–90) – and Italian design was to be seen from London to Petersburg and from Dresden to Copenhagen, it is the charm and delicacy of French Rococo design that marks the most appealing development in the presentation of ballets.

At the same time an interest in the exotic became evident in ballet design; such works as the choreographer Jean-Georges Noverre's first great success *Les Fêtes Chinoises* of 1754 staged at the Opéra Comique in Paris were to echo the fashionable taste for *chinoiserie*. (The decorative influence of the painter Boucher is to be seen in the designing of the period.) As in real life, the elaborate formalism of the seventeenth century had given place to something more subtle, elegant and lightfooted. It is impossible to conceive of the plays

On previous page
Louis René Boquet: costume design for an 'American' in a ballet *entrée*.

Below
31 Giovanni Andrea Gallini: engraving from Gallini's *Treatise on the Art of Dancing*, published in London in 1772. Gallini offers a mandarin procession which would provide a source of decorative ideas for ballet design.

Opposite
32 Charles Cochin the Younger: scene from a performance of Voltaire's *La Princesse de Navarre*, composed in honour of the marriage of Louis the Dauphin (son of Louis XV) to Maria Teresa, Infanta of Spain, in 1745. Combining song, dance and drama, the piece was staged in a theatre that had been erected in the Riding School of the Grandes Ecuries at Versailles. The illustration shows the final scene in which a general dance concludes the action. The elegance of the set and costumes are a natural extension of the court itself.

of Marivaux performed in the same theatrical setting as that which had been given to Racine. So, too, in the ballets of the middle and late eighteenth century, which were to reflect a greater quest for naturalism and freedom of expression – as we know from the writings of Noverre and the polemics of Hildverding and Angiolini – the formal gardens of the seventeenth century were to be replaced by softer and more idyllic landscapes. The taste in the exotic, the use of Chinese, Turkish or Arab decorative ideas, was paralleled by a more realistic representation of nature, though 'realistic' must be considered a relative term. Nature was still carefully ordered, as were the gardens of Versailles; it is not until the next century, with the full flood of Romanticism, that it could be found untamed on stage. Politically absolutism was yielding to the 'enlightenment', although this is reflected in ballet, its design and costume, with rather less force than in the rest of the theatre.

Until well into the eighteenth century the rules governing costume remained very rigid. The categorization of dancers was reflected in their dress. The *danseur noble*, whose style had to be supremely elegant, would appear formally and richly dressed, usually wearing the tonnelet, a costume which owed its inspiration to the undergarments of medieval knights at arms, and became expected dress for the male dancer in the eighteenth century. An extension of the kilted tunic *à la Romaine* of the previous century, it was wired and stiffened and at its largest extent reached further than the outstretched

33 Scene from *Le Turc Généreux*, a ballet pantomime staged at the Theater am Karntnertor in 1758 in honour of the Turkish envoy's arrival at the Hapsburg court. The more naturalistic setting makes use of slanted perspective as well as of a central diminishing colonnade leading to the seaport; the dress of the performers is also notable for its naturalism.

Rococo, Neoclassical, Romantic

34 P. Lior (attributed to): design for a spirit of fire. The illustration shows the continued use of symbolic attributes in stage dress. The fire spirit's tonnelet is decorated with flames all over the tunic; his sleeves are edged from wrist to armpit with simulated flame, and his head-dress also repeats this same fiery motif.

35 Auguste Vestris in the ballet of *Les Amants surpris*, first performed in London at the King's Theatre in 1780. An engraving by J. Thornthwaite after James Roberts. Auguste Vestris's costume here is for a *demi-caractère* dancer. A comparison with a costume designed for his father at this time (plate 38) shows Gaetano much more formally dressed, plumed and garbed as befitted a *danseur noble*.

arms of the dancer. The *danseur de demi-caractère* had costuming which, like his vocabulary of movement, was different from that of the *danseur noble* – lighter, more fantastic. The *danseur comique*, entrusted with grotesque, comic or acrobatic work was to appear on stage, curiously enough, in more obviously naturalistic dress. But even in the tonnelet the male dancer was less restricted than his female counterpart: the predominance of the male dancer as virtuoso was implicit in his greater freedom of dress. Female costume was not to get away from the elaborate skirts of contemporary fashion until the fashion itself changed with the Revolution and the establishment of Napoleon's Empire. Nevertheless, developing ballet technique was to have a marked influence upon costume design, and the first significant move was to be seen in the 1730s when La Camargo shortened her skirts from floor level to a few inches above her ankle to enable her skill in *entrechats* to be appreciated by the audience.

Jean-Baptiste Martin (1659–1735) was chief costume designer at the Paris Opéra. Many of his designs were reproduced and the engravings circulated round Europe to provide design ideas for innumerable performances during

Design for Ballet

36 P. Lior (attributed to): costume design for a *bergère galante*. Boris Kochno attributes this design to Noverre's *Les Petits Riens* (1778). Lior provided designs for the Paris Opéra during the second quarter of the eighteenth century and this drawing displays the conventional outline for the female dancer of the time. It corresponds closely to town dress. Less elaborate than the costuming for noble characters, it still reflects the decorative attitudes that were to culminate in Marie Antoinette's playing at shepherdesses.

the middle of the eighteenth century. The costume design for a *paysanne galante* illustrated in plate 37 is remarkable for its use of a ruched decoration whose pattern is repeated from the skirt to the highly stylized apron and for the pretty use of floral and ribbon decoration at the dancer's throat and in her hat. Originally created for the *Ballet de la Provençale*, the costume is also said to have been used in 'several other ballets of the same genre'.

Louis René Boquet (1717–1814) succeeded Martin at the Opéra and was also chief purveyor of costume for many of the court entertainments at Versailles and the other royal palaces from the middle of the century until the Revolution. A pupil of Boucher, he must be considered as the master of Rococo costuming. In his work we see how Rococo design lightened the stage picture and in many cases took it to an extreme of delicate fantasy. The many designs of his still preserved in theatre collections are testimony to his

Opposite
37 Jean-Baptiste Martin: costume for a *paysanne galante*, created for the *Ballet de la Provençale*, an entrée performed at the Paris Opéra in 1722.

Rococo, Neoclassical, Romantic

Design for Ballet

admirable control of the conventions of the time. It is significant that during the great days of the Stuttgart theatre under the Grand Duke Karl Eugen, whose affection for the theatre made his city one of the most important operatic and dance centres during the middle years of the century, Boquet was invited to design there for several months each year. Boquet's ideas spread throughout Europe by means of engravings and their influence must be adjudged very considerable.

The ballet master and choreographer Jean-Georges Noverre (1727–1810) was one of the major advocates of reform in ballet during the eighteenth century. In his ballets and explicitly in his *Lettres sur la danse et les ballets* (Lyon/Stuttgart, 1760), Noverre called for radical change to free dance from what he saw as excessive artificiality and a denial of naturalism. He is the best-known publicist for the theories of the *ballet d'action*. This was the ideal of dramatic ballet in which the story was carried forward through the dancing and not divorced from it in mimed passages. Consequently, some of the most intriguing testimony about costuming for ballet in the eighteenth century is to be found in his writings.

Left
38 Louis René Boquet: costume design for Gaetano Vestris, the pre-eminent male dancer of his time, celebrated for his noble style. This costume, with its swagged tonnelet, ruched sleeves and plumed headdress is for 'a follower of fortune' in a ballet at the Paris Opéra. Compare with Nijinsky's costume for *Le Pavillon d'Armide*, colour plate 8.

Right
39 Louis René Boquet: costume design for Mlle Allard as a *bacchante*.

In Letter 8 of Cyril Beaumont's translation (London, 1930) Noverre inveighs against the artificiality which in his eyes so detracted from ballet's theatrical force.

> Let us pass to costume; its variety and accuracy are as rare as in music, in ballets and in social dancing. Obstinacy in adhering to outworn traditions is the same in every part of opera; it is monarch of all it surveys. Greek, Roman, shepherd, hunter, warrior, faun . . . tritons, winds, fires . . . all these characters are cut to the same pattern and differ only in colour and in the ornaments with which a desire for ostentatious display rather than good taste has caused them to be bespattered at caprice. Tinsel glitters everywhere: Peasant, Sailor, Hero – all are covered alike. The more a costume is decorated with gewgaws, spangles, gauze and net the greater the admiration it procures the player and the ignorant spectator . . . At the Opéra, few things to be encountered are more curious than the sight of a band of warriors who come to do battle, fight and carry off the victory. Do they bring in their wake all the horrors of carnage? Are their features aflame? Are their looks ferocious? Is their hair dishevelled? No, Sir, nothing of the kind. They are dressed as if going on parade and resemble effeminate men fresh from a perfumed bath rather than survivors of a desperate struggle . . . I would do away with those stiff tonnelets which in certain dancing positions transport, as it were, the hip to the shoulder and conceal all the contours of the body. I would banish all uniformity of costume, an indifferent ungrateful device which owes its origin to lack of taste. I should prefer light and simple draperies of contrasting colours worn in such a manner as to reveal the dancer's figure. I should like them to be airy, but without stinting the material . . . I would give to the dancer that sense of briskness which he cannot attain when clad in the mediaeval armour ordained by the Opéra. I would reduce by three-quarters the ridiculous panniers of our *danseuses*, they are equally opposed to the liberty, speed, prompt and lively action of the dance.

Noverre in later Letters also complains about the continued use of the mask which was worn by dancers. Masks were a survival from the court ballets of the early seventeenth century, and their continued use in the eighteenth century added to the artificiality of dancing at a time when ballet was moving – albeit very slowly – towards a greater naturalism. The abandoning of the mask came only in the later decades of the century when Pierre Gardel refused to appear wearing a mask so that the public might be aware that it was he and not Auguste Vestris who was dancing.

Noverre's observations in Letter 8 about scenery are interesting. He pays tribute to Boquet:

> . . . entrusted with the designing of costumes for the Opéra, he has partly remedied the defects which existed in this branch so essential to illusion. It is to be hoped that he will be permitted to continue his work . . . As for scenery, Sir, I shall not discuss it; At the Opéra the scenes do not err in the matter of taste, they may even be beautiful, because the artists employed in this branch are really talented. But intrigue and a false sense of economy limit the painters' genius and

Design for Ballet

stifle their talents. Besides, at the Opéra, one is never informed of the names of the artists responsible for the scenes, so that there is little glory to be gained and consequently there are few scenes which do not leave much to be desired.

In passing we must note that Noverre's admiration for the English actor David Garrick (the admiration was reciprocated, the men were friends) was aroused by Garrick's search for simplicity and a kind of truthful naturalism rare at this time. Garrick played Hamlet without the customary wig and though his Shakespearean roles found him still dressed in the usual elegant French clothes of the period, additions – like the ermine cloak he wore as Lear – were significant innovations. (Fifty years later the Danish ballet master August Bournonville was scornful of those theatrical performers who appeared as Romeo wearing plumed head-dresses!)

On the technical side, stage machinery was becoming ever more elaborate. It is significant that when Diderot's great *Encyclopédie* appeared in 1772 it gave considerable emphasis in the theatre section to the machinery (plate 41). The care taken to illustrate and explain the whole machinery of the theatre reveals how vivid was public interest in the marvels which the theatre offered by way of transformation and stage effects. The two Dutch prints illustrated in plate 42 are equally informative. They give a remarkably precise indication of the actual appearance of the stage in the later eighteenth century. The flying

Opposite
40 Giovanni Andrea Gallini: frontispiece to *Treatise on the Art of Dancing* (London, 1772). Presumably intended as a portrait of the author in full fig as *danseur noble*, this costume exhibits the complicated and sterile decorative ideas which were so constricting in design, the conventions against which Noverre was to inveigh so strongly in his *Lettres sur la danse et les ballets*.

Below
41 A plate from the *Encyclopédie* (published in Paris in 1772 by Diderot and d'Alembert), showing a theatrical machine. The illustration shows the machinery and two inset panels: that on the left is for the decoration of a forest, showing the machine effect for flying Renaud from the scene: that on the right is a detail of a tree trunk and grass which is used in the same forest scene.

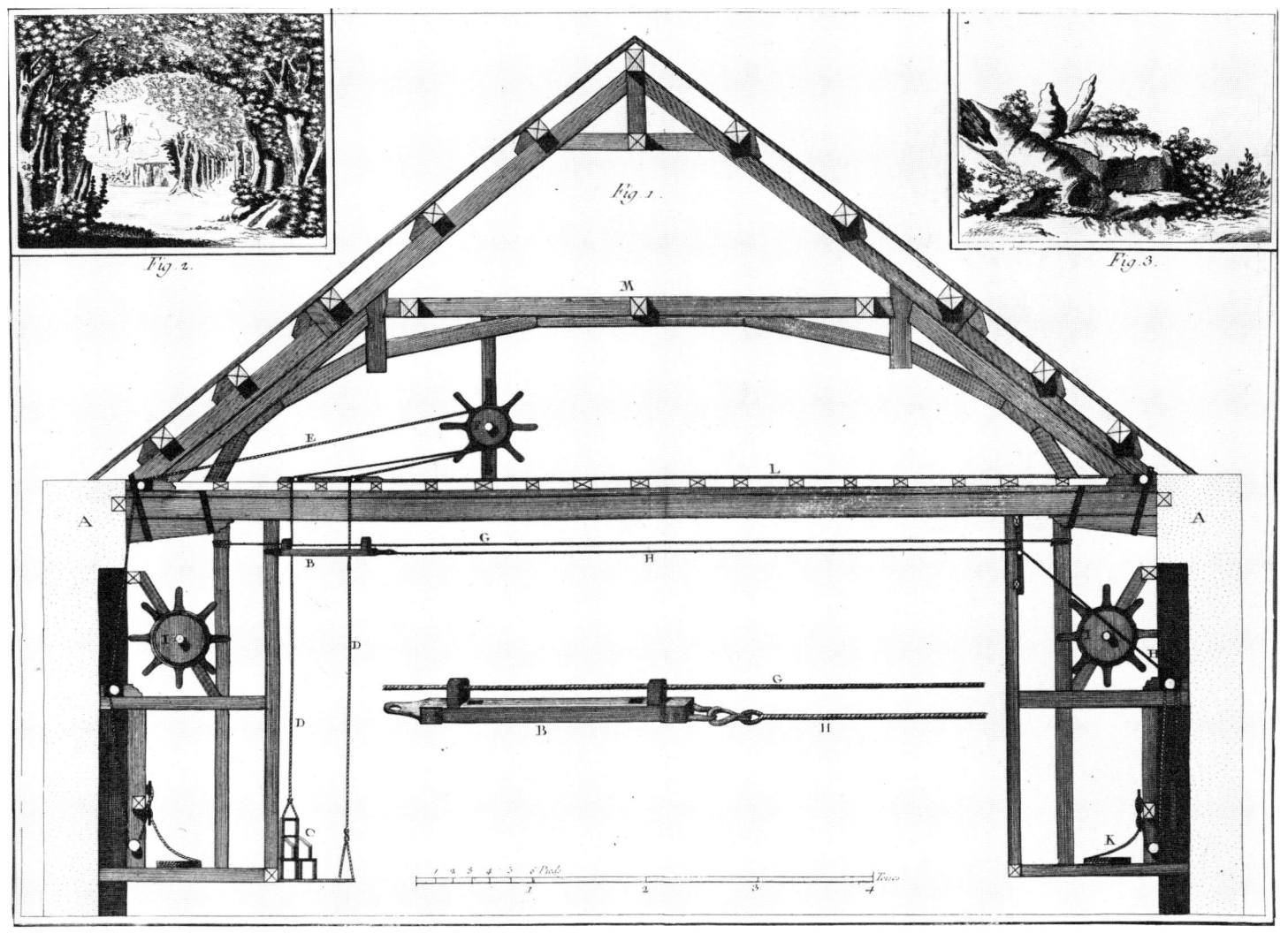

Design for Ballet

Colour 1 Design for a ballet costume, *c*. 1600. This costume may have been used either in Florence or in France, but it is probably Italian in origin as it bears a very close resemblance to those designed for the Florentine *intermezzi*.

42 Two etchings after W. Writs. Above, a scene from *Dido's Death* in the survey *Atlas: van de Stad Amsterdam* (1775, after Writs, 1771): below, a scene from *Phaeton* engraved by S. Fokke (1777, after Writs, 1760).

Design for Ballet

machinery which allows Mercury to appear in the upper illustration and Phaeton to fall from his chariot while being menaced by Jupiter on his eagle in the lower, is very clear. Ropes and pulleys are used with equal ingenuity, whether to fly a single figure or to produce a complicated aerial disaster. The row of tents, like the wooded scene and rocky wings, were long-established conventions of theatrical design by this time. In his valuable *World Theatre: an illustrated history* (London, 1968), Bamber Gascoigne analyses a series of Dutch prints, of which these are two, and shows how an eighteenth-century theatre put setting to a variety of uses. He suggests how, by the dropping in of backcloths and by an adaptation of the wings, a new setting could be devised.

The next major development in stage design came with the Neoclassical period. The return to the grander artistic imagery of antiquity was a reaction against the Rococo and what was felt to be its lightness and frivolity. Its aim was at its best a kind of noble purity and it led to an imitation of the antique which reflected the idealism of the philosophical inquiry which so strongly marked the second half of the eighteenth century. The work of David and Ingres typifies this in painting, while in the theatre designers like Sanquirico reflected this new look.

It was Alessandro Sanquirico (1777–1849) who best displayed the aspirations of Neoclassicism to show an ordered stage picture, and with the

43 One of the most extraordinary theatrical survivals is the little court theatre at Drottningholm, outside Stockholm. Built in 1766, the theatre had fallen into disuse during the nineteenth century and became totally neglected, serving as a painting store in the twentieth century. In 1921 a Danish scholar, researching for a picture, found the complete set of scenery, wings and backcloths, untouched, and the machinery in working order once its ropes had been refurbished. This accident of survival has preserved for us a court theatre of the mid-eighteenth century virtually intact. The illustration shows the theatre as it is today after it has been lovingly restored. The scene, with its draped wings and tenting, after the fashion of the Bibienas, and the backcloth of a military encampment, is immediately recognizable as a continuation of a style first established in the seventeenth century and which persisted unchanged for over a hundred years. Compare with plate 42.

Rococo, Neoclassical, Romantic

Above
44 J. Smit: the Palace of the Sun from a series of engravings which record the interior of the Schouwburg Theatre in Amersterdam, 1772. This final apotheosis of a ballet shows Apollo in his temple surrounded by the four elements of fire, water, air and light. The setting and the costumes are entirely conventional.

Right
45 Pietro Gonzaga (1751–1831): design for *Cinderella*, ballet with choreography by Ivan Valberkh and Auguste Poirot, music by Steibelt, first performed in Petersburg, 1807. Gonzaga was a most prolific decorator and designed more than 300 opera and ballet productions – the majority for the Imperial Theatres of Petersburg. His work reflects the continuing influence of the Italian perspective school of stage design of which he was one of the last and best exponents.

Design for Ballet

Colour 2 Design for the scene of The Birds from *Il Carnevale Languente*, court ballet produced by Count Philippe d'Aglié in Turin in 1647.

Rococo, Neoclassical, Romantic

Design for Ballet

46 Antonio de Pian (1784–1851): setting for Louis Duport's children's ballet *Cinderella* as revived in Vienna in 1817 with new music by Kinsky. Engraving by Norbert Bittner. Antonio de Pian came from Venice and made his career in Austria as a landscape painter and stage designer, producing sets for several Mozart operas in the years following the composer's death. For *Cinderella*, which was performed by no fewer than 176 young dancers, members of the Kinderballett, he devised a piece of heavily draped Neoclassicism.

building of the Teatro alla Scala in 1778 by Giuseppe Piermarini, one of the greatest of the Italian Neoclassical architects, Milan was to become the focal point of this new ideal. Sanquirico's work with the choreographer Salvatore Viganò, represents the finest examples of neoclassical ballet. Viganò's themes, heroic and grandiose – in such works as *I Titani* or *La Vestale* – were elaborate mimed spectacles where dance took a second place to massive theatrical effects which were framed by the tremendous creations of Sanquirico.

In his life of Rossini, published in 1824, Stendhal gives us a very clear picture of the decorative traditions at La Scala:

> Each scene of the opera and each scene of the ballets is set in a fresh décor; and there are invariably a great many scenes, since the author relies to some extent upon the audience's appreciation of new and original sets to ensure the success of his work as a whole. No set is ever used for two distinct spectacles; if the opera or ballet should

Rococo, Neoclassical, Romantic

47 Alessandro Sanquirico: design for a seaport in Meyerbeer's opera *The Crusader in Egypt* as staged at the Teatro alla Scala, Milan, 1826. The statutory ballet sequence in this opera is set amid the magnificence of Sanquirico's harbour scene. The action seems framed beneath the huge Islamic arch and the Bibiena style of diagonal perspective is still cleverly preserved.

prove a failure, the set, which may have been magnificent, is nevertheless ruthlessly painted out on the following day, even if it has only been seen at one single performance; for the same flats are used over and over again for new scenes. All the scenery is painted with size-paint, and the set as a whole is built up on principles which are utterly different from those which are in vogue in Paris today. In Paris, it is all tinselly glitter, everything is a filigree of pretty, witty arabesques, each enamelled in immaculate detail. But in Milan, everything is sacrificed to mass effects of form and colour, and to the *general impression*. It is David's own special genius transposed into the medium of décor. The result is that, sometimes, even the most frivolous sets seem to wear a strange and imposing dignity, which strikes the beholder immediately, and produces a strong impression of beauty.

(Stendhal, *Life of Rossini*, translated by Richard N. Coe, London, 1956)

Design for Ballet

Colour 3

Colour 5

Rococo, Neoclassical, Romantic

Colour 4

On pages 72 and 73
Colour 3 Louis Boquet: costume designs for *Orpheus and Eurydice*, ballet with choreography by Jean-Georges Noverre, music by Deller, first performed in Stuttgart in 1763.

Colour 4 Alessandro Sanquirico: setting for a scene inside a greenhouse from the ballet *Elerz e Zulmida* staged at the Teatro alla Scala, Milan, 1826. At this period the vogue for conservatories was spreading throughout Europe and Sanquirico's design is a magnificent fantasy upon a conservatory.

Colour 5 On 27 January 1821 a gala performance was given at the royal palace in Berlin in honour of the visit of the Grand Duke Nicholas and the Grand Duchess Alexandra Feodorovna of Russia. The production, which combined song and dance, was based upon Thomas Moore's *Lalla Rookh* and its performers – actors, singers, dancers – were members of the Prussian court. The illustration by August Klöber (1793–1864) shows the march from the divertissement as it was recorded for a souvenir album.

Rococo, Neoclassical, Romantic

Anyone wishing to understand the full splendour of Milanese design in the early years of the nineteenth century is referred to the *Raccolto di Scene Teatrali eseguite o disegnate d'al piu celebri Pittori Scenici in Milano*, a collection of 194 settings edited by Stanislas Stucchi and published in 1830. These include no fewer than 117 settings by Sanquirico, 20 by Paolo Landriani and several by Pasquale Canna.

Landriani (1755–1839) was a theatre architect and stage designer whose pupils included Sanquirico and Giovanni Perego, and his *Osservazioni sui difetti proditti nei teatri dalla cattiva costruzione del palco scenico* (Milan, 1815) gives valuable insight into the design attitudes of the time. Canna's designs were to be seen both at the Scala and at the Teatro San Carlo in Naples.

Parallel with Neoclassicism was the emergence of another artistic movement which was in fact to supersede the neoclassical ideal. This was Romanticism. Although both Sanquirico and Canna worked chiefly in the Neoclassical tradition, its rigour is frequently softened by the influence of the Romantic movement. This is particularly evident in Sanquirico's stagings for *Chao-Kiang* (plate 48), and Canna's beautiful recreation of a ruined temple in his design for *Seguaci di Bacco* (plate 50), which may owe something to Piranesi.

Romanticism pervades the work of Lorenzo Sacchetti (1759–1834). Sacchetti was born in Padua but it was in Venice that he first worked most successfully in the theatre for a period of ten years. In 1794 Viganò invited him to go to Vienna where he worked initially as an assistant to the chief designer Josef Platzer at the Hoftheater before becoming designer to the court. The design illustrated in plate 51 is a good example of the style of the Romantic school of theatre design. Gone are the rigid perspectives and formal ordering of the scene; instead there is a gentle naturalism. In this Sacchetti reflects the ideals of his one-time master Platzer, who believed in the importance of theatrical lighting in establishing atmosphere and in a greater naturalism in representation.

The roots of both Neoclassicism and Romanticism are to be found in the eighteenth century. The noble simplicity and grand calmness that were among the chief ideals of Neoclassicism were to reach their culmination during the years of Napoleon. But these ideals, in themselves a revolt against the rigid forms of the eighteenth century, were to find an equally rebellious image in Romanticism which propounded completely different concepts from those of Neoclassicism. The revolt against reason, which was one of the germs of romanticism, can be traced back to several artists of the eighteenth century, to Walpole and to Piranesi, but for ballet the change was to come very late.

At the centre of the European ballet tradition lies the Paris Opéra. Thanks to the intervention of Marie Antoinette, Noverre had been appointed as director of the ballet at the theatre, but his tenure of office was to be brief and the great changes in ballet which might have been anticipated from a lengthy directorate by this master of the *ballet d'action* did not take place. He was succeeded in 1781 by Maximilien Gardel as ballet master. This elder of two brothers had a modest talent which he used to produce a type of ballet pantomime which the public found perfectly agreeable. His sudden death in 1787 brought his younger brother Pierre to power and this remarkable man was to stay there for the next forty years. Through Ancien Régime, Revolution, Directorate, Empire and Restoration, Pierre Gardel remained unshaken in his position, and the works which he produced perpetuated the

48 Alessandro Sanquirico: design for *Chao-Kiang*. Louis Henry (1784–1836) created over one hundred ballets during his career, working in both France and Italy. His *Chao-Kiang* was first performed in Naples in 1820 and it was for an Italian staging that Sanquirico produced this remarkable mountain scene.

On pages 76 and 77
Colour 6 Design by Ciceri after Daguerre for *Aladin ou la Lampe Merveilleuse*, opera by Isouard first performed at the Paris Opéra, 6 February 1822.

Design for Ballet

Rococo, Neoclassical, Romantic

Opposite
49 a, b *Chao-Kiang* as staged in a pirated version in Petersburg in 1832. These illustrations show the charming way in which conventional scenes in the theatre – the palace set, the harbour set – have been adapted to a Chinese theme. In both scenes the perspective traditions of the eighteenth century can be seen breaking down into a more naturalistic style.

Above
50 Pasquale Canna: a scene from the ballet *Seguaci di Bacco* as staged at the Teatro San Carlo in Naples, *c.* 1800.

Right
51 Lorenzo Sacchetti: design for the first act of *Il Diavolo Innamorato in Ispagnia*, *c.* 1800.

Rococo, Neoclassical, Romantic

Colour 7 An engraving by A. E. Chalon of Marie Taglioni as *La Sylphide*. Chalon's portraits of Marie Taglioni are among the most touching and delightful testimonies we have to the greatness of this dancer and to the new image of the Romantic ballerina.

Right
52 Thomas Bruun (1742–1800): drawing showing a ballet by Vincenzo Galeotti at the Royal Theatre, Copenhagen. Thomas Bruun's drawing, which is an expression of the stage picture rather than an actual design, conveys something of both the increasing naturalism of stage scenery towards the end of the eighteenth century – though there is still the use of machines to allow Mercury to appear in the clouds above the stage – and the persistence of the hooped skirt and the tonnelet.

Below
53 Louis Chipart (1764–1825): design for Galeotti's ballet *Lagertha*, staged at the Royal Theatre in Copenhagen in 1801. Chipart, who was employed as a stage artist after Thomas Bruun's death, here provides a charming evocation of northern scenery in which the Romantic view of nature is already beginning to appear.

Design for Ballet

conservative elements in ballet. It was only in 1820 when the younger Jean Aumer was invited to produce ballets at the Opéra that there was any real indication of innovation. Even then Romanticism, which was by now causing such a fever in the other arts in France, as witnessed in the paintings of Géricault or the writings of Lamartine and Hugo, and which had already exerted some influence on stage design in Italy and Austria, had yet to reach the ballet at the Paris Opéra. With the vast change in fashion in dress brought about by the Revolution, the huge panniers and tonnelets had given place to the simplicity and purity of the Empire line, and this gradually softened into the styles of the 1820s. At the same time the work of such decorators as Pierre Ciceri (1782–1868) revealed the new concepts of Romantic design. But it was only with the arrival of Marie Taglioni as a dancer, and with her prodigious

54 Marie Taglioni in *La Bayadère*. In the summer of 1831, before her triumph the next year in *La Sylphide*, Taglioni appeared in London in *La Bayadère*, a ballet by Deshayes adapted from Auber's opera-ballet *Le Dieu et la Bayadère*. The fuller skirts of this costume are an indication of the fashion to come from the Romantic ballerina; the Indian local colour is supplied by the jewels worn in her hair and the sari-like scarf, but little else.

55 Pierre Luc-Charles Ciceri: design for *La Sylphide*, first performed at the Paris Opéra, 1832. Ciceri's design for the second act, a forest glade, is a beautifully atmospheric setting in which Marie Taglioni as the sylphide could drift and float. It is notable also for its clever suggestion of sunlight and deep shade.

success in *La Sylphide* in 1832 that Romanticism came to the ballet stage and took command. It was of its first performance that Gautier made his celebrated observation:

> The twelve marble and gold houses of the Olympians were relegated to the dust of the storehouse and only the Romantic forests and valleys lit by the charming German moonlight of Heinrich Heine's ballads exist . . . Pink tights always remained pink, without tights there is no dance, but now the Greek sandal gives place to the satin shoe. This new style brought a great abuse of white gauze, of tulle and tarlatans and shadows melted into mist through transparent dresses. White was almost the only colour used.

Chalon's engravings of Taglioni (colour plate 6) illustrate the costuming which was to become before long almost a uniform for the goddesses of the Romantic age, the close-fitting bodice leading into the billowing tarlatans of the skirt, the flowery crown and corsage and the pearls both as necklace and bracelets.

Design for Ballet

The design for *La Sylphide* was produced by Ciceri, the first great master of Romantic stage design in France. He worked not only for the Opéra where he was decorator in chief but also for the Comédie Française, the Odéon and several other smaller theatres. His first designs for the Paris Opéra date from 1815 when he decorated Didelot's version of *Flore et Zéphire* (plate 56). This ballet is in itself a work of theatrical importance since when first staged in London in 1796 at the King's Theatre it created a sensation by its flying effects. The dancers were travelled on wires, not as the descending deities of the eighteenth-century ballet but as figures in whom flight was yet another aspect of their dancing. It is, in an odd way, a precursor of the Romantic ideal of the aerial dance which was to crystallize in the appearance of Taglioni in *La Sylphide* thirty-six years later.

In 1822 Ciceri was responsible for the realization of Daguerre's designs for the fairy opera *Aladin ou La Lampe Merveilleuse* (plates 57, 58, colour plate 6).

Left
56 This early print – dating from the late 1820s – shows Fanny Elssler in a version of Didelot's *Flore et Zéphire*, which was first performed in London in 1796 but which persisted in various versions into the heyday of Romanticism. Elssler's costume here is clearly a transitional one: it shows the way in which pre-Romantic dress retained the basic Empire outline until the emergence of Taglioni in her sylphide costume in 1832.

Opposite above
57 Pierre Luc-Charles Ciceri: scene from the second act of *Aladin ou la Lampe Merveilleuse*, opera by Isouard, first performed at the Paris Opéra, 6 February 1822.

Opposite below
58 Costume for Monsieur Montjoie in the first ballet scene of *Aladin*. The Neoclassical tunic for male dancers was a direct reflection of the aesthetics of the 1820s but considerable elaboration was used to denote character and nationality. This beautiful design is for a *danseur noble* and suggests a Persian character (though the absence of shoes indicates that it is more representative of the design than of the interpreter). The use of jewels in Oriental costuming dates back to the splendours of the *ballet de cour* and it persists right through to the work of Léon Bakst for the Diaghilev staging of *Schéhérazade*.

The introduction of gas lighting for the first time on the Opéra stage with *Aladin* revolutionized the stage picture. As Gautier observed, 'The age of purely visual spectacles has arrived.'

Until this time it was not usual at the Paris Opéra to lower the curtain between the acts of a ballet or opera, and so scenery was constructed on the principle that it should be easily manipulated. Also, most of the traditional design attitudes of the eighteenth century still obtained even down to the skilled used of perspective. With the decision that the curtain or a drop-cloth should descend between the acts, there came the possibility of more elaborate, naturalistic setting and it was Ciceri who developed this trend (his décors for Auber's opera *Gustave III*, in which one scene shows three gibbets in a stormy landscape, is an extraordinary piece of naturalistic design). One of Ciceri's outstanding achievements came in 1831 with the staging of Meyerbeer's *Robert the Devil*. This work marks the beginning of the five-year directorate of Dr Véron at the Paris Opéra. Véron, extremely canny in manipulating public opinion, and a man whose tenure at the Opéra was to find the theatre more financially successful than it had been in many years, allowed Ciceri an unlimited budget for his work on the opera, and the celebrated ballet scene in the cloisters was reported to have cost nearly fifty thousand francs. The innovation of gas lighting was now to achieve an added justification: it could reproduce the moonlight which was to be so vital an ingredient of the Romantic ballet.

Design for Ballet

The Romantic period in dance brought an uneven and highly dispersed era in ballet production, and hence in design. For a period of twenty years between 1830 and 1850 the ballet flourished in Paris and London; at the same time the great Bournonville tradition was being established in Copenhagen. (August Bournonville assumed the direction of the Royal Danish Ballet in 1830. At the time of his retirement in 1877 he had created a repertory and a dance style which have sustained the company ever since.) In Imperial Russia ballet started on an upward path which was to lead to Russian ballet's being the sole and magnificent representative of the art at the end of the century.

The favoured themes of Romanticism in ballet were those of mystery and exoticism. The moonlit cloister scene in *Robert the Devil* was the precursor of the first unequivocally Romantic ballet, *La Sylphide* of 1832. From this moment on the light and imponderable figure of Marie Taglioni was a central image of the theatre; her great rival Fanny Elssler reflected the other key aspect of the Romantic woman, the warm and voluptuous 'Spanish' beauty. The Romantic audience's appetite was for the strange and distant – whether in time or place – and the ballets and their settings all capitalized upon this fact. A

59 Nikolay Fydorov: design for L. Maurer's ballet *The Shade*, produced in Petersburg in 1839. This palace setting looks back to the Bibiena style and it shows no trace of the Romantic ideas so common now throughout the rest of Europe.

Rococo, Neoclassical, Romantic

whole catalogue of mysterious heroines, of ghosts and sprites, of gypsies and *bayadères*, now took the stage. The Romantic ballerina, who totally dominated the ballet, was called upon to appear in an extraordinary number of unusual, nationalist guises: but national flavour, be it Bulgarian, Neapolitan or Scottish, was only applied as a decorative addition to the conventional dress by means of embroidered and decorated jackets, jaunty caps and dainty little boots.

The design for such spectacles was able, in the first flush of the Romantic movement, to match the fervour and delight of the ballet's themes. The decoration for *Lalla Rookh* (plate 65), a ballet by Jules Perrot, greatest

60 Mademoiselle Hullin as a bacchante in *Alcide*, a ballet by Deshayes and Albert staged at the King's Theatre, London, in 1821 on the occasion of the coronation of King George IV. The simple Neoclassical line reflects Regency taste but the character of the role is suggested by the leopard-skin and by the dressing of the hair with vine leaves and grapes. Compare with plate 39, Boquet's design for Mlle Allard as a *bacchante*.

Design for Ballet

choreographer of the Romantic period, is a typical flight of fancy. Inspired by Thomas Moore's poem, the ballet described the heroine's journey to Kashmir. *The Times* commented:

> ... it is a splendid spectacle ... The representations of the Oriental courts, the splendour and variety of the costumes, the taste and invention displayed in the novel groupings can hardly be surpassed. The first scene, especially, with Aurungzebe seated on the throne in the form of a peacock's tail, while over his head is a canopy brought forward in bold relief, and his numerous attendants are gathered before him, presents a picture of the most gorgeous magnificence ... The *pas symbolique* of Hindoo girls may be pronounced one of the most elegant scarf dances ever yet contrived, and shows what new combinations are possible in a style apparently so hackneyed. The last figure in this *pas*, in which Cerrito stands as a statue on a pedestal and the girls with pink scarves form a series of steps, is entirely novel in its effect and admirably conceived.

In Copenhagen, where Romanticism was tempered by Bournonville's practical nature, and his concern for a more 'truthful' form of ballet (in which the male dancer remained the equal partner of the ballerina), design was more

Above left
61 Augusta Nielsen in *La Lithuanienne*, a solo created in 1845.

Above right
62 Lise Noblet in the role of Fenella in Auber's opera *La Muette de Portici* in 1828. Lithograph by Lemercier from a drawing by Achille Deveria.

Opposite
63 Amalia Galster, a Berlin dancer who married Paul Taglioni, brother of Marie. Although the addition of flowers, lace, brooches, bangles gives some variety to the costume, this example of a ballerina's dress at the height of the Romantic movement shows how predictable much of the costuming had become for the *danseuse*.

Rococo, Neoclassical, Romantic

Design for Ballet

90

64 Engraving by Andreas Geiger after Schöller showing a setting for Bernardo Vestris's revival of Filippo Taglioni's ballet *The Revolt in the Seraglio* in Vienna, 1839.

Design for Ballet

Rococo, Neoclassical, Romantic

literal. Bournonville was a great choreographer but part of his importance lies in his ability to act as a camera, visiting Spain, Italy, Russia and London and bringing back impressions from his travels which he then translated into ballet. The setting for these ballets often called for very straightforward representation in design: the emergence of dance incident from a completely realistic setting today provides some of their charm. In his historical works, an important aspect of his *œuvre*, Bournonville again asked for literal designing.

By the middle of the century, although new ballets were still being staged throughout Europe, the art was declining towards that ritual of unthinking performance and unenterprising presentation which was to bring dancing into such disrepute by the end of the century. It is dangerous to generalize, but it cannot be denied that any survey of the nineteenth century's dance design will more often than not provide an uninteresting picture. The great days in which distinguished theatrical artists found opportunities for innovation and splendid display were gone. The bourgeois theatre of the nineteenth century was often to view ballet as a feeble dependant upon opera.

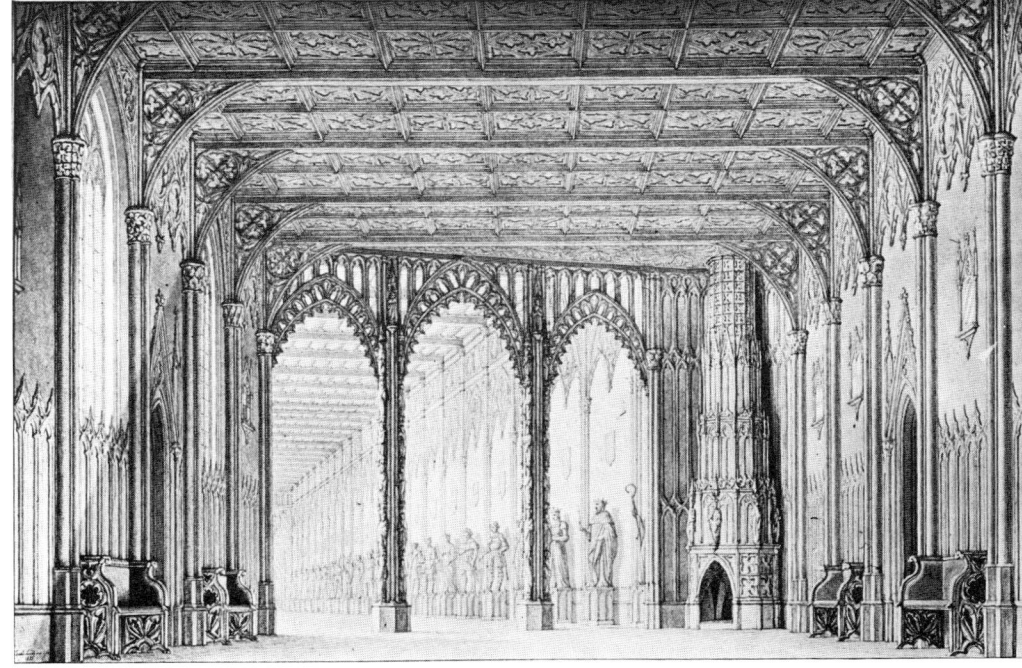

Opposite
65 Charles Marshall (1806–90): design for the *pas symbolique* of Jules Perrot's ballet *Lalla Rookh*, first performed at Her Majesty's Theatre, London, on 11 June 1846. Engraving from the *Illustrated London News*.

Above
66 Troels Lund (1802–67): sketch for *Valdemar*, ballet by August Bournonville, depicting the Knights' Hall at the castle of Roskilde. This is a fine example of the revival of interest in Gothic architecture which is here combined with a use of the *scena per angolo*.

Design for Ballet

Because ballet in the nineteenth century was to find its permanent home in the opera house, the design attitudes which were to frame it were those dictated by the traditions of opera itself. Ciceri's often brilliant decorative ideas, the example of Neoclassical grandeur provided by Sanquirico and his school, were to yield to an increasingly laboured Romantic fantasy which would in time decline into routine. By the end of the century the Italian ballet stage was almost entirely occupied by such wildly complicated spectacles as *Sieba* (1876), *Excelsior* (1881), *Amor* (1886) and *Sport* (1897). Most were based on topical themes and relied upon massive stage effects – including the appearance of elephants. *Excelsior* celebrated the triumphs of science and featured scenes in the 'Palace of Telegraphy' in Washington; the desert; the Suez Canal and the Mont Cenis tunnel. The scene illustrated in plate 70 shows a square in Washington in which Obscurantism is defeated by the light of Electricity. The dogged bad taste of the entire affair is all too typical of the period and is equally well illustrated by Anton Brioschi's design for a ballet at

Above
67 Drawing by Antoni Zaleski, lithographed by P. Gavarni in Petersburg, 1852, for *Cracow Wedding*, the most celebrated of all Polish ballets. This type of genre ballet offered a far more literal view of stage costuming; the men's dress in particular seemed remarkably naturalistic.

Opposite
68 A page of photographs of typical costumes of the mid-nineteenth century from *Den Danske Ballets Histoire* by Elith Reumert, Copenhagen, 1922. Although the two girls' costumes now seem dated and improbable and both their ballets have long since disappeared from the repertory, the men's costumes have not altered radically and their ballets have remained in regular performance. Indeed, Gennaro's costume in *Napoli* is almost sacred and has been retained unaltered since the first performance in 1846.

Valdemar Price som Junker Ove i „Et Folkesagn"

Valdemar Price i „Napoli"

Daniel Krum i „La Ventana"

Marie Westberg i „Valkyrien"

Anna Tychsen i „Aditi"

Dekoration tegnet af C.F. Christensen til
Førsteopførelsen af "Fjernt fra Danmark"
20 April 1860.

Opposite
69 a, b Christian Ferdinand Christensen (1805–83): décor for *Far from Denmark*, ballet by August Bournonville, first performed on 20 April 1860. Part of the action is a ball set on a Danish frigate in Buenos Aires harbour, and Christensen's design is a literal re-creation of the deck of a ship. (b) shows how in 1945 the set for this scene had been scrupulously preserved: a tribute to the original design.

Above
70 *Excelsior*, a ballet by Luigi Manzotti first performed at La Scala, Milan, 1881: the Electricity quadrille from a 1910 staging at La Scala.

Left
71 Anton Brioschi (b. 1855): design for a ballet at the Vienna Hofoper, 1899. This is a prime example of ballet in its appalling decadence at the end of the nineteenth century.

Below
72 C. Wilhelm: costume design for *High Jinks*, first produced at the Empire Theatre, Leicester Square, London, 1904. This illustration is for a standard bearer and is obviously intended for a pretty girl.

the Vienna Hofoper (plate 71) with its false palm trees, gasoliers, girandoles, pendant lights and girls dressed as sunflowers. In France, too, improbability and a quite obvious sexual allure were what was required by the audience – and given to them. The male dancer had disappeared, to be replaced by the well-corseted charmers of the *corps de ballet*. A similar state of affairs in London was somewhat alleviated by the talent of C. Wilhelm, the principal designer at the Empire, who excelled particularly in the provision of fantastic costumes (plates 72, 73), 'ballet' for the London audience having come to mean the lightweight if charming entertainments to be found at the Empire and the Alhambra and other music halls.

The other side of the Romantic coin was turgid literalism, a debasing of the authenticity of setting sought by such choreographers as Bournonville, Saint-Léon and Petipa for their geographically exotic or historically remote themes. Carefully researched historical design, lacking any imagination, was to prove stultifying in the extreme. The tradition of literal representation, of designs created according to formula in the workshops of an opera house rather than involving exceptional decorators in their own right, was finally to bring ballet design to a low ebb.

Our illustrations, albeit they seek to be representative, are dictated by the material that survives, and it is noticeable that the charm and imaginative spirit of the Romantic decoration soon gives way to a perpetuation of these accepted ideas with no attempt at novelty. This reflects exactly the image of ballet in the public mind: a pretty and often mindless spectacle in which attractive (and all too available) young women could be admired and in which thought, dramatic tension, or any nobility of ideals were sadly lacking. For an unthinking art there was an unthinking decoration. The ritualization of the ballerina's appearance is but one example of this: her *persona* on the stage was not that of the role she played but the more permanent and easily recognizable figure of the ballerina as star dancer, corsetted, bejewelled and typecast in the

Opposite
73 Adeline Genée in *The Pretty Prentice* at the London Coliseum, 1916. In his biography of Adeline Genée (London, 1958), Ivor Guest describes the costume as being of 'many-coloured silk, the skirt, composed of panels resembling large feathers outlined in silver, being worn over black and silver trousers. The bodice which glittered with sequins of every colour, had a snake like effect, and the fantastic feathered head-dress might have been designed for Gaby Deslys.'

Rococo, Neoclassical, Romantic

74 a, b Two engravings from contemporary Petersburg journals showing the designs for Act I and Act V of Petipa's ballet *La Bayadère*, first produced at the Bolshoy Theatre, Petersburg, 1877. The story of *La Bayadère* was set in India and the illustrations show the type of elaborate, literal settings which were so common in ballet during the latter part of the nineteenth century. Neither décor has much theatrical merit beyond establishing a locale against which an exciting dramatic ballet took place, but it is only fair to note that the design for the (now suppressed) fifth act, in which a temple was destroyed by a thunderstorm and very satisfactorily crushed everyone beneath it, shows how such *coups de théâtre* were an often necessary part of the ballets of the time. The storm and shipwreck in *Le Corsaire* is another famous example of the use of stage machinery at this period.

75 Mathilde Felixovna Kshessinskaya, *prima ballerina assoluta* of the Imperial Russian Ballet in Petersburg. Her costume reflects both the opulence and the stereotyping of the ballerina's image at the turn of the twentieth century.

gradually shortening tarlatans, pink tights and satin point shoes. Just as Camargo had shortened her skirts in the eighteenth century, so in the 1880s and 1890s the Italian ballerina Virginia Zucchi and her successors, in order to show off such newly mastered feats of virtuosity as intricate pointe work and multiple turns, abbreviated the Romantic tarlatans to the knee-length tutu. This became standard dress for the ballerina roles for the next three decades. Even in Imperial Russia, where at least the ballet was under the direct supervision of a great master, Marius Petipa, this institutionalization of the art and of the ballerina was almost as commonplace as in the moribund opera houses of Western Europe. The petal-cut bodice and gold fish-scales on the skirt of Kshessinskaya's costume illustrated in plate 75 represent as much as was allowed to identify the character to the audience. The jewels which Kshessinskaya is wearing are very remarkable. A woman of great beauty and charm, she had been loved by the Tsarevitch (later Nicholas II) and several Grand Dukes – hence the legend that they referred to her not as 'Mathilde' but as 'Notre-thilde' – and she mentions in her memoirs that if a stage head-dress was particularly becoming one or other of her admirers would 'have it copied by Fabergé' for subsequent performances. She is seen wearing a fair part of a king's ransom in diamonds and it was expected of the ballerina to appear on stage heavily jewelled if the role offered the least excuse for it – and if she could muster the requisite pieces.

Design for Ballet

Left
76 Julia Siedova in the title role of Petipa's ballet *Pharaoh's Daughter*, as staged at the Maryinsky Theatre, Petersburg, c. 1900. The head-dress and decoration on the tutu were all the concessions the wardrobe was required to make towards suggesting historical accuracy or local colour.

Opposite
77 Anna Pavlova as the heroine and Mikhail Mordkin as the hero (Lord Wilson) in *Pharaoh's Daughter* as staged at the Bolshoy Theatre, Moscow, 1905. Mordkin's costume is naturalistic to a degree – the character is that of an English milord travelling in Egypt during the middle of the nineteenth century who is transported back in time to the Egypt of the Pharaohs. Pavlova, as the Egyptian heroine, is allowed to proclaim her identity in head-dress and in the Egyptian motif that is applied to the front of her tutu. Beyond that she remains quintessentially a ballerina.

Rococo, Neoclassical, Romantic

Design for Ballet

Above
78 David: design for the setting of Act II, scene I of *King Candaules*, ballet by Marius Petipa first produced at the Bolshoy Theatre, Petersburg, 1868. Act II of this ballet, a mythological work about the King of Lydia, took place in an arena with a triumphal arch. Cyril Beaumont records that in the background of the setting there was a statue of Venus Victrix and tiers of seats on either side.

Left
79 Members of the Bolshoy Ballet, Moscow, in Gorsky's ballet *Gudule's Daughter*, inspired by Victor Hugo's *Notre Dame de Paris* (which had earlier been the source for Perrot's *Esmeralda*). Designed by Konstantin Korovin, the work was first performed in 1902 as a mimo-drama with dances. The elaborate naturalism of the costuming for the mime scene shown here illustrates again the points made by Fokine.

Rococo, Neoclassical, Romantic

80 a, b (a) Alfred Bekeffi in the Indian dance from Petipa's *Bluebeard*, Petersburg, 1896. Bekeffi, one of the most distinguished character dancers of the Imperial Ballet, is seen here in a very acceptable evocation of Indian costume. But, as the photograph of Nicholas Legat (b) in *Raymonda* shows, the *premier danseur noble* had to appear in conventional ballet dress.

Mikhail Fokine, one of the greatest innovators in choreography of the twentieth century, records his disgust with the decorative routines of the Imperial Ballet in Petersburg, when he joined it at the beginning of this century, and his comments reflect a long-established tradition.

In his *Memoirs of a Ballet Master* (New York, 1961) he speaks of:

> the tasteless and anachronistic forms. I recall (Pavel) Gerdt in *King Candaules*. After pushing the statue of Venus off its pedestal in the temple, he would place his sweetheart on it instead, and she would assume the position of the goddess, but – in a short ballet *tutu*! Everything – the costumes of the ballerina, the appeal to the audience, the continuous interruption of the action – led me to conclude that the ballet lacked its most essential element: presentation to the spectator of an artistically created image ... When I played a mime role, I represented an authentic image of the period. But when I danced a classic part, I portrayed a leading dancer – outside the confines of place or time, with marcelled hair, pink cheeks, and ballet

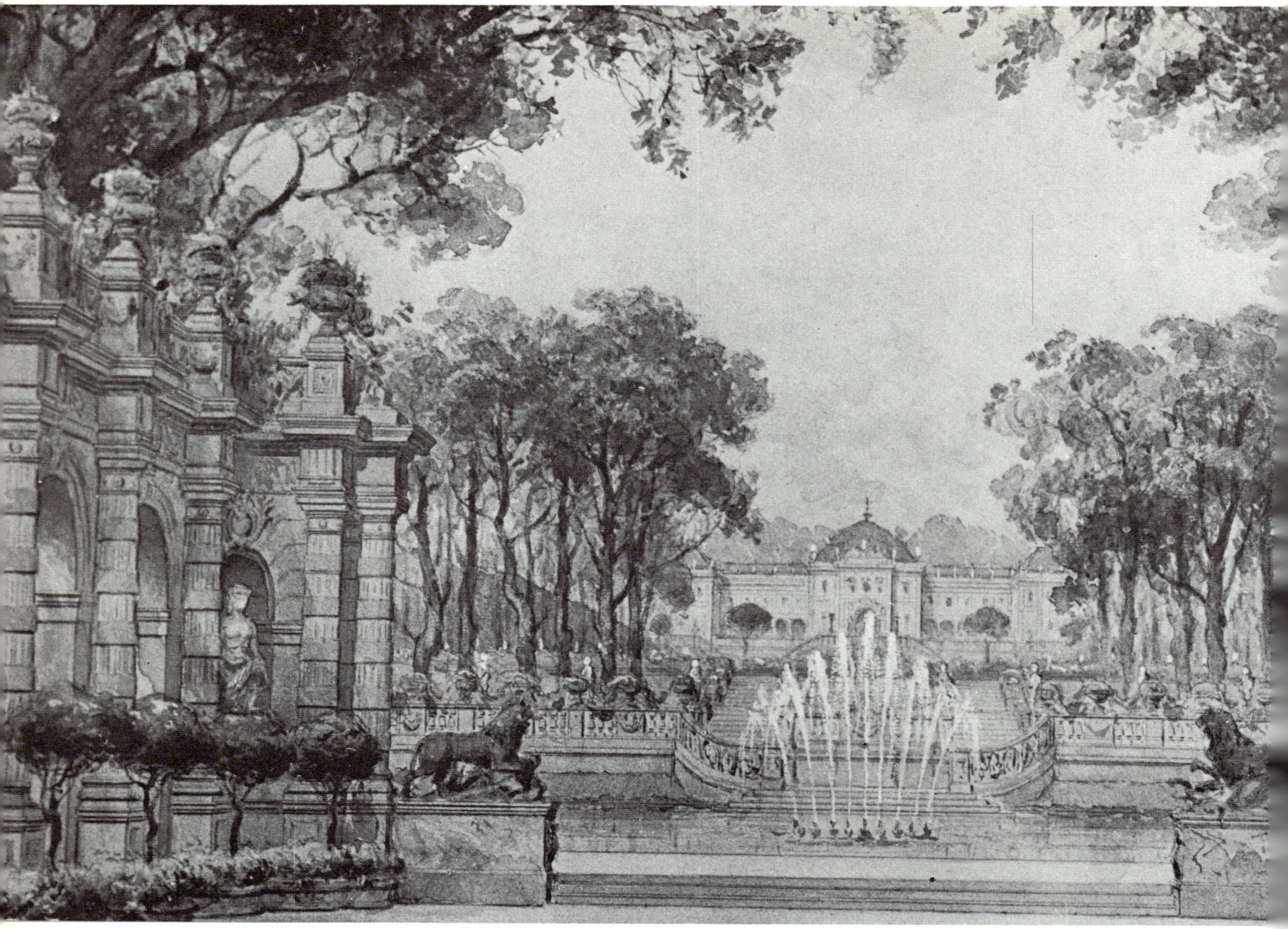

Апоѳеозъ
бал.
Спящей
Красавицы

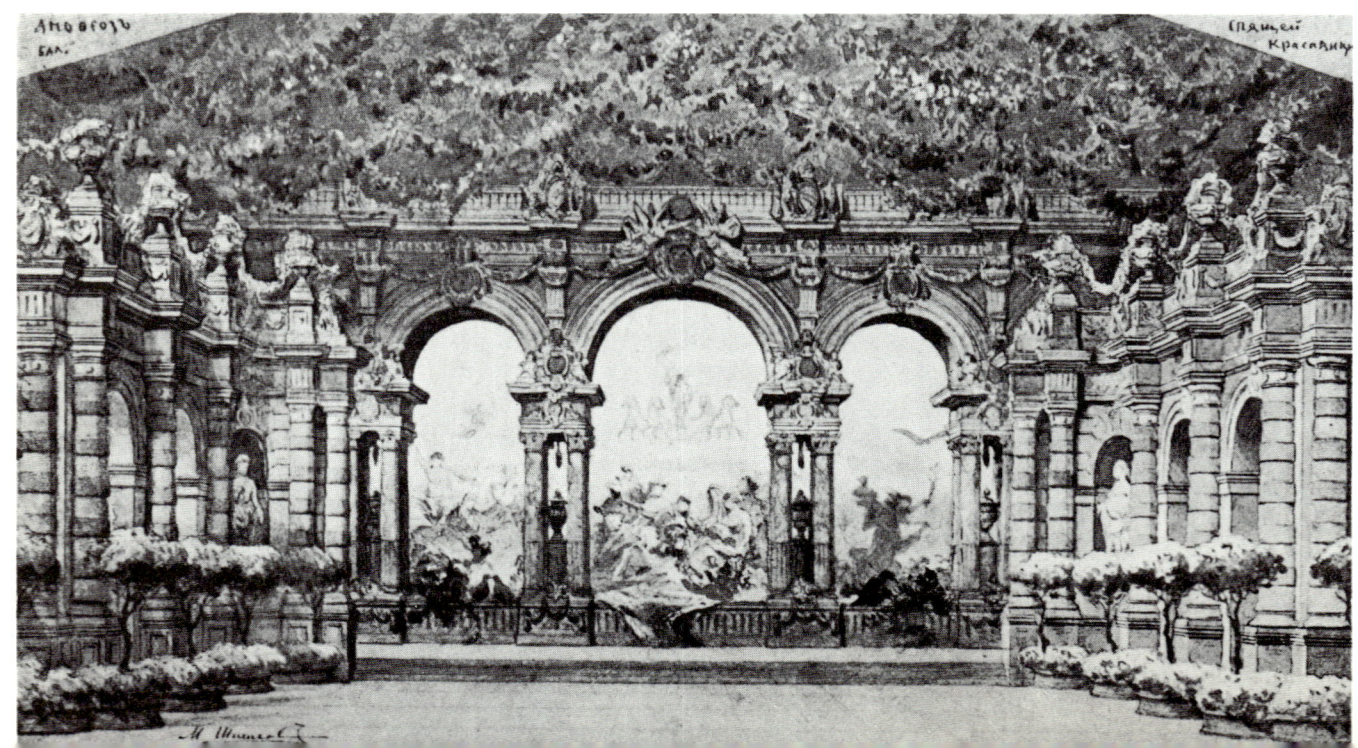

81 a, b M. Shishkov: two designs for *The Sleeping Beauty*, ballet with choreography by Petipa and music by Tchaikovsky first performed at the Maryinsky Theatre, Petersburg, 1890. (a) the garden scene for Act I; (b) the final scene.

tights. Sometimes in the very same role – such as that of Jean de Brienne in *Raymonda* – I appeared in the second act and in the beginning of the third as a Knight Crusader, attired in an historically correct costume, because there was no dancing in these scenes, only pantomime, sword play, rescue of a lady, and so on; but in the middle of the third act I removed my wig and hastily waved my hair into sheeplike curls, thus preparing myself for my forthcoming variation. As soon as the time for the dance approached, everything else lost its meaning. I felt that, the more historically authentic were the costumes of the mimes, of the performers of the character dances and of the supers, the more idiotic we, the classical dancers, must have appeared in the midst of them. On the same stage appeared ladies in long dresses with trains and with high ornaments on their heads side by side with dancers in pink tights and short skirts looking like open umbrellas.

However, it was in Russia that the noteworthy exception obtained, in the designs of M. A. Shishkov, who produced designs which managed to transcend both the rigid demands of the Imperial Ballet and the debased style of decoration of the time. His settings for *The Sleeping Beauty* – the costuming was the work of I. A. Vsevolozhsky, director of the Imperial Theatres and inspirer of the ballet – were far more stylish than might have been expected. *The Sleeping Beauty* was intended as a glorious evocation of the France of Louis XIV; Shishkov's first act (plate 81a) bears not a little resemblance to the vistas and architecture of Versailles. Expansive, elegant, it enhances this masterpiece of ballet. It is worth noting that the later work by Alexandre Benois for *Le Pavillon d'Armide* (plate 82) continues this felicitous Petersburg tradition of looking towards France for cultural inspiration. Shishkov's design for *Beauty's* last act (plate 81b) owes something to the Baroque traditions at the beginning of the eighteenth century; the backdrop behind the triple archway was required to show, as Petipa's production notes for the ballet indicate, an apotheosis in which Apollo was seen in a costume of Louis XIV's time. The implied homage to the Tsar was obvious and Shishkov's hint of a backcloth shows a heroic figure in a quadriga with, beneath it, some exuberant allegorical figures.

But despite such a magnificent exception, the general picture was bleak. The conventions of presenting dance to the audience were ossified: in the great opera houses the ballet looked moribund and emptily grandiloquent. In the popular theatre it was vulgar and of ill repute. The remarkable experiments in theatrical naturalism associated with the production of plays in the Saxe Meiningen court theatre during the 1870s, and the parallel work of Antoine in Paris – even the developments of the Moscow Arts Theatre – were not to make the least impact upon ballet stagings.

It was as a reaction against the stale traditionalism in opera decoration that the wealthy Muscovite merchant Savva Mamontov invited the easel painters whom he patronized to decorate operas. These he staged in his private opera house during the 1890s and his example was to be an initial inspiration for Diaghilev. And it is to Diaghilev that we are indebted for the rebirth of ballet and its design at the beginning of the twentieth century.

THE DIAGHILEV ERA

Although the rebirth of ballet in the West is very properly associated with the arrival of Serge Diaghilev and his troupe of Russian dancers in Paris in 1909, the seeds of the artistic renaissance linked to the Ballet Russe and to Diaghilev's aesthetic attitudes were sown during the preceding decades.

In his early years Diaghilev owed everything to his friends. The young provincial who arrived in Petersburg in 1890 at the age of eighteen was to fall on his feet thanks to the education which he received by joining the group of young intellectuals who surrounded his cousin Dima Filosofov. Their acknowledged leader was Alexandre Benois: Benois in turn was to introduce Léon Bakst into the group of 'Neva Pickwickians'. Armed with a new understanding of the arts and his own colossal charm and drive, Diaghilev found himself within a decade a markedly influential figure in the new wave of artistic endeavour that was sweeping through Russia.

But he was in no way an initiator at this time. For the most important developments in art and in stage design we must look away from Imperial Petersburg to wealthy bourgeois Moscow, and to the estate of the railway millionaire Savva Mamontov at Abramtsevo, outside Moscow.

Here, in the 1870s and 1880s, Mamontov surrounded himself with a colony of artists whom he supported in their rejection of the stale academic traditions which were typified by the work of the Petersburg Academy. Their movement had started in 1863 when a group of painters calling themselves the 'Wanderers' had begun to take itinerant exhibitions round the countryside. In their art they sought a revival of a national culture which would feed from the vital traditions of folk art and indigenous Russian painting. In the summer Mamontov's colony of artists discussed and painted at Abramtsevo, and in the winter in Mamontov's Moscow home there were amateur theatricals which made use of the painters to provide décor and costumes. From this developed private operatic productions for which Mamontov provided the funds while his artist friends provided stage designs. In his operatic enterprise, which had been made possible by an edict rescinding the monopoly of opera stagings held by the Imperial Theatres, Mamontov gave an extraordinary impetus to the Russian-ness of opera and its production. The artists who came under his patronage – men of the stature of Vasnetsov, Vrubel, and Korovin – were urged to look at stage design as an extension of their easel painting. Instead of the staid traditionalism of the 'official' operatic performances in the Imperial Theatres where the stage workrooms produced, like sausages from a machine, temples or gardens or forests, theatre décor was suddenly seen to be relevant in painterly terms to the work presented. Operas by Rimsky-Korsakov, Dargomizhsky, Mussorgsky and Borodin were receiving performances that they would otherwise have been denied, and the great Russian bass Fyodor Shalyapin was given his best and earliest chances in these productions.

Mamontov's operatic venture reflected the strong nationalistic feeling in Moscow at that time: his cousin Konstantin Stanislavsky was just starting his Art Theatre in Moscow – yet another example of the burgeoning interest in new forms of stage presentation. The Mamontov operas were important forerunners of the stage picture of the twentieth century: the debt owed to Diaghilev must in no small part be referred back to Mamontov whose example Diaghilev and his collaborators were to copy.

In his *Reminiscences of the Russian Ballet* (London, 1941) Alexandre Benois acknowledges this debt:

> In 1898 Mamontov's company paid a visit to St Petersburg and it was there that we all (I had just come from Paris for a short stay) were able to see for ourselves just how original and interesting was Korovin's treatment of scenic painting. I did not like everything; I thought the planning was rather poor at times, and there was a certain roughness in the technique – but these shortcomings would have been explained by the very modest means that the private enterprise had at its disposal. On the whole Korovin's décors amazed us by their daring approach to the problem and above all by their high *artistic* value – the very quality which was so often missing in the elaborate productions of the Imperial stage.

When in 1895 the young Diaghilev met Mamontov he found an immediate inspiration. Mamontov's patronage of new artists reflected Diaghilev's emerging awareness of a need to focus his energies upon art. The painters of the Mamontov circle were a starting point for his own desire to further the cause of the new art in Russia and this was to culminate, initially, in the foundation of a magazine, *The World of Art*, which appeared in 1898. It was a journal inspired by the intellectual energy of the Neva Pickwickians, and its financial backing was provided in part by Mamontov and in part by the Princess Tenisheva, another patron of Russian crafts. At the same time Diaghilev embarked upon the annual series of exhibitions which he organized in Petersburg, showing contemporary Western art to the Russian public and offering exhibition opportunities to the Mamontov group of painters. *The World of Art* itself became associated with the exhibitions which in due time showed such contrasting works as those of Arnold Böcklin, Louis Tiffany and James McNeill Whistler.

The World of Art as a magazine lasted until 1904 by which time it had acted as propagandist both for contemporary European art and for the new generation of Russian painters. Its influence was considerable and taken in conjunction with Mamontov's operatic performances it is small wonder that the Imperial Theatres were obliged to update their ideas of stage design.

In 1900 Diaghilev had been invited to work at the Maryinsky Theatre, Petersburg, as supervisor of a new production of the ballet *Sylvia* in which Benois and Bakst were both to be involved. The powerful conservative rearguard in the Theatre were able to abort the enterprise and Diaghilev was obliged to resign. (Shortly after, the Director of the Imperial Theatres himself, Prince Serge Volkonsky, was dismissed. Significantly, his successor Telyakovsky was a 'Moscow man' and it is to him that we owe the first introductions of painterly design into the Imperial Theatres.) For Diaghilev, the years up to 1905 were occupied with *The World of Art* and culminated in his great 1905 exhibition of Russian historical portraiture. This was a final

On previous page
A photograph showing the original production of *Soleil de Nuit* **(Leonid Massine seated right).**

gesture towards Russia; thereafter his energies seem devoted to the publicising of Russian arts in Western Europe. In 1906 he organized an exhibition of Russian art at the Grand Palais in Paris; in 1907 Paris heard a series of concerts of Russian music, which led in 1908 to a season of Russian opera at the Opéra.

In 1909, for what had been decided should be an annual event, Diaghilev proposed a combined opera and ballet season. That financial problems had to limit the operatic participation was unfortunate; happily the ballet was properly represented and it is from this 1909 season that we may date the birth of the Diaghilev company and Diaghilev's final and total commitment of himself to a single cause.

It is not our purpose here to rehash the twenty glorious years of the Diaghilev Ballet. Suffice it to say that it is entirely due to the Ballet Russe experience that the art of ballet in the West was awakened from the long sleep into which it had fallen. The example of Diaghilev, of his creative ideas, his constant quest for the new, his conviction that ballet was a major artistic force – and his revelation to the world that this was in fact so – have provided ideals that many later companies have failed to maintain. Today ballet companies around the world still feed off the fat of the Diaghilev repertory. There are few who have managed to achieve anything of comparable excellence. It must be stated, though, that Diaghilev's was an itinerant and ultimately rootless enterprise. The greater achievements of ballet in our time in the West have been those of the establishing of permanent national troupes – companies like the British Royal Ballet and the New York City Ballet. Although they were animated by creators associated with Diaghilev, the path those creators took was very different from that of Diaghilev: none the less, it was Diaghilev who set them on the path and who armed them with the skills which they were to use.

Diaghilev's ballet company did not exist as a permanent entity until 1911. Its first two seasons in 1909 and 1910 were nothing more than visits abroad by dancers of the Imperial Theatres organized and masterminded by Diaghilev. The Nijinsky scandal during the winter of 1910, when the dancer – beloved of Diaghilev – was dismissed by the Imperial Theatres for an infraction of the costume rules of the Maryinsky Theatre, impelled Diaghilev into the positive action of setting up a permanent company. This company would in effect continue the artistic achievements already made in the first two seasons in which major works of art had been created by the choreographer Mikhail Fokine and the designers employed by Diaghilev, notably Benois and Bakst, and a first major score, Stravinsky's *The Firebird*, had been commissioned.

From 1911 onwards the Ballet Russe was Diaghilev's company. The history of the company divides most conveniently into three periods: the first, an essentially Russian period up to 1914; the second, a time of transition and of extraordinary changes of fortune during the years of the First World War and the immediate post-war period up to the production of *The Sleeping Princess* in 1921; the third covers the final seven years of the troupe's existence and is dominated by the fact of a base in Monte Carlo, by the influence of French taste and fashion, but also by the need to try to live up to a reputation that had been so effortlessly won by Diaghilev in the pre-war years.

From his arrival in Petersburg in 1890 Diaghilev had had the good fortune to fall in with counsellors and friends who were both better educated and more cosmopolitan than he. His rise to eminence in the group is a tribute as much to the extraordinary psychic energy which Benois ascribes to him as to

The Diaghilev Era

82 Alexandre Benois: design for the second scene of *Le Pavillon d'Armide*, 1909. Originally staged at the Maryinsky Theatre, Petersburg, in 1907, *Le Pavillon d'Armide*, with choreography by Mikhail Fokine and score by Nikolay Cherepnin, was revived for the first Diaghilev Ballet Russe season in Paris in 1909 where it featured in the opening programme.

Design for Ballet

his developing awareness and his eagerness to impose himself upon the world. In all his enterprises from 1895 onwards – the exhibitions, *The World of Art*, and the Paris excursions that preceded the Ballet Russe's first appearance – Diaghilev acted 'in committee'. His chief guide was at first Alexandre Benois (1870–1960), to whose cosmopolitanism (he was of mixed French, German and Venetian blood and was essentially francophile) he owed so much, and whom he acknowledged as his artistic adviser. A no less important visual influence was Léon Bakst (1866–1924). Diaghilev had initiated *The World of Art* with Benois's assistance, and it is through their association with this magazine and the artistic movement that it represented that both Benois and Bakst were to work initially for the Imperial Theatres in Petersburg.

These two artists were to remain Diaghilev's mentors and conscience for several years. No small part of the success of the original Paris visit of the Ballet Russe can be attributed to the decorative excellence of the ballets. Benois's designs for *Le Pavillon d'Armide* (plate 82, colour plate 8) were a

Left and opposite
84 a, b (a) Léon Bakst: costume design for the fiancée in *Le Dieu Bleu*, ballet with choreography by Fokine, music by Reynaldo Hahn, scenario by Cocteau and de Madrazo, first performed by the Diaghilev Ballet Russe in Paris, 1912. (b) the costume, worn by Karsavina who created the role.

Opposite
83 Ida Rubinstein as Zobeide in *Schéhérazade*, a photograph taken by Bert in Paris, 1910. Bakst was obsessed by Ida Rubinstein's extraordinary glamour, by her lean silhouette and the russet hair which framed her aquiline features. In his design for this character, who has little dancing to do, Bakst was able to present a figure of great sensual fascination, as exotic as the image he had created of her the year before when she made her entrance in *Cléopâtre*, revealed to the public beneath a series of veils which were unwound from her body on stage.

superb evocation of French Rococo (the ballet's argument was of a tapestry coming to life and it was subtitled *Le Gobelins Animé*); the visual excitement of Bakst's *Cléopâtre* was a first indication to Paris of the revolution in colour and design which was to be associated with his name thereafter.

From the 1909 Paris season until the middle of the First World War – by which time the Diaghilev Ballet had gone through several convulsions – virtually all the design was by Russian artists. This fact is of exceptional interest. Despite his willingness to encourage the most far-seeing experiments in dancing – witness his desire that Nijinsky should take choreography along completely new paths – and despite his eagerness for a new and cosmopolitan ideal in music for ballet, Diaghilev made no attempt to use painters of the Post-Impressionist and Fauve schools. Although the great collectors in Moscow – the wealthy merchant families like the Ryabushinskys and Shchukins and Morosovs – had been collecting vast numbers of canvases by (among others) Matisse and Picasso and Cézanne, Diaghilev showed no inclination to make use of French artists and painters at this time. He might employ Jean Cocteau as an artistic antenna to keep him in touch with all the latest events of the Parisian avant-garde, and would entrust this *prince frivole* with making a libretto for the utterly derivative piece of orientalism *Le Dieu Bleu*, but Diaghilev remained resolutely nationalist in his taste for stage design.

The artists associated with *The World of Art* were to provide every stage picture. To Bakst fell the lion's share and in 1910 *Schéhérazade* (plate 83, colour plate 9) banished the fustiness and literalism that had so afflicted the ballet stage in the west.* Bakst's taste for fierce yet complementary colours, his understanding of the sensuous and psychologically powerful effects to be obtained from the combinations of what Arnold Haskell calls 'Macaw-feather

*That in recent years it has returned with a vengeance, is to be deplored. The swing of history's pendulum has brought back to ballet design stage pictures of niggling fussiness and the dingiest pseudo-Romanticism.

Design for Ballet

85 Léon Bakst: set for *Thamar*, ballet with choreography by Fokine, music by Balakirev, first performed by the Diaghilev Ballet Russe in Paris, 1912. This photograph shows a revival of the ballet by the de Basil Ballet Russe in the 1930s with Lyubov Chernichova as Thamar.

colouring', brought a new beauty to stage design. It is difficult for us over sixty years later to understand not only how daring was the theme of *Schéhérazade*, but also how important it was to the eyes of the Western world to see a vibrant and powerfully emotive palette of colour. It was designing of genius.

Karsavina in her book of memoirs, *Theatre Street* (London, 1930), describes Bakst: 'He was exotic, fantastic – reaching from one pole to another. The spice and sombreness of the East, the serene aloofness of classical antiquity were his.' To Bakst's understanding of the Orient was added a remarkable feeling for classical antiquity, which was to present the West with magnificent designs for the three Greek works *L'Après-midi d'un faune*, *Daphnis and Chloe* and *Narcisse*. His sense of an interior was no less potent in the rooms he designed for *Le Spectre de la Rose* and *Le Carnaval* (a masterpiece of economy

116

The Diaghilev Era

achieved with two sofas and a dado-ed wall), and his feeling for the exotic could encompass the sensual in *Cléopâtre* and *Schéhérazade*, in *Le Dieu Bleu* and *Thamar*.

Thamar (plate 85) was the story of a Queen of Georgia who summoned travellers to her presence, and, after having entertained them, stabbed them and disposed of their bodies through an oubliette. Bakst's setting was described by Cyril Beaumont (in *The Diaghilev Ballet in London*, London, 1946) as 'a great room with walls coloured mauve and purple, and slanted ceiling painted green. The lighting was subdued save for the dull glow of a dying fire. The scene was dominated by a huge divan set against the far wall . . .' Bakst's use of bricks to create an effect of soaring height, and the adaptation of Georgian decorative motifs, is typical of his ability to absorb and rework 'national colour' into his design vocabulary.

Fokine's account of the creation of the design for *Daphnis and Chloe* (plate 86) reveals something of Diaghilev's attitude to his designers. Diaghilev had commissioned the score for this ballet from Ravel during the first Russian season in Paris in 1909 but the meticulously careful composer did not

86 Léon Bakst: setting for the first tableau of *Daphnis and Chloe*, ballet with choreography by Fokine, music by Ravel, first produced by the Diaghilev Ballet Russe in Paris, 1912.

Design for Ballet

complete the orchestration until 1911. Fokine did not start work on the ballet until 1912. He then discovered, as he puts it in his memoirs,

> that much of the material of his ballet had already been utilized the preceding season in *Narcisse*: the same style, the same shepherds and shepherdesses and nymphs, the same scenery and even a similar use of a backstage chorus.
>
> What angered me greatly and seemed to me most inartistic was Diaghilev's use in *Narcisse* of the Bakst scenery designed for *Daphnis*. All the paraphernalia I needed for *Daphnis* – the green meadow, the grove with the statues of three nymphs; wreaths, sacrificial offerings of the shepherds – were all in *Narcisse* . . . Since his scenery for *Daphnis* had been used for *Narcisse*, Bakst had to design a second set. Not to repeat himself, he disregarded my stage action and moved the nymphs to the opposite side of the stage, placing them on trees rather than in a grove.

The case of Alexandre Benois is curious. In his *Reminiscences of the Russian Ballet* Benois provides some of the very best insights into the genesis of both *The World of Art* and the Ballet Russe, in which his ideals were manifest to the world. Benois was, in many ways, the most important formative influence upon Diaghilev, but his urbanity and traditionalism were gradually to be outstripped by the more questing spirit of Diaghilev himself. It is significant that it was at Benois's insistence that *Giselle* was taken to Paris in 1910, and despite his beautiful designs and the charming thought of bringing back a French masterpiece which the French had forgotten, the ballet was one of the few failures of the early seasons: the Paris public was eager for sensation and *Giselle* was sensational only to those who understood the artistry of Karsavina and Nijinsky in the principal roles. In *Le Pavillon d'Armide* and *Les Sylphides* Benois's exquisite taste brought a great deal to the productions; it was to bring even more to *Petrushka* (plate 87, colour plate 10), in whose creation and realization he was most intimately concerned. First staged in Paris in 1911 with music by Stravinsky and choreography by Fokine, *Petrushka* is generally acknowledged as being the most perfect of all the Diaghilev ballet creations, by reason of its unified concept and the close collaboration existing between its creators during the period of its preparation. Benois's sense of the past was triumphantly deployed in this evocation of the Petersburg Butterweek Fair of 1840 in the Admiralty Square and even today his designs can be seen as inspired exercises in the revival of an historical period in stage terms.

Although Diaghilev had named Benois as artistic director of his company – a generous acknowledgement of the artist's importance – the two men were to fall out over a minor incident concerned with the portrait of the Charlatan in Petrushka's cell and this effectively severed Benois's connection with the Ballet Russe. He returned once more to work with the company when he designed *Le Rossignol*, Stravinsky's opera with ballet, in 1914, but two months after this production the First World War broke out and Benois was never again to share in the achievements of Diaghilev's Ballet Russe. His lengthy career – he lived until 1960, dying full of years and honours – was to find him designing plays, operas and ballets throughout the world. His style retained its aristocratic and refined feeling for the past.

Of the other designers employed by Diaghilev in this first, Russian, period, all but one (José-Maria Sert) were part of the *World of Art* circle: Rerikh

87 Alexandre Benois: costume design for the Charlatan in *Petrushka* as redrawn for the Royal Ballet's staging in 1956. The drawing also shows the Charlatan's street clothes which he wears for the last scene.

(1874–1947), Golovin (1863–1930), Korovin (1861–1939), Anisfeld (b. 1879), Sudeikin (b. 1883), Dobuzhinsky (1875–1957), Goncharova (1881–1962) and Larionov (1881–1964). Of these, the most in accord with Diaghilev's developing ideals were Natalia Goncharova and Mikhail Larionov. Golovin and Korovin were accepted and honoured figures in stage design. Anisfeld produced only the *Sadko* designs (colour plate 11) – handsome, traditionally Russian work for a ballet with choreography by Fokine which, as Grigoriev records, 'Provided just what the Paris audience wanted – a rousing display of Russian temperament; and its final ensemble produced much the same effect as the dances from *Prince Igor*.' Sudeikin provided the neo-Beardsley decoration for *La Tragédie de Salomé*. Karsavina, the first Salome, writes that the ballet was a

> highly sophisticated, visually effective, and I should say interesting production, in the style of Aubrey Beardsley. Exceptionally Beardsleyesque was the descent of Salome from the top of a very high dais. As she came down step by step, a black and gold cloak enveloped her and as she descended the train unfolded behind until it covered the whole flight of steps. And when she threw if off her shoulders, the exiguous tunic revealed a full blown rose painted on her thigh.

The work was short-lived and during its run Sudeikin painted the rose on Karsavina's thigh at each performance.

Nikolay Rerikh, with his archaeological knowledge, was an obvious choice for the two 'archaic' works *The Polovtsian Dances from Prince Igor* and *Le Sacre du Printemps* (colour plate 13). His fascination with the past and his interest in folk art made him particularly well-suited to evoke the primitive Russian ritual which Stravinsky and Nijinsky sought to create in *Sacre*. But Richard Buckle in his biography of Nijinsky records that Rerikh's décor for *Sacre* 'attracted little notice in comparison with the music and choreography . . . Rerikh was not made much of and returned to Russia feeling he had not been given his due. (He later became a recluse in the Himalayas, and died in 1947.)'

In Goncharova and her husband, Larionov, Diaghilev found younger artists who typified the new adventurousness in painting inside Russia itself. Both were associated with avant-garde painting in Moscow – they were the orginators of the 'rayonnist' style of painting – and in her earliest work for Diaghilev, *Le Coq d'Or* of 1914, Goncharova produced designs in which the naïve vitality of peasant art was preserved despite the extreme sophistication of theatrical convention. Henceforth Goncharova and Larionov were to be the staunchest of Diaghilev's Russian collaborators.

With the outbreak of war in 1914 there came both a death and a re-birth of the Ballet Russe. The troupe that had existed was scattered; many of the dancers returned to Russia, while Diaghilev with a few associates remained in Europe. Diaghilev had already broken with Fokine and Nijinsky as choreographers, and his new protégé, Leonid Massine, had proved himself only as a dancer in *La Légende de Joseph*, which had been produced in May 1914. Yet after the initial shock of the outbreak of war Diaghilev set about reassembling a company around Massine as dancer. During 1915 dancers were engaged and in neutral Switzerland a small 'committee' assembled comprising Stravinsky, Larionov and Goncharova, and Massine. A good deal

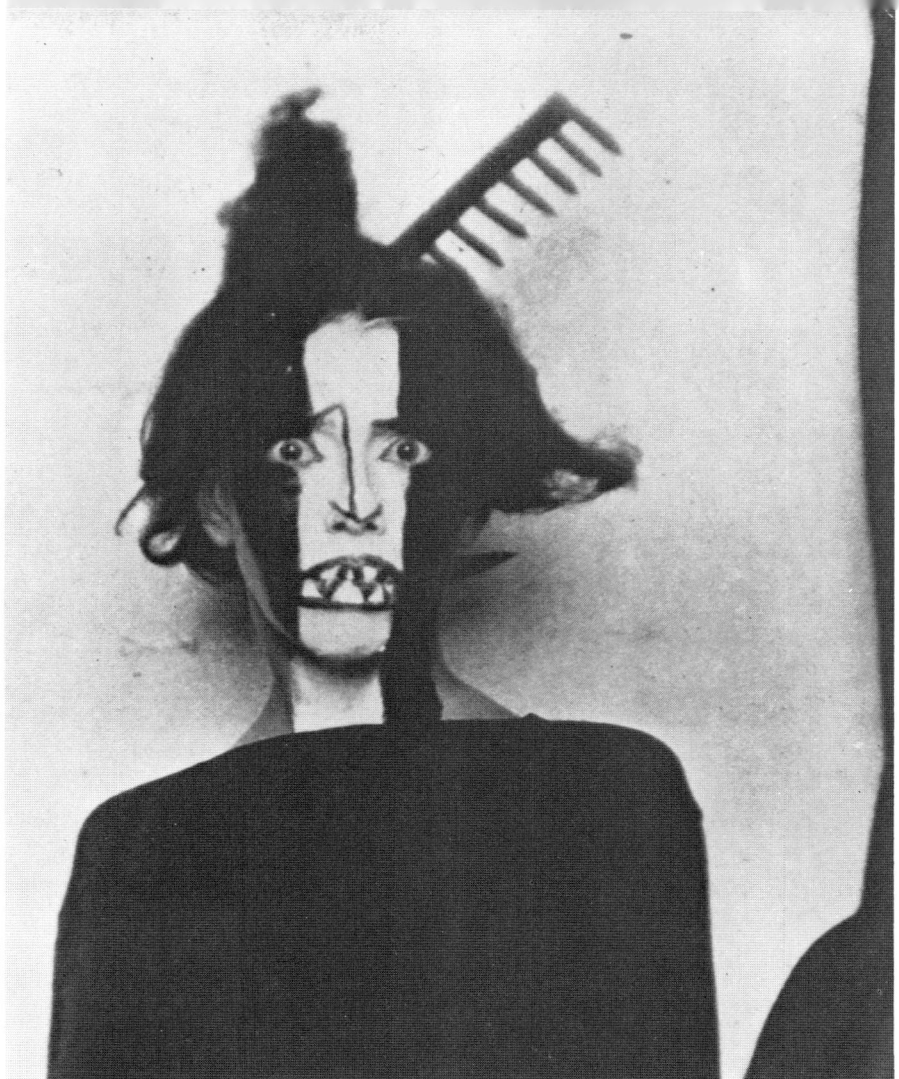

88 Mikhail Larionov: make-up devised for Kikimora, the witch (Lydia Sokolova) in *Contes Russes*, ballet with choreography by Massine, music by Lyadov, décor and costumes by Larionov, first performed by the Diaghilev Ballet Russe in Paris, 1917.

of work was planned and Diaghilev invited Larionov, a man of very considerable working knowledge of theatrical production, to assist Massine first of all in an unperformed work called *Liturgie*, and then in 1915 with the staging of *Soleil de Nuit* (colour plate 12).

The importance of Larionov in these early years of the 'second' Diaghilev period is very significant. Arnold Haskell, who knew him well, says that Larionov brought

> ... an entirely fresh point of view. He could follow and at times anticipate Diaghilev, who was able to select from and guide his many exciting ideas. These were so many and so exciting that he was never to receive his due as a painter. He lacked the necessary concentration to advance in any one phase. The constant bustle of the theatre was his true milieu. Larionov was one of the very few of Diaghilev's inner circle to do him full justice.

Haskell records that Diaghilev had first met Larionov at the time of the last *World of Art* exhibition in 1904. He had been vastly amused by Larionov's gesture in walking round Moscow one day with his face brightly painted (a fact that is worth recalling in the light of the elaborate maquillage for Kikimora in *Contes Russes* (plate 88), which Larionov designed in 1916). In 1906 Diaghilev had sent the young painter to Paris with the exhibition of

Russian art, and Larionov was greatly excited by the Fauve and the Ecole de Paris styles. With his intense interest in theatre and dancing, and in the art of the circus, Larionov also responded with enthusiasm to popular art as exemplified by graffiti, the pictorial style of peasants, and of soldiers whom he knew during a brief spell of military service. His adaptations of peasant design to the theatre were to catch not just the decorative ideas but the spirit of folk art.

Soleil de Nuit, Massine's first choreographic essay to reach the stage, owed much to the inspiration and guidance offered by Larionov. The piece was designed by Larionov, and he also provided the costumes and set for short dance numbers which were composed during these years, and eventually assembled as *Contes Russes* in 1917.

As a sidelight to the artistic climate of these years, Richard Buckle's admirable *In Search of Diaghilev* – an account of the preparation of the great Diaghilev exhibition he organized in 1954 – contains the following comment about Larionov:

> No one is more devoted than Mikhail Larionov to the memory of Diaghilev; and he revered him for exactly what Benois disapproved of – the determination to be contemporary and up to date. Larionov praises Diaghilev for outgrowing his admiration for the kind of sensitive pastiche of the baroque and Romantic stage design in which Benois and his friends excelled; Benois thinks that Diaghilev was completely taken in by Larionov's combination of folk art with Cubism and other revolutionary elements.

The determination to be contemporary and up to date was an idea that was ultimately to become obsessive during the post-war years. Cut off from Russia and in his mid-forties, Diaghilev found himself stranded in a Europe in torment, whose turmoil was reflected (as it had been predicted) in the evolution of music and painting. In music, Diaghilev could be accounted 'up to date' in his discovery of Stravinsky, and in his use of Prokofiev; otherwise his concern during the 1920s was largely to be with the fashionable and agreeable music typified by Les Six. (There is not the least evidence that he contemplated, let alone appreciated, the truly 'new' music that was being created in Vienna by Arnold Schoenberg.) In design, the first flirtations with 'the new' come with *Fireworks* and *Parade* in 1917 – and here we sense something of Diaghilev's renewed enthusiasm for his company amid the disasters of war. *Fireworks* was not a ballet but a performance of Stravinsky's early score with what Grigoriev (the company *régisseur* throughout its existence) calls

> a setting ordered from the Cubist painter Balla. It consisted of various geometrical structures, such as cubes and cones, made of some transparent material which allowed of their being lit from within in accordance with the complicated lighting plot which Diaghilev devised and worked himself. He maintained that it interpreted the music; and this Cubist fantasy proved much to the taste of his advanced artistic friends.

In the mid-seventies the use of lighting and the designs by the Futurist Giacomo Balla seems a very remarkable portent of some of the light shows of today, and even of the 'ballet without dancers' idea which has teased producers for many years.

Parade probably represents the most deliberate attempt by Diaghilev to break with his past. The novelty of the work of Larionov and Goncharova was that of a generation younger than Bakst and Benois, but one still identifiably attached to the *World of Art* ethos. Their art had been born long before they left Russia; they were Russian *émigrés* set in their ways, for all the novelty and vigorous anti-naturalism of their work and their wonderful sense of theatre.

With *Parade* and *Fireworks* Diaghilev accepts for the first time the challenge of European painting's avant-garde, and makes a decision to look to Europe rather than back to Russia for the design of his repertory. This is a decision to be confirmed in the post-war years, when his pursuit of fashion seems an almost feverish quest to keep up with youth and his own pre-war image.

Parade (plates 89a, b, colour plate 14), the collaboration of Satie, Picasso, Cocteau and Massine, is an extraordinary work to find created in the midst of a war, but it remains one of the most far-seeing pieces of its time, suggesting a good deal about the tone of the art of the twenties. Its often humorous reference to the popular art of the music hall, its delight in the absurd qualities of modern life and the surroundings of the modern world – as in the appearance of skyscrapers in the costuming – suggest how strong indeed was Cocteau's influence in the devising and creation of this piece. Diaghilev in effect acted more as midwife than as parent.

The structures worn by the Managers hint at the subjugation of the dancer to decorative ideas, a fact which was to become increasingly prominent with the Ballet Russe during the twenties. Diaghilev had met Picasso in 1916 in Paris, and had commissioned the designs for *Parade* then. The Cocteau-Satie collaboration was already established and the three went to Rome to join the Ballet Russe and set to work with Massine on the choreography. The resultant *ballet réaliste* was called by Cocteau 'a simple, rough action that combines the charms of the circus and of the music hall'. It could also be described as the *Petrushka* of the avant-garde: this time the old Charlatan becomes the two preposterous Cubist structures of the Managers and the hapless dolls of Fokine's ballet become the rejected figures of the *Parade*. (A *Parade* is a comic 'trailer' to a travelling theatrical performance and the whole point of *Parade* is that despite the entreaties of the Managers and the appearance of the dancers nobody goes to see the show.) The most immediately striking element of the staging was of course the two pieces of animated scenery that are the Managers, whose 'awkwardness of movement underneath their wooden frames, far from hampering the choreographer, obliged him to break with the ancient formulae and to seek inspiration not in the things that move, but in the things round which we move, and which move according to the rhythm of our steps' (Jean Cocteau, *Le Coq et l'Harlequin* translated by Rollo Myers, London, 1921). Elsewhere Cocteau describes the figures of the Managers as 'wild, uncivilized, vulgar, noisy creatures harming whatever they praised and arousing (as it actually happened) the hatred, laughter and scorn of the public by the strangeness of their appearance and behaviour'. These Managers bear an interesting relationship to the symbolic costuming and the *habits de métiers* engravings of the seventeenth century.

The Satie score, with its deliberate echoes of music hall style and the introduction of naturalist sound – from typewriters and a siren – was a shock to the public, but the importance attached to the ballet in 1917 is best

89 a, b Pablo Picasso (1881–1973): (a) the French Manager in *Parade* as performed by the Diaghilev Ballet Russe and (b) *right* the American Manager in *Parade* as revived by Massine for London Festival Ballet in 1974. First performed in Paris in 1917 with choreography by Massine, music by Satie, libretto by Cocteau, *Parade* introduced the ideas of Cubism to the ballet stage for the first time.

conveyed by Apollinaire's programme note which said that Picasso and Massine had

> forged the alliance of painting and dance, of music and the plastic arts, which is the sign of a more complete art. From this new alliance has resulted something beyond Realism. Picasso's sets and costumes are proof of the realism of his art. This realism, or Cubism, call it what you will, has stirred the arts more deeply than anything else during the past ten years. The sets and costumes of *Parade* show more clearly Picasso's determination to extract from an object the utmost aesthetic emotion which it is capable of yielding . . . the supreme purpose is to produce a translation of reality.

Parade's design is probably the most extreme example of the designer's ballet. As revived today it looks haunted: the sets and costumes amazing, the score intriguing, the dance action minimal. (The same in a sense is true of

Design for Ballet

Schéhérazade, that other seminal stage picture. Bakst's luxuriant colours still excite the mind while the drama, when not frankly ludicrous, looks staid to a degree.)

The other wartime works were far more traditional, with the exception of the *Tyl Eulenspiegel* (plate 90) staged in New York by Nijinsky with fine designs by Robert Edmond Jones (1887–1954), which Diaghilev never saw or had any connection with. The Diaghilev Ballet's American tours during the First World War were fraught with disaster, not least because of the unpredictability of Nijinsky who had insisted upon complete authority. His *Tyl* was, according to the several accounts available, a brilliant ballet which was destroyed by the fact of being hastily prepared and presented only half completed to the public. Carl van Vechten, the distinguished American critic, notes in his collected dance writings (New York, 1974) that:

> The scenery and costumes by Robert E. Jones of New York, were decidedly diverting ... over a steep, spreading background of ultramarine, the crazy turrets of medieval castles leaned dizzily to and fro. The costumes were exaggerations of the exaggerated fashions of the Middle Ages ... The colours were oranges, reds, greens and blues, those indeed of Bakst's *Schéhérazade*, but so differently disposed that they made an entirely dissimilar impression. The effect reminded one spectator of a Spanish omelet.

Above
90 Robert Edmond Jones: design for a market woman (Lydia Sokolova) in *Tyl Eulenspiegel*, ballet with choreography by Nijinsky, music by Richard Strauss, performed by the Diaghilev Ballet Russe in New York, 1916.

Left
91 Léon Bakst: costumes for *The Good-Humoured Ladies*, ballet with choreography by Massine, music by Scarlatti orchestrated by Tommasini, first performed by the Diaghilev Ballet Russe in Rome 1917. This photograph shows Lyubov Chernichova as Constanza and Stanislas Idzikowski as Battista in the original staging.

The Diaghilev Era

Of the three important Massine ballets either created or conceived and planned during the war only one – *The Good-Humoured Ladies* – had designs by one of the old guard, Léon Bakst (plate 91). This ballet originally had an extraordinary setting by Bakst which showed an Italian street scene, its buildings leaning inwards as if seen in a convex mirror. Diaghilev, however, could not understand Bakst's vision and the setting was redesigned with the buildings shown in correct perspective. The costumes were superb confections, superbly executed.

The other two ballets, *The Three-Cornered Hat* and *La Boutique Fantasque*, looked to Europe, and even the redesigning of *Cléopâtre* in 1918 made use of Robert Delaunay (1885–1941) and his wife Sonia (b. 1885), whose brilliantly toned Cubism produced a setting of vibrant colours, and a costume for Cleopatra which consisted of bold strips of colour, very different from the sensuous archaism of Bakst. Picasso was commissioned to do *The Three-Cornered Hat* (plate 92) and his masterly design was to be one of the sensations when the piece was eventually staged in London in 1919. However, in his *Picasso Theatre* Douglas Cooper interestingly observes that although Picasso had obviously a great natural affinity to the task of designing *The Three-Cornered Hat* he did not arrive at the final version of the setting easily. It would seem that he made some twenty alternative versions of the décor and it was only by a process of elimination that he finally achieved the magnificent simplicity of the setting we know. In it the Spanish landscape is reduced to its very essence and it provides an ideal background for the dazzling regional costumes.

For *La Boutique Fantasque* the choice was André Derain (1880–1954), whose

92 Pablo Picasso: set design for *The Three-Cornered Hat*, ballet with choreography by Massine, music by de Falla, first performed by the Diaghilev Ballet Russe at the Alhambra Theatre, London, 1919.

Design for Ballet

93 José-Maria Sert: design for the last scene of *Le Astuzie Femminili*, opera-ballet with choreography by Massine, music by Cimarosa, first performed by the Diaghilev Ballet Russe at the Paris Opéra in 1920 and revised in Monte Carlo in 1924 under the title of *Cimarosiana*. The set is of a perspective from a terrace overlooking Rome.

Fauve style was tamed in the service of this enchanting ballet. It is significant that Diaghilev rejected Bakst's proposed designs for this work; his draft setting looked frankly old-fashioned – harking back to his designs for *Die Puppenfee* at the Maryinsky Theatre in 1903.

Of the other works in the immediate post-war years, a revival of *Le Rossignol* was undertaken by Massine, and Henri Matisse (1869–1954) was invited to provide sets and costumes, though their *chinoiserie* could hardly be considered innovative. More impressive were the two further Picasso creations – for *Pulcinella* and the *Cuadro Flamenco* – while the staging of the opera-ballet *Le Astuzie Femminili* (plate 93) had décor by José-Maria Sert (1876–1945), the Spanish artist who was married to Diaghilev's greatest woman friend, Misia Edwards. (Sert had also provided the scenery for *La Légende de Joseph* in 1914 and the costumes for *Las Meninas*, a divertissement by Massine given in Spain in 1916.) When Massine left Diaghilev in 1921 the impresario took the exceptional step of asking Larionov to help prepare the young dancer Tadeusz Slavinski as a choreographer, since he had previously helped Massine. Their combined talents however could do little for *Chout*, although both design (by Larionov) and score (by Prokofiev) were admired.

The departure of Massine and the unsuitability of Slavinski as a choreographic talent impelled Diaghilev into one of the most unexpected undertakings of his career: the decision to stage *The Sleeping Beauty*. Inspired

Colour 8 Alexandre Benois: costume design for Vaslav Nijinsky as Armida's favourite slave in *Le Pavillon d'Armide*. This illustration shows the original costume for the version given in Petersburg in 1907. For the later Paris production the claret-coloured silk was changed to yellow.

La Papillon d'Armide
1ère version
Théâtre Marie
1907.
Costume
de Nijinsky
(L'esclave favori
d'Armide)

Alexandre Benois

Le bineux
suit à
pieds joints!

94 Léon Bakst: design for *The Sleeping Beauty* as produced by Anna Pavlova in New York, 1916. This design for the last scene was to be slightly reworked by Bakst for the Diaghilev staging in London, 1921, which looked less effective than this first, Bibiena-inspired fantasy.

by the London run of the musical comedy *Chu Chin Chow* (which he learned with amazement had been playing for over three years) Diaghilev realized that a success of a similar nature would give him a wonderful breathing space. He would be able to recoup his forces, discover a new choreographer, and also accumulate some much-needed funds – the post-war years were haunted by unrelenting financial problems for Diaghilev. Thus he decided that London should see a full scale, glorious version of the greatest of the old Imperial Russian ballets. With superlative dancers engaged for the principal roles, with the score edited and in part reorchestrated by Stravinsky, and with Diaghilev himself in constant supervision of the production, *The Sleeping Princess*, as the work was renamed, was put under way. For the designs, Diaghilev turned to Bakst, although it might have seemed that Benois was a more obvious choice and Grigoriev states that Diaghilev badly missed Benois. Fortunately Bakst had already had experience in designing the work since he had provided the scenery and costumes for a version that Anna Pavlova danced with her company in a revue on Broadway in 1916 (plate 94). Bakst's designs had been commissioned while he was in Europe and they were sent to New York with explicit instructions for their execution. Although Pavlova's *Beauty* failed to please the New York audience – having started off as a forty-eight minute condensation it was gradually reduced during the run of the show to a mere eighteen minutes – the designs seem to have won particular favour and Bakst sent them to London for exhibition at the Fine Art Society in 1917. These designs formed the basis for the vast amount of work the ailing Bakst accomplished – five sets and over one hundred costumes in the space of two months. The result was sumptuously beautiful, magnificent in every respect (plates 95, 96) but it failed to satisfy the public, who understood nothing of the

Right
95 Léon Bakst: design for a Mazurka Dancer in the last act of *The Sleeping Princess*. Midnight blue, gold and white and peacock green are the colours for this *corps de ballet* costume – no less splendid than those designed for the principal characters. The costuming is as brilliant a fantastication of Polish court dress as were any of the Oriental extravagances in *Schéhérazade*.

Below
96 Léon Bakst: design for the second act in the Diaghilev Ballet Russe production of *The Sleeping Princess* performed in London, 1921. Bakst's fantastic garden has a very sound dramatic purpose. The pillared colonnade along which the King and Queen are seen walking also provided a wonderful first entrance for the Princess Aurora. Against settings such as this the miracle of Bakst's costuming, beautiful both in outline and in colour, could take full effect. When seen in isolation, as preserved in theatre museums or shown in exhibitions, the costumes inevitably lose much of their impact.

The Diaghilev Era

Colour 9 Léon Bakst: design for *Schéhérazade*, ballet with choreography by Fokine, music by Rimsky-Korsakov, first performed by the Diaghilev Ballet Russe in Paris, 1910.

grandeur of Petipa's choreography, and who showed little taste for Tchaikovsky (Bloomsbury being notably vociferous in denigrating the score).

The blow to Diaghilev was cruel. Hopes of financial stability vanished, and in the spring of 1922 the Ballet Russe limped from London leaving behind debts and, for perceptive members of the public, the memory of one of the most beautiful examples of stage design in this century.

From the disaster of *The Sleeping Princess* there came one good thing; ironically it was to be another choreographer. Diaghilev had engaged Bronislava Nijinska, sister of Nijinsky, as a dancer with his company once again – she had featured in the early seasons of the Ballet Russe – and she now showed enough imaginative ability to be asked to rearrange certain sections of the Petipa text. Most significant, she was responsible for that very popular aberration 'The Three Ivans', a trio of peasant boys whom Diaghilev insisted upon introducing to dance to the music of the coda to the great last act duet (Diaghilev's taste was not always impeccable). The success of this number made Diaghilev realize that he had another choreographer to be exploited, and for the next three years Nijinska was to create the new repertory. It is this repertory which indicates the final acceptance of French taste to guide the decoration and much of the music of the last period of the Ballet Russe, a state of affairs which was confirmed by the invitation to become the resident ballet company in Monte Carlo in 1922. The establishment of the Ballet Russe as a permanent winter troupe for six months every year in the then ultra-fashionable setting of Monte Carlo is indication enough of the new aesthetic surroundings of the company.

The musical scores and the designing now largely reflected the most modish Parisian taste; the ballets often proved ephemeral, lightweight, and 'amusing' novelties which seize on the pleasure of a moment for their existence and then disappear. That this artistic climate could in fact produce a major piece is witnessed by the beautiful *Les Biches* of 1924 with its pallidly enchanting Laurencin designs, delicious music and supremely well made choreography. It is Diaghilev's *Sylphides* of the 1920s. But many of the subsequent works were evanescent to a point of invisibility.

Le Train Bleu is the prime example: inspired by Cocteau's sight of Anton Dolin performing handstands it had a setting by Henri Laurens and oh-so-chic clothes by Chanel. Diaghilev tried to give it a little more weight with the addition of a Picasso front-cloth but this could not save the piece any more than Braque's designs could rescue the *Zéphire et Flore* of 1925.

In the context of this frivolity *Les Noces* of 1923 is almost shocking in its seriousness. The score had been written during the war – Diaghilev, when he heard it, had wept at its power to evoke the lost Russia of his youth – but its staging did not materialize until Nijinska had proved herself. Goncharova who with Larionov had the previous year decorated Nijinska's first ballet *Le Renard* (plate 97) produced some brilliantly coloured examples of peasant art as a realization of Stravinsky's text. However, these signally failed to capture the hieratic beauty of Nijinska's choreography and she persuaded Goncharova to remove all colour except for the earthy tones of the costuming. (For a full account of this collaboration see Appendix in Clarke/Crisp, *Making a Ballet*, London and New York, 1975).

With the middle and late years of the 1920s, there came an almost feverish quest for the new. In saying this we must insist though that the 'new' for Diaghilev also implied the best. Between 1924 and his last year, 1929,

97 Mikhail Larionov: costumes for the Cat, the Cockerel and the Goat in *Le Renard*, ballet originally staged by the Diaghilev Ballet Russe at the Paris Opéra in 1922 with words and music by Stravinsky, choreography by Nijinska, scenery by Goncharova; revived by Diaghilev in 1929 with choreography by Lifar. This photograph shows the three characters danced by Hoyer I, Efimov and Lissanevich. The identification of the characters by their stencilled names foreshadows the procedures of Pop Art forty years later.

On pages 136 and 137
Colour 10 Alexandre Benois: design for the fair scene in *Petrushka*, ballet with choreography by Fokine, music by Stravinsky, first performed by the Diaghilev Ballet Russe in Paris, 1911. Although Benois redesigned this ballet many times for various companies, he made only minor changes of detail, and this watercolour, dated 1911, represents his first thoughts.

Colour 11 Boris Anisfeld: costume design for the King of the Sea in Rimsky-Korsakov's opera *Sadko*. Diaghilev presented the Kingdom of the Sea scene from this opera as part of the first programme of his Paris season in June 1911.

Colour 12 Mikhail Larionov: setting for *Soleil de Nuit*, ballet with choreography by Massine, music by Rimsky-Korsakov, first performed by the Diaghilev Ballet Russe in Geneva, 1915. This was Massine's first ballet, and also Larionov's first design for Diaghilev.

Colour 13 Nikolay Rerikh: design for a group of elders for *Le Sacre du Printemps*, ballet with choreography by Nijinsky, music by Stravinsky, first performed by the Diaghilev Ballet Russe in Paris, 1913.

The Diaghilev Era

Colour 10
Colour 11

136

Colour 12
Colour 13

Design for Ballet

98 Leopold Survage (1879–1968): design for *Mavra, opera buffa* by Stravinsky presented by Diaghilev in 1922. Survage's design is a very clever adaptation of the 'indoor-outdoor' set with a prospect of fields and trees and green-roofed houses to be seen through the lace-curtained windows of the heroine's house.

The Diaghilev Era

Diaghilev employed as designers the following artists: Georges Braque, Juan Gris, Marie Laurencin, Henri Laurens, Pedro Pruna, Henri Matisse, Maurice Utrillo, Max Ernst, Joan Miró, André Derain, Pablo Picasso, Naum Gabo, Anton Pevsner, Pavel Tchelitchev, André Bauchant, Giorgio de' Chirico, Georges Rouault and Yuri Yakulov.

The list is prodigious. It indicates, if nothing else, the power of the Ballet Russe to popularize and to act as propagandist for modern painting. But it also indicates a far more uneasy attitude towards the overall aesthetic of the company. Diaghilev could no longer proclaim any definitive policy other than that of catholicity. He was providing magnificent wrappings for ultimately unworthy concoctions. *Les Matelots* might be designed by Pruna,

Right
99 Juan Gris (1887–1927): costume for Louis XIV in La Fête Merveilleuse, gala organized by Diaghilev at Versailles in 1923. This design is a faithful reworking of correct historical costume with the addition of an ermine-tailed cloak. As the King mounted to his throne at the top of the staircase the cloak unfurled behind him to cover the entire staircase. The costume was used again in 1924 in Les Tentations de la Bergère.

Design for Ballet

Above
Colour 14 Pablo Picasso: frontcloth for *Parade*, ballet with choreography by Massine, music by Satie, libretto by Cocteau, first performed by the Diaghilev Ballet Russe in Paris, 1917. This photograph shows the curtain as it was re-created for Massine's revival of his ballet for London Festival Ballet in 1974.

Opposite
Colour 15 Natalia Goncharova: designs for the backcloth in the last scene of *The Firebird*, ballet with choreography by Fokine, music by Stravinsky. When originally staged by the Diaghilev Ballet Russe in Paris, 1910, *The Firebird* had a setting by Golovin and costumes by Bakst and Golovin. In 1926 Diaghilev revived the ballet and had it redesigned by Natalia Goncharova. Her backcloth suggests a fantastic medieval Russian city in accord with the fairy tale quality of the ballet.

The Diaghilev Era

Design for Ballet

The Diaghilev Era

100 Pablo Picasso: scene from *Mercure – Poses plastiques*, ballet with choreography by Massine, music by Satie, first staged for Count Etienne de Beaumont's Les Soirées de Paris in 1924 and first performed by the Diaghilev Ballet Russe in Paris, 1927.

101 André Derain (1880–1954): design for *Jack-in-the-Box*, ballet with choreography by Balanchine, music by Satie, first performed by the Diaghilev Ballet Russe in Paris, 1926.

Opposite above
Colour 16 Georges Braque: projected design for *Les Fâcheux*, ballet by Boris Kochno with choreography by Bronislava Nijinska, music by Georges Auric, first performed by the Diaghilev Ballet Russe in Monte Carlo, 1924.

Opposite below
Colour 17 Theodore Steinlen: design for the first act of *Iberia*, ballet with choreography by Jean Börlin, music by Albeniz, first performed by the Ballets Suédois, 1920.

Barabau by Utrillo; *Roméo et Juliette* might involve the Surrealists Ernst and Miró, and provoke a satisfactory scandal to titillate the box office, but these were not works to bear comparison with the creations of ten or fifteen years before.

Tamara Karsavina who created the role of Juliette, writing in *The Dancing Times* in March 1967 observed that when she attended her first rehearsal the dancers

> were all in practice dress on the bare stage; that is, there was a backcloth of washy blue, with a large disc in the middle, which, I was told, represented the sun. When the rehearsal began, some small flats were moved on to the stage by the artists . . . Only Romeo and Juliet wore costumes for the rehearsal part, the rest had yellow practice tunics. The two leading lights of the Surrealist movement, Max Ernst and Joan Miró, made the décor and costumes. Considering the output, it seems that the job was over-manned.

The ballet was subtitled 'A rehearsal without scenery in two parts' and the décor was listed as 'curtains and scenic adjuncts' by Ernst and Miró.

This is very much the period of the designer's ballet. Balanchine who had just joined the company from Russia, Nijinska and Massine who returned to work, were not producing choreography of much merit and it was to counterbalance this apparent weakness that Diaghilev was to insist upon the importance of the decoration of his ballets. Two examples – *Le Pas d'Acier* and *Ode* – were to come in the last years of the company. With *Le Pas d'Acier* (plate 102), Diaghilev was playing with Communism, seeking to produce a Soviet

102 a, b Yury Yakulov (1884–1928): costumes for *Le Pas d'Acier*, ballet with choreography by Massine, music by Prokofiev, first performed by the Diaghilev Ballet Russe in Paris, 1927.

Design for Ballet

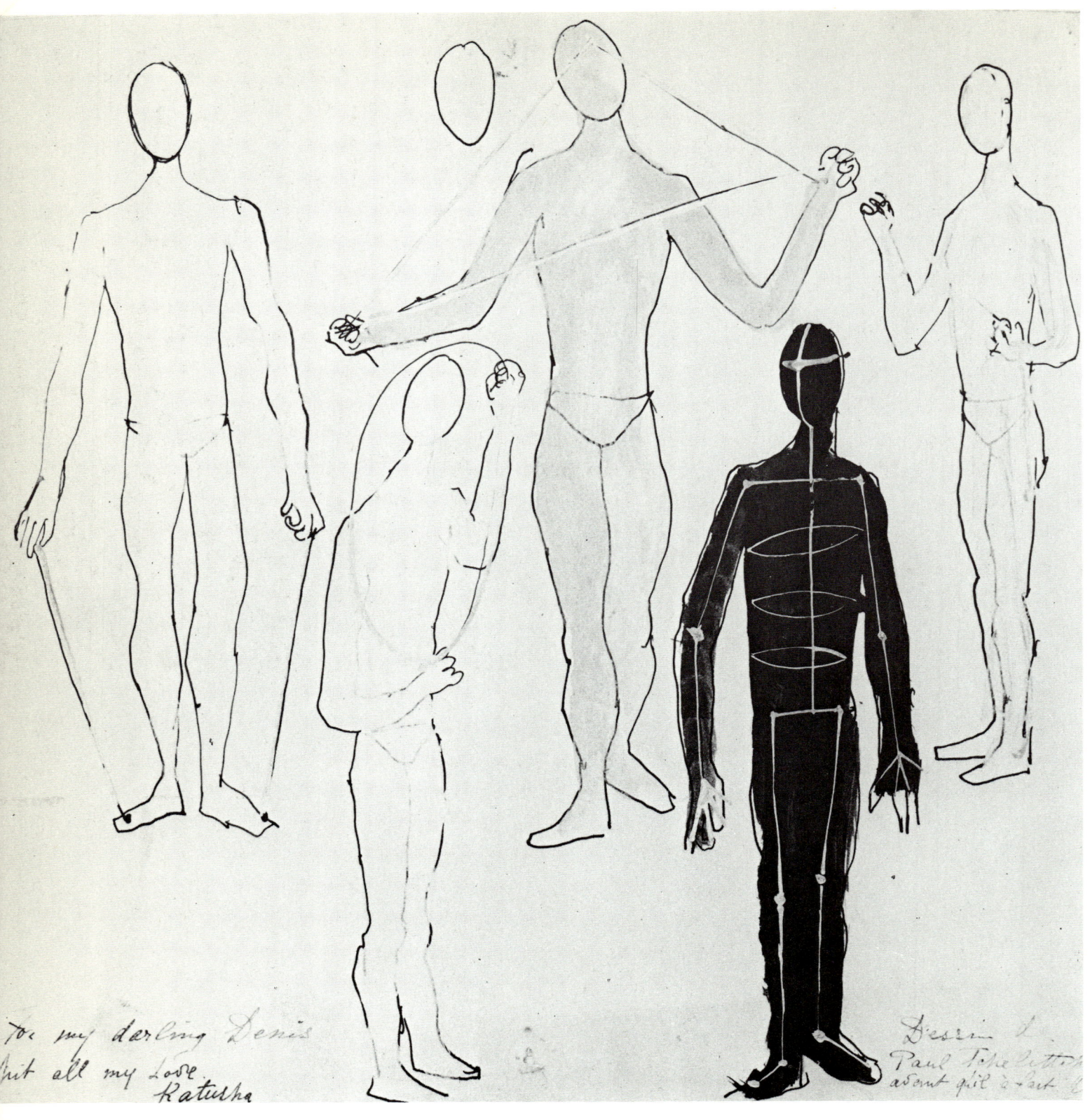

The Diaghilev Era

103 a, b Pavel Tchelitchev: design for *Ode*, ballet with choreography by Massine, music by Nabokov, first performed by the Diaghilev Ballet Russe in Paris, 1928. (a) shows working sketches by Tchelitchev for the male costumes and (b) is a general view of the stage when the ballet was first produced.

ballet in the improbable surroundings of Monte Carlo. Diaghilev had been cut off from Russia since the outbreak of the First World War and he was fascinated by the artistic developments that had come with the early years of the Soviet régime. When in 1923 Tairov's Kemerny Theatre visited Paris from Moscow, Diaghilev was excited by the productions and their Constructivist décor by Alexandra Exter and Yakulov. Diaghilev decided to stage a 'Soviet' ballet; he commissioned a score from Prokofiev and invited Yakulov to provide the designs and further hoped to involve Tairov and Meyerhold. Their refusal to collaborate meant that eventually the production was a compromise. It was an unworthy piece, but Yakulov's designs were at least authentically Soviet, and allowed Diaghilev to present Russian Constructivism to the Western public.

Ode – 'an evening meditation on the majesty of God on observing the Aurora Borealis' – was a setting of an eighteenth century ode by the Russia émigré composer Nicholas Nabokov, which Diaghilev decided to use for a ballet (plate 103). Boris Kochno, who was the scenarist and was responsible for the staging, records in his *Diaghilev and the Ballet Russe* (New York, 1970 and London, 1971) the troubles that ensued when Pavel Tchelitchev was intent upon using film, neon lighting and phosphorescent costumes to update the basic idea of a spectacle inspired by Russian court festivities of the eighteenth century. The use of a vista of dolls of diminishing size to create a mysterious

Design for Ballet

Left
104 Naum Gabo (1890–1977) and Anton Pevsner (1886–1962): setting for *La Chatte*, ballet with choreography by Balanchine and music by Henri Sauguet, first performed by the Diaghilev Ballet Russe in Paris, 1927. The mica and talc shapes devised by the Constructivist sculptors were set off by a stage-cloth and backdrop of black American cloth. The novelty of the production lay in the beautiful effects obtained by the play of light upon the transparent mica constructions.

perspective and the addition of cords held and pulled by the anonymously clothed dancers produced extraordinary effects which foreshadow some of the work of Alwin Nikolais forty years later. The late A. V. Coton in his *A Prejudice for Ballet* (London, 1938) provides a perceptive account of the visual effect:

> One's strongest remaining impression is of the unearthly beauty created in most of the scenes by a revolutionary use of light never before seen in any form of Theatre – floods, spots, panoramic effects, projections against a screen and great burst of light suggesting the sudden animation of pyrotechnical set pieces, as the groups of dancers and static figures were bathed in pools of glowing illumination, swiftly dimmed and flooded again, almost imperceptibly changing colours.

Amid the variety of schools of painting Diaghilev was unwilling to make any definitive choice. Surrealism, Victorian naïveté – the use of Pollock's toy theatre designs for *The Triumph of Neptune* – Constructivism, the later developments of Fauvism, all served their purpose. This bolstering of the weaker repertory by a kind of decorative *legerdemain* is understandable: Diaghilev's own taste in dancing was often conservative and he preserved, where possible, a balance within the repertory by maintaining established classical and Fokinian successes. It is only in 1928 when Balanchine was entrusted with Stravinsky's *Apollo* that the return of choreography to some

Opposite
105 Pedro Pruna (b. 1904): costume for Felia Dubrovska as the Film Star in *La Pastorale*, a comedy-ballet with choreography by Balanchine and music by Georges Auric, first performed by the Diaghilev Ballet Russe in Paris, 1926. *La Pastorale*, a joke about a film company on location, was a lightweight, ephemeral piece. Costuming included both modern dress – for the director and film crews – and historical costume for the actors in the supposed film. Dubrovska's costume with its sweeping train is supposed to evoke the sixteenth century but has all the chic of the 1920s.

The Diaghilev Era

form of pre-eminence is evident. (In the following year *The Prodigal Son* confirmed Balanchine's genius, though in very different fashion.)

It is a sign of Diaghilev's taste that *Apollo* should be entrusted to a Sunday painter, André Bauchant (1873–1955), who specialized in flower-pieces and landscapes. For Diaghilev he produced the charming front curtain illustrated in plate 106a, and also a setting showing Mount Olympus to which Apollo leads the Muses in the ballet's closing moments. The clarity and classic harmony of Balanchine's choreography has long outgrown such decorative fancies and the ballet is now best seen in a completely austere and functional setting which imposes no bounds on the choreography's dignity. Bauchant was unable to provide costume designs for the first production and Kochno records that Diaghilev adapted dress from figures in Bauchant's paintings. Again, costuming has altered very considerably since then: Balanchine would probably now feel these costumes (plate 106b) are 'too fancy' but it is undeniable that Nikitina's very simple tutu is the epitome of elegance and Lifar's belted tunic and gold wig, gold shoes and lacings suggest the glamour of the young god.

Le Bal (plate 107) was staged in 1929 towards the very end of the Diaghilev Ballet Russe's existence, with choreography by Balanchine and designs by Giorgio de' Chirico (b. 1888). *The Times* newspaper, reviewing the first London performance in July 1929, records

> The ballet is remarkable for the beauty of its décor ... under the various pastel shades lies white as a foundation; white often comes to the surface, though the prevailing tone is biscuit brown; elaborate tracery in black adds linear interest. All the dancers wear black and white wigs, looking rather uncomfortably like those convolutions of the brain that are found in textbooks of psychology. But their formal significance is greater than their chance representation suggests, and they help to harmonize the whole scene.

106 a, b André Bauchant: front curtain and costumes for *Apollon Musagète* (*Apollo*), ballet with choreography by Balanchine, music by Stravinsky, first performed by the Diaghilev Ballet Russe in Paris, 1928. (b) shows Alicia Nikitina as Terpsichore and Serge Lifar as Apollo in the original production.

Design for Ballet

Le Bal was a mysterious work whose second scene (plate 107a) was set in a ballroom in Sicily wherein a young officer went in pursuit of a young woman. The designs by the Surrealist de' Chirico repeated the architectural motifs of the set – temples, columns and brickwork – in the costuming.

In August 1929 Diaghilev died in Venice, and with him died the Ballet Russe. It was impossible that the company should continue, inconceivable that there should be anyone to replace him. As we look back over the twenty years of the enterprise we can see how vital a transformation the Ballet Russe had made in the artistic ideals and awareness of Western man. Diaghilev had acted as a catalyst, as a guide and as an inspiration to both artists and public. In everything his company had reflected his taste. If, in certain years, that taste seemed to falter there is no gainsaying that this great man had shown that ballet, as an amalgamation of all the arts, could command the services and the respect of the greatest creators of the epoch. For the first time in European history since the glorious days of Louis XIV ballet had engaged the finest

107a, b Giorgio de' Chirico: designs for *Le Bal*, ballet with choreography by Balanchine and music by Vittorio Rieti, first performed by the Diaghilev Ballet Russe in Monte Carlo, 1929. (a) shows the ballroom set for the second scene in a revival by Massine for the Ballet Russe de Monte Carlo in 1935. (b) is the costume design for the young woman, a role created by Alexandra Danilova.

Design for Ballet

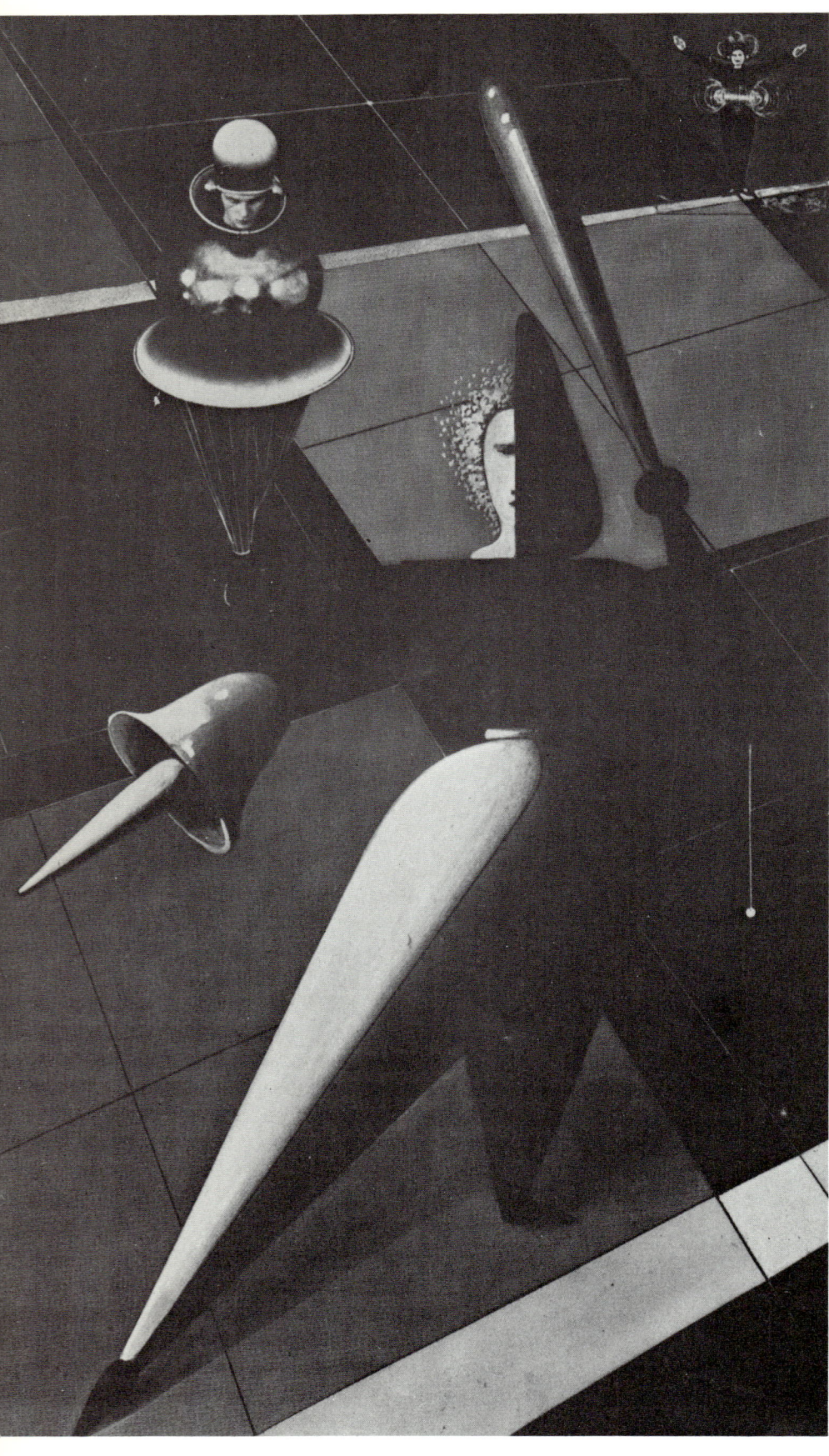

108 Oskar Schlemmer (1888–1943): costume design for *The Triadic Ballet*, with choreography by Oskar Schlemmer with Albert Burger and Elsa Hoetzel, music by Paul Hindemith, staged as an example of the work of the Bauhaus at the Landestheater, Stuttgart, 1922. Though not in a true sense a ballet, it was an attempt by the aestheticians of the Bauhaus to give expression in movement to their theories about the underlying shapes of the human body and its relation to space. Schlemmer's designs must have owed something to the Managers in *Parade* (see plates 89a, b): the human body was shown in a state of metamorphosis and the costumes were padded and exaggerated in outline through the use of papier mâché and cloth.

The Diaghilev Era

achievements of the arts in its own period. It had initiated rather than followed fashion. From the Diaghilev era can be traced nearly every subsequent development in stage design. That no one thereafter has been able to command the allegiance of major artists to such a degree, nor been so able to reveal them to the world, is the most extraordinary comment upon Diaghilev, who, rootless and without subvention, could impose his genius upon two decades of Western civilization.

A note on the Ballets Suédois

The Ballets Suédois was a company which lasted from 1920 to 1925 and one in which it is not too fanciful to cast Rolf de Maré as Diaghilev and Jean Börlin as Nijinsky. The company had started as a result of Mikhail Fokine's friendship with Rolf de Maré, an extremely wealthy Swede, a man of the arts, collector of paintings, an admirer of folk art and especially of folk dancing. Fokine and

109 Andrée Parr: costume designs for *L'Homme et son désir*, with choreography by Jean Börlin, music by Darius Milhaud, first performed by the Ballets Suédois in Paris, 1921. The two female figures are dressed as bells and the male dancer represents pan-pipes.

The Diaghilev Era

110 Fernand Léger (1881–1955): design for *Skating Rink*, dance poem by Riciotto Canudo with choreography by Jean Börlin and music by Arthur Honneger, first performed by the Ballets Suédois in Paris, 1922. *Skating Rink*, with brilliantly coloured décor and costumes by Léger, was an attempt to capitalize on the new 'poetry' of popular entertainments, of music hall and sport.

Design for Ballet

The Diaghilev Era

his wife Vera stayed with de Maré in Sweden, and during conversations the idea of starting a company which might act as a showcase for modern ideas in painting and dance was formulated. De Maré knew Paris, was friendly with Picasso, Léger, Braque, and many more of the painters of the avant-garde. Fokine's several visits to Sweden following his breach with Diaghilev were to act as an inspiration for Swedish ballet. He staged his ballets and taught; among his pupils were Jenny Hasselquist, Carina Ari, and Jean Börlin, all later to dance with the Ballets Suédois. Eventually Fokine recommended Börlin to de Maré as dancer and choreographer for the new company, Les Ballets Suédois, Swedish in name but essentially French in decorative outlook and in aspirations. The company, formed in 1920, involved the talents of Cocteau, Canudo, Claudel, and Blaise Cendras as librettists; the twenty-four works which eventually comprised the repertory had Börlin as sole choreographer, but a multiplicity of designers and composers – these last included Honneger, Satie, Cole Porter (orchestrated by Charles Koechlin!), Alfven, five of Les Six for *Les Mariés de la Tour Eiffel*, and Casella.

The internationalism of the company was most evident in the design; with the exception of a few Swedish works, which used Nils von Dardel, Einer

111 Fernand Léger: setting for *La Création du Monde*, ballet with choreography by Jean Börlin, music by Darius Milhaud, first performed by the Ballets Suédois in Paris, 1923.

112 Gerald Murphy (1888–1964): setting for *Within the Quota*, ballet with choreography by Jean Börlin, music by Cole Porter, first performed by the Ballets Suédois in Paris, 1923, it dealt with an immigrant's view of the US.

Design for Ballet

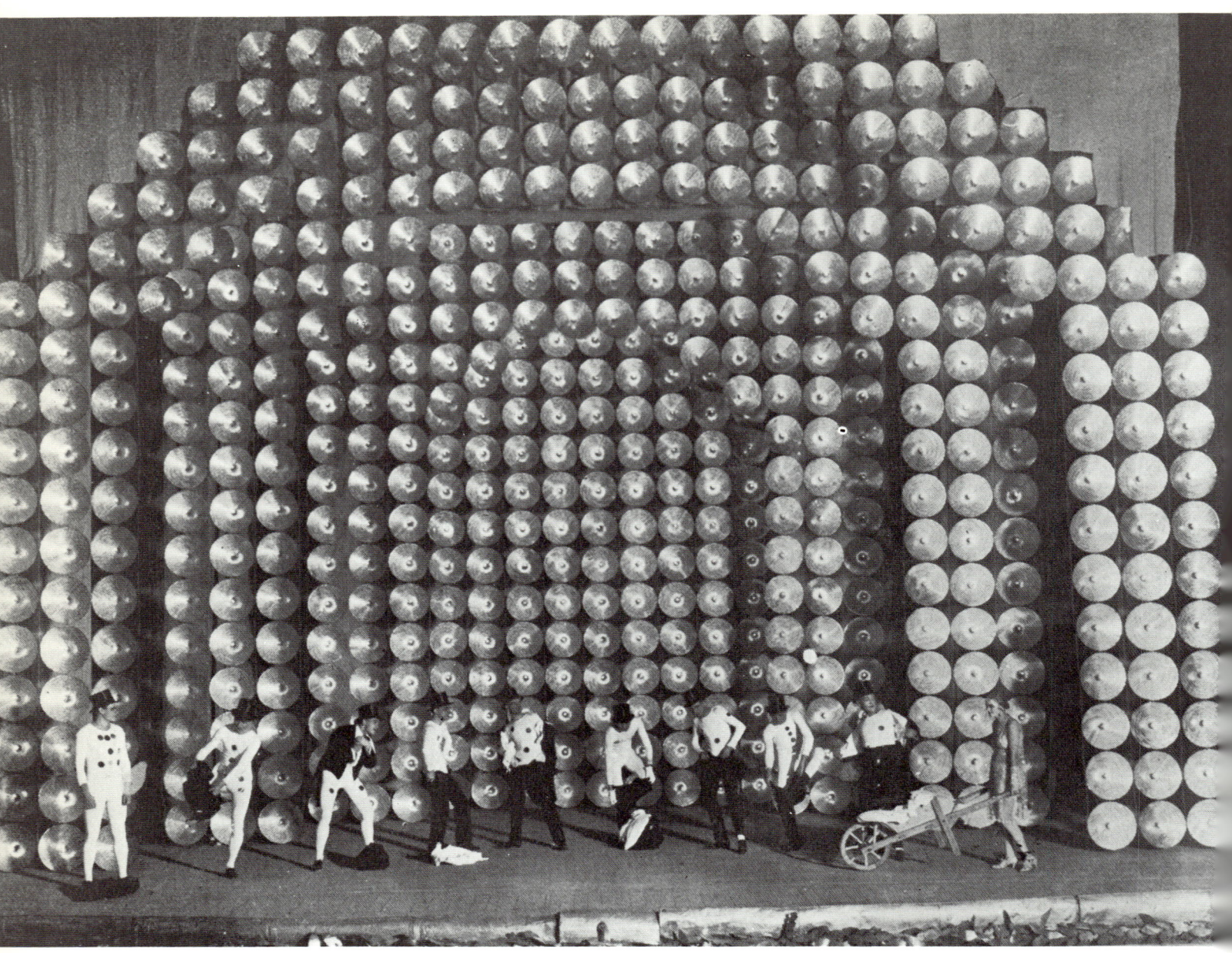

113 Francis Picabia (1879–1953): setting for *Relâche*, ballet with choreography by Jean Börlin, music by Satie, first performed by the Ballets Suédois in Paris, 1924.

Nerman and Gunar Hallstrom, the majority were decorated by Steinlen, Foujita, Pierre Laprade, André Hellé, Andrée Parr, Irène Lagut, Jean Hugo, Léger, Hélène Perdriat, Gerald Murphy, Giorgio de' Chirico, Francis Picabia and Pierre Bonnard. Among the most original of the ballets was *La Création du Monde*, in which the décor moved and became in effect a gigantic mobile, and the 'anti-ballet' *Relâche* (plate 113), with its anarchic disregard of the nice boundaries between stage and auditorium, stage reality and everyday reality, and its filmed interlude – René Clair's *Entr'acte*. *Relâche* (the French for 'theatre closed') was an experiment largely devised by Picabia to shock the audience by

> ... life, life as I like it; life without a morrow, the life of today, everything for today, nothing for yesterday, nothing for tomorrow. Motor headlights, pearl necklaces, rounded and slender forms of

women, publicity, music, motor-cars, men in evening dress, movement, noise, play, clear and transparent water, the pleasure of laughter, that is *Relâche* ... Erik Satie, Börlin, Rolf de Maré, René Clair, Prieur, and I have created *Relâche* a little in the same way that God creates life. There are no scenes, no costumes, no nudity, only space, space in which our imagination loves to roam.
(Cyril W. Beaumont, *Complete Book of Ballets*, London, 1937.)

The undoubted fun of *Relâche* lay in the determination of its collaborators to produce a very 'different' spectacle. It is the forerunner of some of the more outrageous manifestations of the 1920s, owing perhaps something to the

114 Alexandra Exter (1882–1949): design for a Bach ballet staged by Bronislava Nijinska in Paris, 1925. Alexandra Exter was one of the most distinguished members of the group of Russian-born artists who worked in the theatre in Russia before and just after the Revolution. Her initial interest in Cubism led Exter to view the theatre as a place for exciting Cubist experiment. She became involved with the experiments of Alexander Tairov at the Kamerny Theatre in Moscow and their joint productions during the war years were radical attempts at an entirely new form of theatrical presentation.

Dadaist desire to shock the comfortable public in any way possible. Picabia called it 'a lot of kicks in a lot of backsides, sacred or otherwise'.

Jean Börlin, exhausted by a most punishing schedule of creation and performance, was unable to continue working after 1925 and the company disbanded. During its brief years it had offered an interesting rivalry to the Diaghilev enterprise. Visually most distinguished, its ballets lacked any great choreographic merit; none have survived and what remains is the amazingly rich collection of design material formed by de Maré and now preserved in the Dansmuseet in Stockholm.

It is ironic that the Ballets Suédois paid only one brief visit to Sweden and were much disliked there.

AFTER DIAGHILEV

Design for Ballet

THE BALLET RUSSE companies of the 1930s were started in emulation of the Diaghilev troupe. Their ideal was, if not to cash in on an illustrious title, at least to try and revive the public success of the Russian Ballet. What was lacking, of course, was Diaghilev's taste, his drive for the new, his assumption that the ballets he presented were there because he wished to see them. They were examples of private whim rather than public consideration. He did not always like certain of his later pieces or certain of his later collaborators but his quest for new forms of expression, new boundaries for the art, were at least consistent. The decision to revive the Ballet Russe came in 1932 with the amalgamation of two companies: the Ballet de l'Opéra de Monte Carlo, directed by René Blum and the Ballet de l'Opéra Russe à Paris, administered by Colonel W. de Basil. With de Basil as director and Blum (a man of real taste) as artistic director, the new company called upon many former Diaghilev dancers and part of the former Diaghilev repertory (cared for by Serge Grigoriev), with Balanchine as choreographer. The company was successful, more so than had been thought possible, and when Balanchine left in 1933 to direct Les Ballets 1933 (financed by Edward James, the connoisseur and collector, as a showcase for his wife, the Austrian dancer Tilly Losch), Leonid Massine became chief choreographer. The subsequent struggles for power, for the right to stage certain ballets, for the magic title 'Ballet Russe' and the equally magic words 'Monte Carlo' are part of a gordion knot of amalgamations and splits, of changes of title and lawsuits, which lasted through the middle of the decade. Blum and de Basil each

On previous page
Dorothea Tanning (b. 1910): costumes for three 'guests' in *Night Shadow*, ballet with choreography by Balanchine and music by Bellini arranged by Rieti, first produced by the Ballet Russe de Monte Carlo in New York, 1946.

115 **André Derain: two costumes for *Les Songes*, ballet with choreography by Balanchine, music by Darius Milhaud, first performed by Les Ballets 1933, in Paris, 1933.**

After Diaghilev

acquired a company; each company toured extensively, feeding off the old repertory and staging new works as the years went on. In 1939 the de Basil company went to Australia and thence via South America to the USA, and after the war staggered to Europe where it ceased operations.

Blum remained in Europe – and died in Auschwitz. His company settled in the USA and became the Ballet Russe de Monte Carlo directed by Serge Denham, which after an increasingly tenuous existence in the late 1950s ceased to perform in 1962. Other companies formed at the war's end – Ballet International in New York, the Nouveaux Ballets de Monte Carlo, and the Grand Ballet du Marquis de Cuevas – perpetuated something of the Ballet Russe atmosphere as itinerant, big-star companies with a certain amount of glamour but few roots. It would, however, be idle to pretend that much of the creative force of the Diaghilev company could be found in these offspring. The tragedy of the Ballet Russe companies of the 1930s was that they aped Diaghilev's procedures without ever understanding the reason behind them. As the climate of Western life changed in the shadow of war, and as Diaghilev's progeny – Balanchine in the USA, Lifar at the Paris Opéra, Ninette de Valois and Marie Rambert in London – established their pattern of work, so the Ballet Russe became feebler and more self-parodying.

The Diaghilev enterprise had to end – it had prepared the ground for what was to come in France, Britain and the USA: the development of authentically national companies. The itinerant Ballets Russes of the 1930s still had a great deal of theatrical vitality and they contained dancers of brilliance who could best keep the old Diaghilev repertory alive. But they had no homes and they were increasingly at the mercy of public taste. The most interesting achievements of the 1930s were the symphonic ballets of Leonid Massine. Throughout his long career Massine has continued the Diaghilev manner in inviting distinguished creators to work with him. The décor of his ballets from the 1930s to the 1940s involved Joan Miró for *Jeux d'Enfants* (plate 116); Marc Chagall for *Aleko*; Salvador Dali for *Bacchanal*,

116 Joan Miró (b. 1893): scene from *Jeux d'Enfants*, ballet with choreography by Massine, music by Bizet, first performed by the Blum-de Basil Ballet Russe in Monte Carlo, 1933.

COL. W. de BASIL's BALLETS RUSSES Scene from "Jardin Public."

Opposite above
117 Jean Lurçat (1892–1966): scene from *Jardin Public*, ballet with choreography by Massine, music by Vladimir Dukelsky, first performed by the de Basil Ballet Russe in Chicago, 1935.

Opposite below
118 Raoul Dufy (1877–1953): setting for *Beach*, ballet with choreography by Massine, music by Jean Françaix, first performed by the Blum-de Basil Ballet Russe in Monte Carlo, 1933.

Above
119 Mariano Andreù: setting for *Don Juan*, ballet with choreography by Fokine, music by Gluck, first produced by René Blum's Ballet Russe de Monte Carlo in London, 1936. The Spanish painter Mariano Andreù produced a very skilled evocation of sixteenth-century Spanish dress and architecture for one of Fokine's last major ballets. Part of the action was given on a forestage masked by the large curtains which are seen here pulled back to reveal the main setting.

Labyrinth and *Tristan Fou* (plate 125); Matisse for *Rouge et Noir*; Derain for *La Valse* and *Mam'zelle Angot*; Bérard for *Symphonie Fantastique* (colour plate 20), *Seventh Symphony* (plate 120) and *Clock Symphony* (plate 121); André Masson for *Les Présages*; Balthus for *Le Peintre et son Modèle*; Tchelitchev for *Nobilissima Visione* (plate 124); Jean Lurçat for *Jardin Public* (plate 117); and Raoul Dufy for *Beach* (plate 118).

The prestige of the Ballet Russe companies was sufficient to maintain the 'painterly' aspect of design for new works well into the 1940s. In certain cases this meant that ballets were danced against paintings by well known artists; more rarely it meant that artist-designers of the quality of Bakst and Benois were involved.

Three figures of this period have a particular importance: Christian Bérard (1902–49), Eugene Berman (1899–1972), and Pavel Tchelitchev (1898–1957). A most perceptive assessment of Bérard's importance comes from an artist and designer of no less importance, Michael Ayrton. Writing in *Ballet Annual*, he provided an obituary in which he declared:

> It must surely be generally agreed that Christian Bérard, was, of his generation, the most subtle, exquisite and elegant designer both for the ballet and the drama, in France or indeed elsewhere. His costumes

Design for Ballet

are the most becoming and his sets remain both simpler and in more perfect taste than those of his scarcely less distinguished rivals and one time colleagues, Pavel Tchelitchev and Eugene Berman. His work was French where theirs was Russo-Parisian or quasi-Italianate; his skills and his sensitivity were the pure product of his native land unalloyed either by the superstitious metaphysics of Tchelitchev or the morbid archaism of Berman, and he surpassed them, not unnaturally, in just those qualities of subtlety and chic which have been the particular heritage of France since the days of Antoine Watteau. He was never cursed with the fabulous and essentially cerebral invention of Tchelitchev nor moved to the despairing expression of decay with which Berman has concerned himself. Bérard chose a gentle territory and, in attempting less profundity, he achieved a greater and apparently effortless perfection within his chosen orbit ... a man must be allowed to choose his own path and perhaps Bérard realised that the breathtaking speed and lightness of his touch and the lyrical effervescence of his colour were more suited to the transitory illusion of the theatre and even the flippancy of the fashion journal than to the more ruthless permanency of the easel picture. The most perfect of his theatrical creations were the least grandiose: *Cotillon* was superior to *The Seventh Symphony* and *Symphonie Fantastique* was finer than *The Clock Symphony*. Bérard's genius was for the nostalgic evocation of an unattainable world as fragile as a flower and as intangible as smoke in the evening air. In this delicate achievement, both in his rare paintings and in his justly famous work for the theatre he has not been surpassed in our day.

120 Christian Bérard: scene from *Seventh Symphony*, ballet with choreography by Massine, music by Beethoven, first performed by the Ballet Russe de Monte Carlo in Monte Carlo, 1938.

After Diaghilev

121 Christian Bérard: costume designs for the Duke and the Lizard in *Clock Symphony*, ballet with choreography by Massine, music by Haydn, first produced by the Sadler's Wells Ballet at Covent Garden, 1948. Although the ballet had little to recommend it, the designs at least had the merit of Bérard's exquisite taste.

Bérard's initial introduction to the ballet stage came with his designs for *La Nuit*, a ballet in a Cochran revue, but his first important designs were two Balanchine ballets, *Cotillon* for the Ballet Russe de Monte Carlo in 1932 and *Mozartiana* for Les Ballets 1933. There followed two works for Massine, the *Symphonie Fantastique* (colour plate 20) of 1936 and *Seventh Symphony* (plate 120) of 1938. His subsequent work, which contributed so much to the renaissance of French ballet after the war, will be discussed later.

Eugene Berman was born in Petersburg and studied art in Russia before leaving for Paris after the Revolution. But it was the Italian landscape with its expansive sky, its architectural felicities and its ruins which inspired his work. His love of architecture in design and his feeling for perspective can be dated from his first trip to Italy in 1922. He particularly admired the concepts of the Renaissance stage scene and was eager to adopt them for his own imaginative

122 Eugene Berman: setting for *Icare*, ballet with choreography by Lifar, rhythms by Lifar orchestrated by Szyfer, as revived for the Ballet Russe de Monte Carlo, in New York, 1938.

world. His paintings of this period contain scenes that were like vistas from the Renaissance and Baroque theatre. During the 1920s he became associated with a group of painters who were classified as Neo-romantics; they included Bérard, Tchelitchev and Berman's brother Leonid. Eugene Berman greatly admired Bérard and wished to work in the theatre too, but it was not until 1936 that he made his first designs for *L'Opéra de Quatre Sous* in Paris. Then after his arrival in America came the chance to work for the ballet in 1938 and 1939. He designed *Icare* (plate 122) and *The Devil's Holiday* (plate 123) for the Ballet Russe de Monte Carlo – in the latter work in particular he was able to use the Italianate manner he so adored. Edwin Denby in his review of the first performance wrote:

> Berman, from whom we had wonderful drops for *Icare* last season, has given us five more which are as brilliant as any baroque Burnacini, but full of contemporary intimate and personal sentiment and also scenically discreet; and his costumes are the most wonderful imaginable.

As a tribute to the landscape he loved, Berman designed several settings for a projected ballet to be danced to Mendelssohn's Italian Symphony. In 1941 he designed a version of *Giselle* which he was later to use in 1946 for Ballet Theatre New York.

In 1941 he also designed Balanchine's *Concerto Barocco* for American Ballet Caravan. Allison Delarue in his excellent monograph on Berman (Dance Index, volume 5, no. 1, New York, January 1946) describes this setting as

> ... of almost austere simplicity. A sense of infinity grew from Berman's use of architectural arches in receding perspective towards

After Diaghilev

the backdrop, pursued, as it were, with the relentlessness of a Bach fugue. In contrast was the sumptuousness of the rich, nostalgic blue backdrop and of the white clouds which, in the wonderful illusion of space, seem suspended between the arches. How often Berman defines a shape or a gesture in painting, or balances weights, as eloquently as ballet!

In 1943 came one of Berman's greatest achievements in designing, Antony Tudor's *Romeo and Juliet* for American Ballet Theatre. And from this point Berman's contribution to design may more properly be considered in a later section of this book.

Pavel Tchelitchev had attempted an almost impossible task in *Ode* – the creation of a world of light whose poetic sensibilities and resonances were hard for an audience to grasp in 1928. Like Berman and Bérard he did not decorate a great many works, but each remains an important contribution. Tchelitchev's obsession with a form of alchemy of the senses is very well

123 Eugene Berman: costume design for the Hat-seller in *The Devil's Holiday*, ballet with choreography by Frederick Ashton, music by Paganini arranged by Tommasini, first performed by the Ballet Russe de Monte Carlo in New York, 1939.

Design for Ballet

174

124 a, b Pavel Tchelitchev: working drawings and set design for *Nobilissima Visione* (*Saint Francis*), ballet with choreography by Massine, music by Hindemith, first performed by the de Basil Ballet Russe in London, 1938.

summed up by Lincoln Kirstein in his *The New York City Ballet* (New York, 1973):

> Pavel Tchelitchev has suffered from an ambiguous reputation. In life and after, he was admired, feared and envied as a ferocious wit and fantastic decorator. Since he was a sworn enemy of official Surrealism, he never shared in the scandal or prestige of its politics as a clique or academy; yet his free-floating, serious, whimsical rhetoric fatally suggested some likely connection. It accentuated a systematic derangement of the senses, as he said, *sur mesure et par commande*, fantasy by formula, hysteria on demand; substructures touched the rational and metaphysical, while academic Surrealism 'comes out of the tube; lies flat on the brush' ... In an age of haphazard improvisation, his fantasy fed continually on vividly observed anatomies of animal, vegetable, mineral, and celestial worlds. To be sure, he was 'impossible'; he loved impossible colours, the gorgeous chromatics of sunsets, autumn leaves, orchids, jewels and hummingbirds. He liked dancers and loved to dress them, chiefly by undressing them, but cared little for their dancing once he had costumed them for the stage.

In 1933 he worked for Les Ballets 1933 on *Errante*, a ballet by Balanchine in which he again played light into a white setting. Balanchine was to use him for the staging of Gluck's *Orpheus and Eurydice* at the Metropolitan Opera House, New York, in 1936. This was a remarkably beautiful staging which displeased all but a few perceptive members of the audience and created a scandal – not surprising in view of the socialite, barnacled canary-fanciers who made up the audience at the old Met. (The production is fully discussed in Kirstein's *The New York City Ballet*: entry for December 1935.)

In 1938 Tchelitchev worked with Massine on *Nobilissima Visione* (plate 124) for the de Basil Ballet Russe. In this work the Italian landscape banished much of Tchelitchev's gloom and the settings – which were painted scenery – were

Design for Ballet

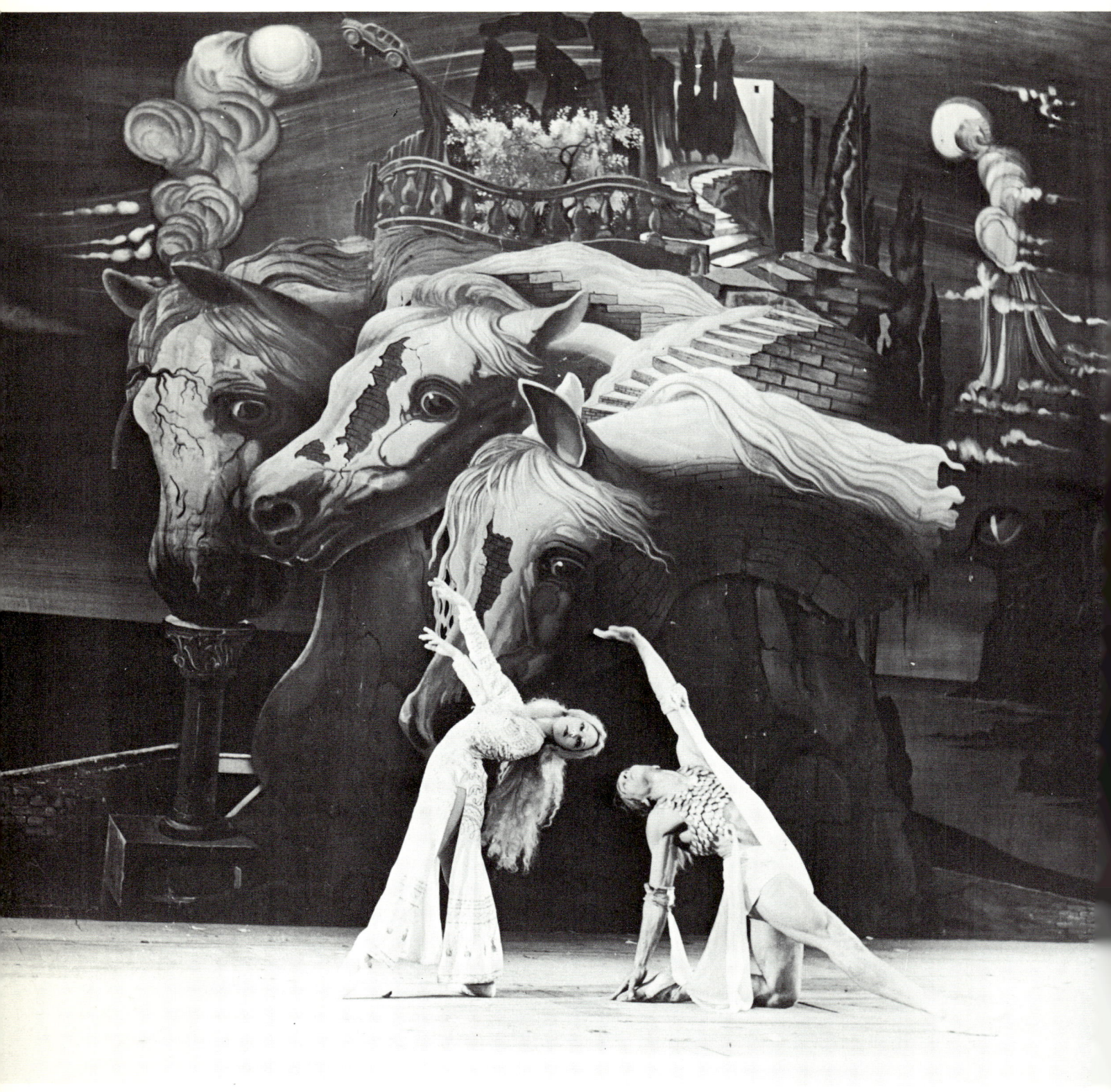

125 Salvador Dali: scene from *Tristan Fou*, ballet with choreography by Massine, music by Wagner, first produced by Ballet International in New York, 1944, and here seen in the revival by the Grand Ballet du Marquis du Cuevas, 1948.

After Diaghilev

filled with southern light. The association with Balanchine continued with *Balustrade*, danced to Stravinsky's Violin Concerto, and staged by the Original Ballet Russe in New York in 1941. A black stage was marked out by a white balustrade and the fantastic costuming made use of sequins which caught the light and suggested something of the glittering, mysterious world of insects and birds which was evoked by Tchelitchev's extraordinarily beautiful designs. In the same year Tchelitchev worked on an important project for Balanchine, *The Cave of Sleep* to a score by Hindemith: this was never realized in performance, but in the following year his designs for *Apollo* and for *Concerto* were used on South American tours by the then Kirstein/Balanchine American Ballet Caravan.

The attraction of Surrealism had also brought Salvador Dali (b. 1904) to the ballet stage and his three works for Massine, and the *Colloque Sentimentale* which he decorated in 1944 for André Eglevsky, brought all the well known paraphernalia of his nightmare world into ballet. Dali's imagery was to prove overpowering. In *Tristan Fou* (plate 125) the engulfing and disturbing designs dominated the choreography – though the work was an extraordinary visual sensation. *Colloque Sentimentale* (plate 126) was memorable for its backcloth, and for the dressmaker's dummy mounted on a tortoise and the draped bicyclist who crossed the stage. But the central *pas de deux* was lost amid the Surrealist flummery.

126 Salvador Dali: scene from *Colloque Sentimentale*, ballet with choreography by André Eglevsky, music by Paul Bowles, first staged by Ballet International in New York, 1944, and subsequently revived by the Grand Ballet du Marquis de Cuevas, 1948.

Opposite above
127 Giorgio de' Chirico: design for *Protée*, ballet with choreography by David Lichine, music by Debussy, first produced by the de Basil Ballet Russe in London, 1938.

Opposite below
128 Alexandre Benois: design for the first scene of *The Nutcracker* as revived by Alexandra Fedorova for the Ballet Russe de Monte Carlo in New York, 1940.

Below
129 André Derain: setting for *Salade*, ballet with choreography by Lifar, music by Darius Milhaud, first performed at the Paris Opéra, 1935.

Balanchine's *Night Shadow* in its first appearance with the Ballet Russe de Monte Carlo in 1946 was also given Surrealist treatment. In a conventional setting the 'guests' were clothed in some distinctly unconventional outfits (see page 165).

Parallel with the Ballets Russes activities of the 1930s, recognition must go to Serge Lifar for the rebirth of ballet at the Paris Opéra which he brought about when he was appointed principal dancer and ballet master in 1930. Under Lifar's powerful guidance the ballet company was reorganized and Lifar himself produced a massive body of work until his final departure in 1958. To him we owe the re-establishment of the Paris Opéra as a major European ballet house. As choreographer, dancer and polemicist Lifar made an extraordinary contribution to the ballet of our time: his works may not always have found favour with the public outside France, but it is ungrateful and unjust to ignore his achievement. He brought with him to the Opéra very

After Diaghilev

130 Fernand Léger: project for a setting for *David Triomphant*, ballet with choreography by Lifar, music by Debussy and Moussorgsky, first performed at the Théâtre de la Maison Internationale des Etudiants, Paris, 1936.

Design for Ballet

After Diaghilev

Opposite above
131 Mikhail Larionov: model for a setting for *Sur le Borysthène*, ballet with choreography by Lifar, music by Prokofiev, costumes by Goncharova, first performed at the Paris Opéra, 1932.

Opposite below
132 Giorgio de' Chirico: setting for *Bacchus et Ariane*, ballet with choreography by Lifar, music by Albert Roussel, first performed at the Paris Opéra, 1933.

Above
133 Paul Larthe: design for the first act of *Coppélia* as revived at the Paris Opéra, 1936.

considerable glamour and also an understanding of how Diaghilev had worked. Lifar rehabilitated the male dancer, and his ballets of the inter-war years had a heroic dignity which was also reflected in their visual presentation. He called upon designers of the calibre of de' Chirico, Pruna, Goncharova and Larionov, and made particular use of such French designers as Colin, Derain, Dignimont, Larthe, Léger, Brianchon, Cassandre, Brayer and Delfau.

As an historical postscript to the 1930s it is interesting to note that the emergent British ballet of this time attracted some very distinguished designers. Despite the pre-eminence of the Ballets Russes, the Sadler's Wells Ballet under Ninette de Valois and the Ballet Rambert guided by Marie Rambert were putting down the firm roots that were to make British ballet so strong in the post-war period. We have chosen to illustrate eight works which indicate something of the exceptional quality of design during these years. As

Design for Ballet

After Diaghilev

early as 1931 and 1932 the Vic-Wells ballet used Duncan Grant and Vanessa Bell, and by the mid-1930s the company could claim also to have employed George Sheringham, Edward Burra, Rex Whistler, E. McKnight Kauffer, Sophie Fedorovitch, Cecil Beaton, and in 1938 they turned to André Derain for Ashton's *Harlequin in the Street*.

Rex Whistler, who was killed in action in Normandy in 1944 at the age of thirty-nine, was one of Britain's few designers of genius. An artist with an extraordinary natural affinity for the eighteenth century, he made an indelible mark on the art of his time as illustrator, muralist and stage designer. For the straight theatre he produced designs for eight plays during the decade 1933–43, and for the ballet he designed six works: further, he produced designs for *Fidelio* and *The Marriage of Figaro* and décor for a variety of revues. In everything he did there was a consummate sense of period style in which a historical era was brilliantly re-created within the terms of Whistler's own poetic and eloquent manner. The only designs that now survive in the theatre are for Ninette de Valois's masterly and enduring study of Hogarthian London, *The Rake's Progress* (plate 135). After more than forty years the ballet has not dated and nor have Whistler's designs. They are among the finest achievements of British design.

E. McKnight Kauffer (1890–1954), the American-born artist, was one of the most influential graphic designers of the inter-war years. Posters and illustrations by him typify the excellence of much of the graphic design of the period and his work for *Checkmate* (plate 136) is still vividly exciting in the theatre. The conventions of the chess board and the costuming of chess pieces were adapted to the ballet stage with complete success.

The Russian-born Sophie Fedorovitch (1893–1953) came to London in 1920 and, through her friendship with Marie Rambert and especially with Frederick Ashton, was to play a very important role in the development of British ballet. Her designs were distinguished by their elegance and economy of means; they are difficult to illustrate since the subtlety of nuance which is their particular distinction in the theatre cannot be caught in a photograph. Plate 137 shows *La Fête Etrange*, one of her finest achievements, in a 1971 revival by the Scottish Ballet. Fedorovitch captures with extraordinary skill the sense of adolescent suffering in the hushed wintry landscape where a mysterious betrothal party takes place.

The war years, during which Sadler's Wells Ballet continued a policy of new creations, brought the magnificent designs of Graham Sutherland (b. 1903) for Ashton's *The Wanderer* (colour plates 24, 25), but it is Robert Helpmann to whom we owe a particular debt. As principal dancer and choreographer Helpmann was of crucial importance to the company at this time. For his ballets he turned first to Oliver Messel for *Comus* and then to Leslie Hurry, whom he introduced to the theatre with the phenomenal *Hamlet* designs in 1942 (jacket illustration). In the same year he used the Chinese artist Chiang Yee for *The Birds*, and in 1944 Edward Burra (1905–76) was invited to decorate *Miracle in the Gorbals*. One of the finest English painters of his time, Edward Burra had early made a name for himself by his drawings and paintings of the European underworld, its sailors' cafés and brothels. During the 1930s his imaginative treatment of the horrors of the Spanish Civil War produced an intensification of his style, which came to encompass a fierce sense of revulsion. His wartime paintings continued to reflect this mood and *Miracle in the Gorbals*, his finest achievement as a theatrical designer, dates from this period. He recorded with a minute skill the brutish squalor of the locale

134 George Sheringham (1884–1937): set for *The Lord of Burleigh*, ballet with choreography by Frederick Ashton, music by Mendelssohn, first performed by the Camargo Society, London, 1931 and the following year taken into the repertory of the Vic-Wells Ballet.

Design for Ballet

135 Rex Whistler: drop-curtain for *The Rake's Progress*, ballet with choreography by Ninette de Valois, music and scenario by Gavin Gordon, first performed by the Sadler's Wells Ballet in London, 1935.

136 a, b E. McKnight Kauffer: (a) costumes for *Checkmate*, ballet with choreography by Ninette de Valois, music by Arthur Bliss, first performed by the Sadler's Wells Ballet in Paris, 1937. (b) costume design for the Red Knight as revised in 1947 when the ballet was restaged at the Royal Opera House, Covent Garden.

Above
137 Sophie Fedorovitch: setting for *La Fête Etrange*, ballet devised by Ronald Crichton from Alain-Fournier's *Le Grand Meaulnes*, with choreography by Andrée Howard and music by Fauré, first performed by the London Ballet, in London, 1940, and here seen in a revival by the Scottish Ballet in 1971.

Below
138 Edward Burra: design for the set for *Miracle in the Gorbals*, ballet with choreography by Robert Helpmann, music by Arthur Bliss, first performed by the Sadler's Wells Ballet, in London, 1944. Helpmann's fourth ballet told the story of the return of Christ to the slums of Glasgow and his betrayal.

After Diaghilev

and, in addition to the set (plate 138), he provided a magnificent drop-curtain showing a ship in dry dock which effectively placed the ballet in its social and emotional milieu.

Two other works of the wartime repertory were admirably designed. Frederick Ashton, on leave from the RAF, created *The Quest*, which was decorated by John Piper (b. 1903), and Andrée Howard made her first ballet for the company, *The Spider's Banquet*, with designs by Michael Ayrton. Whatever the surrounding difficulties of performing and touring ballet in wartime, the Sadler's Wells Ballet enjoyed at this time its decorative peak.

In Russia

In the years following the Revolution of 1917 the identity of ballet in Russia inevitably underwent a complete change. From being a court entertainment dependent upon the Tsar's purse, the companies in Moscow and Petrograd were faced with the harsh realities of existence in a society eager to destroy everything appertaining to the monarchy. The efforts of Anatoly Lunacharsky, People's Commissar for Education, and a trusted friend of Lenin, were

139 The second act of *Giselle* as it looked in Moscow *c*.1920 in the production by Alexander Gorsky. The novelty of dressing the Wilis in gravecloths and veils rather than in the traditional Romantic tarlatans is symptomatic of the new approach to the classics of ballet which was part of the ideals in production at this time. Natalia Roslavleva in her *Era of the Russian Ballet* (London, 1966) records that Gorsky's production of *Swan Lake* in 1920 had soloists and *corps de ballet* dressed 'in loose tunics in the Duncan style rather than in the traditional tutu'. Other ballets, including *The Nutcracker*, were similarly updated. But these experiments did not last long and today the presentations of the classics by the great Soviet companies are entirely traditional in appearance.

Design for Ballet

to be vital in the battle which ensued during the early 1920s to preserve the ballet and to force it to respond to its new responsibilities in a Soviet state. This story is very interestingly told in Mary Grace Swift's *The Art of the Dance in the USSR* (Indiana, 1968) and her narrative highlights the remarkable experiments in dance and design which at first made the early post-Revolutionary years so stimulating in the USSR. With the emergence of a new style of 'Soviet' ballet there came new design ideas, of course, but the imposition of the doctrine of Socialist Realism under the Stalin régime was to prove inhibiting to anything but the most staid 'official' art. The massive size of the stages in Leningrad and Moscow, the new heroic aesthetic which was propounded from the lyric stage, imposed a pictorial style which during the 1940s and 1950s looked, to Western eyes at least, sterile and old-fashioned. It is difficult for Western observers to obtain any overall judgement of Soviet ballet during these years: our illustrations are offered as some indication of the varied styles to be seen in a country where ballet is an art honoured and revered more than anywhere else in the world.

140 Boris Erdman: scene from *Joseph the Beautiful*, ballet with choreography by Kasyan Goleizovsky, music by S. Vasilenko, first produced in Moscow, 1925. The extraordinary experiments which took place in the arts in Russia in the immediately post-Revolutionary years were witness to the aesthetic vitality of the period. Goleizovsky, a notable innovator, aimed at the acrobatic and sculptural plastique and in *Joseph the Beautiful* he and Erdman painted the dancers' bodies in a colour scheme which was then displayed upon a Constructivist ramp in the Experimental Theatre in Moscow.

After Diaghilev

Above
141 Mikhail Kurilko: design for the Vision Scene of *The Red Poppy*, ballet with choreography by Lev Lashchilin and Vassily Tikhomirov, music by Glière, first performed by the Bolshoy Ballet in Moscow, 1927. *The Red Poppy* is celebrated as the first authentically Soviet ballet to be produced after the Revolution. Its theme of Russian sailors coming to the aid of oppressed Chinese workers in a Treaty Port was ideologically correct and its richness of dance incident was guaranteed to hold the audience's interest from the very beginning. In the second act the heroine, Tao-Hoa, dreams of the ancient China which is so clearly indicated in the design. Kurilko himself devised the scenario for the ballet.

Right
142 B. Matrunin (b. 1895): setting for the second scene of *The Three Fat Men*, ballet with choreography by Igor Moiseyev, music by V. A. Oransky, first performed by the Bolshoy Ballet in Moscow, 1935. It was an ideologically suitable four-act ballet about workers delivered from the oppression of three fat men, and the illustration shows the setting for the bloated capitalist palace of these villains. Its style, and that of the costumes, is properly satiric and grotesque.

Design for Ballet

Colour 18 Pierre Bonnard (1867–1947): design for a set for *Jeux*, ballet with choreography by Jean Börlin, music by Debussy, first performed by the Ballets Suédois in Paris, 1920. Bonnard's only contribution to the ballet stage was made for the first season of Rolf de Maré's company.

Design for Ballet

143 L. F. Fedorov: setting for *The Footballer*, ballet with choreography by Lev Laschilin and Igor Moiseyev, music by V. A. Oransky, first performed by the Bolshoy Ballet in Moscow, 1930. The story concerns the mismatching of a bourgeois couple and a pair of working-class figures. The setting with its use of different levels is supposed to represent the decadent West and it has a certain Art Déco charm.

After Diaghilev

Colour 19 André Derain: design for *L'Epreuve d'Amour*, ballet with choreography by Fokine, music by Mozart, first performed by René Blum's Ballet Russe de Monte Carlo, in Monte Carlo, 1936.

Colour 20 Christian Bérard: costume designs for two revellers in *La Symphonie Fantastique*, ballet with choreography by Massine, music by Berlioz, first produced by the de Basil Ballet Russe in London, 1936.

Colour 21 Natalia Goncharova: setting for *Cinderella*, ballet with choreography by Fokine, music by d'Erlanger, first produced by the de Basil Ballet Russe in London, 1938. This illustration is taken from the souvenir programme.

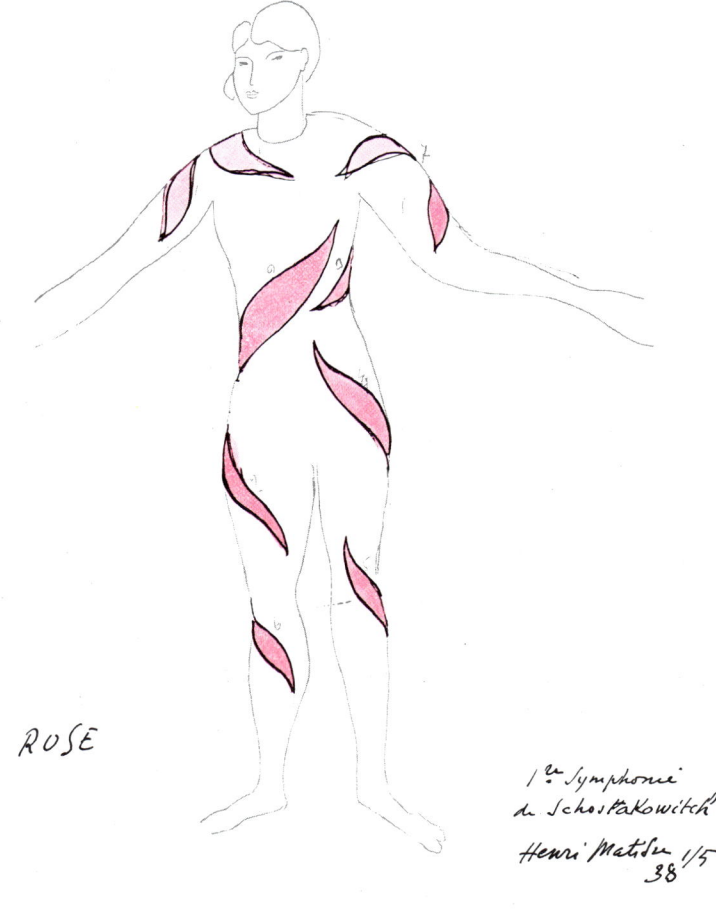

Colour 22 Henri Matisse (1869–1954): costume design for *L'Etrange Farandole* (*Rouge et Noir*), ballet with choreography by Massine to the Shostakovich first symphony, first performed by the René Blum Ballet Russe de Monte Carlo in Monte Carlo, 1939. Dame Alicia Markova remembers Matisse himself painting the pink sections on to her tights.

200

After Diaghilev

Opposite
144 a, b I. Rabinovich (b. 1894): settings for *The Sleeping Beauty*, as produced by the Bolshoy Ballet in Moscow, 1936. (a) The airy fantasy of this set for the Prologue is typical of the period. The size of the stages in Moscow and Leningrad imposes a certain decorative manner upon the ballets which, when not carefully realistic, are given charming though rather lightweight treatment of this kind. (b) Again for the first act a kind of Hollywood fantasy has taken over from any sense of historical accuracy or a desire to place the ballet in an accepted period setting. Soviet productions have sometimes avoided the sort of literalism that is part of the Western view of staging the nineteenth-century masterpieces.

Above
145 Gusztav Olàh (b. 1901): setting for *The Wooden Prince*, ballet with choreography by Jan Cieplinsky, music by Béla Bartók, presented by the Hungarian State Ballet in Budapest, 1935. The distortion, and slightly Constructivist style, is an example of mid-European design of this period.

Above
Colour 23 Kenneth Rowell (b. 1922): setting for the storm in *Le Baiser de la fée*, ballet with choreography by Kenneth MacMillan, music by Igor Stravinsky, first performed in this version by the Royal Ballet at Covent Garden, 1960. This work is notoriously difficult to design because its last scene takes place in a fantasy-world, but Rowell, an Australian painter and designer, produced designs which are among the most poetically beautiful ever commissioned by the Royal Ballet.

Opposite above
Colour 24 Graham Sutherland: backcloth for opening scene of *The Wanderer*, ballet with choreography by Frederick Ashton, music by Schubert, arranged by Liszt, first performed by the Sadler's Wells Ballet in London, 1941.

Opposite below
Colour 25 Graham Sutherland: backcloth for the final scene of *The Wanderer*.

DESIGN OF TODAY

Design of Today

In selecting and arranging the design in this, the most historically recent section of the book, we are conscious of many problems; of being too close to our subject – of not seeing the outline of the artistic wood for the trees of individual talents; of being over-influenced by the current popularity of certain types of design; of, inevitably, not being able to take a total view; of not being able to show certain designs because of the appalling lack of adequate records of performance – it is not usual to find full-stage photographs of ballets that give a proper idea of set and costumes as an entity. We have suffered here, as elsewhere, from the loss and dispersal of designs and from the inability of companies and individuals to answer requests, no matter how urgently expressed or how often repeated, for material relative to a certain company or even a certain country. We admit, of course, to personal preference. It is also hard to disassociate the design for a ballet from our response to its choreography. Certain magnificent ballets have minimal design; much of the New York City Ballet repertory is given in the simplest practice dress since Balanchine's choreography is entirely self-sufficient and requires no decorative aids. Certain utterly worthless ballets were given value by the excellence of their decorative element. Many, many fine ballets have disappeared, taking with them design as rewarding as their choreography. The achievements of lighting designers have, in recent years, brought a real enhancement to the staging of ballet. Diaghilev, asked what he 'did' in the Ballet Russe, would sometimes reply that he was in charge of the lighting. Kochno's testimony to the skill and untiring energy with which this great man would spend hours lighting a ballet is evidence enough of the importance he attached to this aspect of theatre. When the New York City Ballet came to Covent Garden after the war the lighting by the late Jean Rosenthal excited much comment: the company were thought to have brought with them extra batteries of lamps. Jean Rosenthal observed that she was quite simply using the lights in the theatre. One of the most visually stimulating dance performances known to us was given by the Nederlands Dans Theater at the Opera House in Ottowa's National Arts Centre: a work seen several times in Europe was transformed because of the immense contribution made by the lighting designer and the technical crew.

Lighting, a vital ingredient of design in the dance theatre, is, alas, impossible to illustrate in book form. We must however record that the force of light, its evocative and atmospheric power, is too rarely felt in the generality of ballet productions. It is Alwin Nikolais who has best shown what light can do; too few ballet companies seem interested in benefiting from his achievements.

Traditional Design

Because design is dictated by the type of theatre in which it is seen, and hence by the type of audience who will see it, we have sought a division of the designs we illustrate after 1945 into groupings which reflect both aesthetic ideals and performing locales.

Design for Ballet

On previous page
Victor Vasarely (b. 1908): setting for *Kraanberg*, ballet with choreography by Roland Petit, music by Xenakis, first staged by the National Ballet of Canada in Ottawa, 1969. Roland Petit's choreography found little favour but the dizzying optical effects devised by Vasarely were most exciting.

Colour 26 Nicholas Georgiadis: design for the ballroom scene in Act I of *Romeo and Juliet* in the version choreographed by Kenneth MacMillan, first performed by the Royal Ballet at Covent Garden, 1965; seen here in the film production by Paul Czinner, 1966.

Design of Today

Design for Ballet

Design of Today

Dominating this section are the great opera houses which are the home theatres for the national companies and large touring organizations: troupes like the Royal Ballet, the major Russian companies, the New York City Ballet and American Ballet Theatre, London Festival Ballet and the companies based on the state opera houses of Europe.

There is an inevitable bias towards a traditional and 'operatic' style of design. Innovation is rarely the ideal: the established classical ballets of the nineteenth century are the foundation stone of many of these repertories. An interesting facet of this branch of the dance theatre is a comparison between national approaches and the differing attitudes to historical representation over the years. The changing shape of dancers as well as the changing outline of the ballerina's tutu, the refurbishing and updating of the classical repertory, and the whims of dancers and producers who distort both choreography and the aesthetic principles of the old ballets in order to gratify their particular egos, are all contributory factors to the periodic new look that is given to the 'classics'.

Occasionally an artist like Carzou or Berman can provide a setting for *Giselle* (see plate 152) in which personal style becomes one with the period nature of the ballet itself. But for the most part the traditional approach is preferred, above all by opera house audiences. Such satisfactory designs as those by Simon Virsaladze for the Leningrad State Kirov Ballet's productions of *Swan Lake* and *The Sleeping Beauty* (plate 146) are examples to be honoured for their discretion and suitability to the ballets as presented by that great company.

The achievement of the Greek-born designer Nicholas Georgiadis (b. 1925), with his grandeur of effects, is a no less pleasing way of dealing with the classic repertory and also with its extension today in such major contemporary pieces as Kenneth MacMillan's *Manon*, for which Georgiadis has produced designs of great distinction and very positive dramatic power. Georgiadis was first introduced to the ballet stage by MacMillan, whose first professional ballet, *Danses Concertantes*, he designed in 1955. Thereafter MacMillan and Georgiadis collaborated on a sequence of outstanding productions which includes, as well as *Manon*, *Noctambules*, *The Invitation*, *Romeo and Juliet* and *Las Hermanas*. Georgiadis has also designed several productions for Rudolf Nureyev: notably *The Nutcracker* and *The Sleeping Beauty* (plate 151). In all Georgiadis's design there is a very solid architectural reason which supports his imaginative work. Like his settings, his costumes are sustained by a sound historical understanding and he remains one of the most influential designers of today.

The Royal Ballet's policy of producing full-length ballets which continue and develop the attitudes of the nineteenth-century classics has been responsible for some exceptional design on the grand scale. The reopening of the Royal Opera House, Covent Garden, after the war brought the then Sadler's Wells Ballet to its rightful home. The enormous success of the opening production of *The Sleeping Beauty* was testimony not only to the

146 Simon Virsaladze: setting for the first act of *The Sleeping Beauty* as performed by the Leningrad State Kirov Ballet, 1961. This production was shown in London in 1961 when it was acclaimed for its visual elegance.

210

Design of Today

147 Alexandre Benois: design for the first act of *Giselle* as performed at the Paris Opéra, 1948. In his seventy-eighth year, when he redesigned *Giselle* for the Opéra, Benois could still show his mastery of design and his ability to make the traditional setting for a scene seem both touching and apposite. There is nothing novel in this design, but it remains an almost ideal evocation of the period of the ballet and setting for the drama. Younger designers may have sought a variety of innovations: Benois's vision seems both wise and right.

212

Design of Today

Opposite above
148 Oliver Messel: setting for the third act of *The Sleeping Beauty* as performed by the Sadler's Wells Ballet at the reopening of the Royal Opera House, Covent Garden, 1946.

Opposite below
149 Lila de Nobili and Henry Bardon: setting for the Prologue of *The Sleeping Beauty* as performed by the Royal Ballet at Covent Garden, 1968.

Right
150 Peter Farmer: setting for the first act of *The Sleeping Beauty* as performed by the Royal Ballet at Covent Garden, 1973.

Below
151 Nicholas Georgiadis: model for the Prologue of *The Sleeping Beauty* as performed by London Festival Ballet, London, 1975.

classical distinction of the company and the affection in which it was held by the audience, but also to the fairy-tale allure of the designs (plate 148) by Oliver Messel (b. 1905). After the austerities of the war the Bibiena fantasy of Messel's settings seemed like a promise of the pleasures of peace. In some miraculous way the company managed to dispel all thoughts of rationing and clothing coupons and revealed to audiences that British ballet could be as glamorous as the pre-war Ballets Russes. Oliver Messel's *Beauty* designs remain one of the most influential examples of ballet décor in the past thirty years. The elegance of his invention was excellently suited to showing off the diamond flash of Petipa's dance. It is interesting to note that the Royal Ballet subsequently had *The Sleeping Beauty* redesigned by other artists (see plates 149, 150), but the Messel designs were used in 1976 when American Ballet Theatre mounted a production.

Michael Ayrton (1921–75), famed as painter, sculptor and writer, produced some exceptional designs for the theatre. Two of the most remarkable were for the Sadler's Wells Ballet: *The Spider's Banquet* in 1944 and *The Faery Queen*, an opera-masque by Henry Purcell first performed by the Covent Garden Opera Company and the Sadler's Wells Ballet in 1946 (plate 154). Writing about the production of the Purcell masque, Ayrton stated that he had based his scenery and costumes upon the work of Inigo Jones and he notes

> Jones's own method of masque staging approached far nearer to the ballet scenery of today than did the more primitive processions which

Above
152 Jean Carzou: setting for the second act of *Giselle* as performed at the Paris Opéra, 1954. Carzou's style resulted in a fresh and dramatically convincing approach to the old classic. Compare with the Benois setting, plate 151.

Opposite above
153 Osbert Lancaster (b. 1908): backcloth for *Napoli* as staged by Harald Lander for Festival Ballet at the Royal Festival Hall, London, 1954. The artist, cartoonist and writer Osbert Lancaster is probably best known to ballet audiences for his designs for *La Fille mal gardée* and *Pineapple Poll*, but his topographical skill was also wonderfully deployed in the setting he provided for *Napoli*. It is designing marked by the characteristic wit that has made Lancaster one of the most delightful and truly entertaining artists of our time.

Opposite below
154 Michael Ayrton: design for the act drop, *Ballet of the Birds*, Act III, Scene 2, in *The Faery Queen*, opera-masque by Henry Purcell adapted and arranged by Constant Lambert with choreography by Frederick Ashton and produced by Malcolm Baker-Smith, first performed by the Covent Garden Opera and the Sadler's Wells Ballet at Covent Garden, 1946.

Design of Today

Design for Ballet

characterised the pre-Jacobean masque or the austere conventions of Shakespeare's playhouse. From the point of view of spectacular conjuring, the transformation and the 'discoverie', theatrical invention has scarcely progressed to this day, and the devices which Jones learnt from Italy and to which he himself added were ... as complex as anything in the twentieth century theatre.
(Michael Ayrton, *The Faery Queen*, London, 1948.)

The distinguished painter Leslie Hurry (b. 1909) was introduced to ballet by Robert Helpmann for whom he designed *Hamlet* in 1942. The following year Ninette de Valois asked him to redesign the company's production of *Swan Lake*. It was an immediate success but subsequently Hurry admitted that 'he had found great difficulty in subordinating his personal vision as a painter to the traditions attached to the ballet, and had seen it all through the eyes of von Rothbart' (Mary Clarke, *The Sadlers Wells Ballet*, London, 1955). Nevertheless the designs had the rare distinction of poetic sensibility allied to sound dramatic sense: Hurry's very personal graphic idiom is nowhere sacrificed to dull functionalism and his setting for the lakeside scenes (plate 155) with its swan motif, caught and held the imagination of the audience. Hurry was later to work extensively and with distinction in the theatre:

Below
155 Leslie Hurry: setting for *Swan Lake* Acts II and IV, the lakeside, as performed by the Sadler's Wells Ballet at Covent Garden, 1946.

Opposite above
156 John Craxton (b. 1922): setting for the first scene of *Daphnis and Chloe*, ballet with choreography by Frederick Ashton, music by Ravel, first performed by the Sadler's Wells Ballet at Covent Garden, 1951.

Opposite below
157 Edward Burra: drop-curtain for *Don Quixote*, ballet with choreography by Ninette de Valois, music by Roberto Gerhard, first performed by the Sadler's Wells Ballet at Covent Garden, 1950. Burra 'designed sets of a grandeur and bareness that matched the arid Spanish landscape' (Mary Clarke, *The Sadler's Wells Ballet*) and provided two remarkable drop-cloths in which his own very personal imagery of bird-masked figures and a world of often nightmare menace was admirably apt to the ballet's theme.

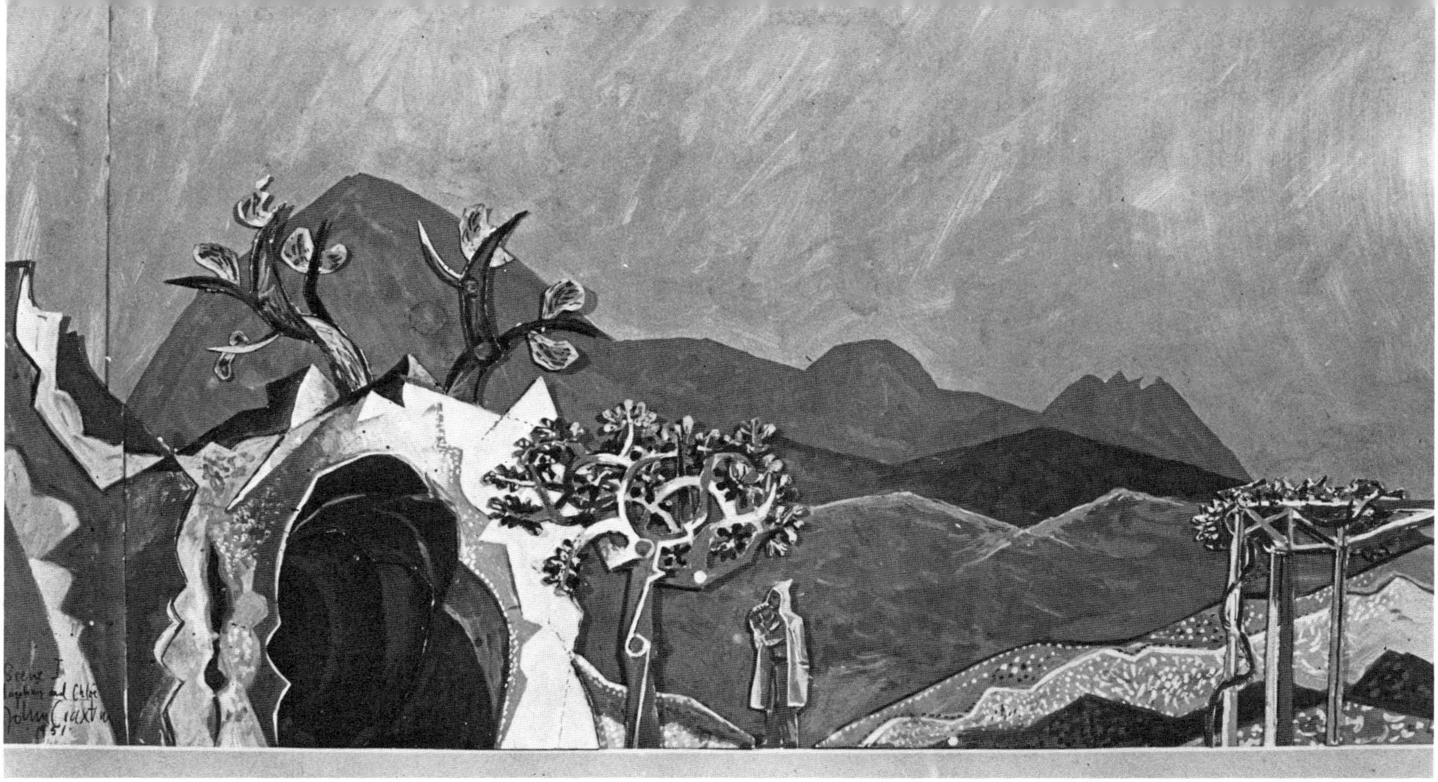
Scene I
and Chloe
John Craxton

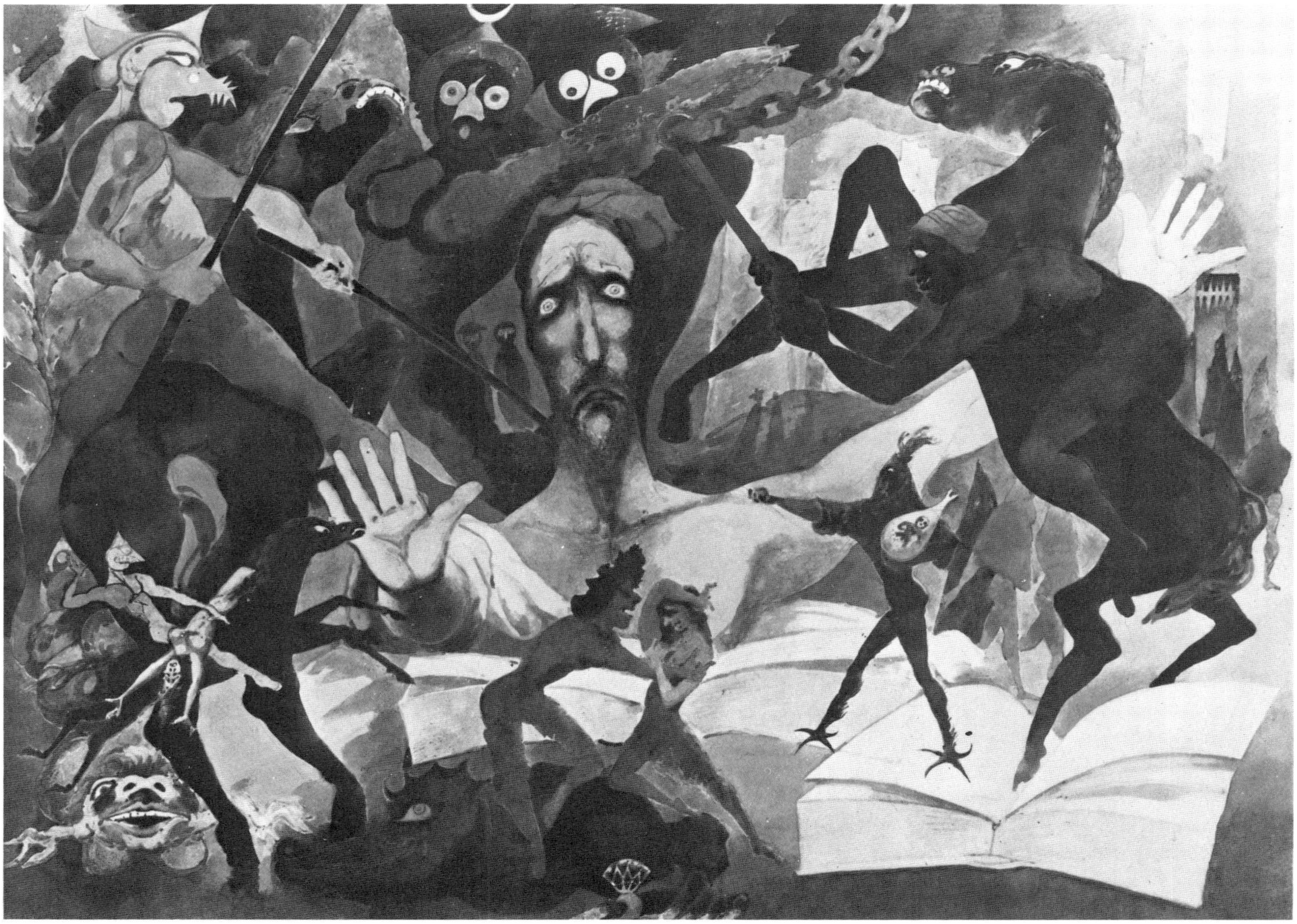

218

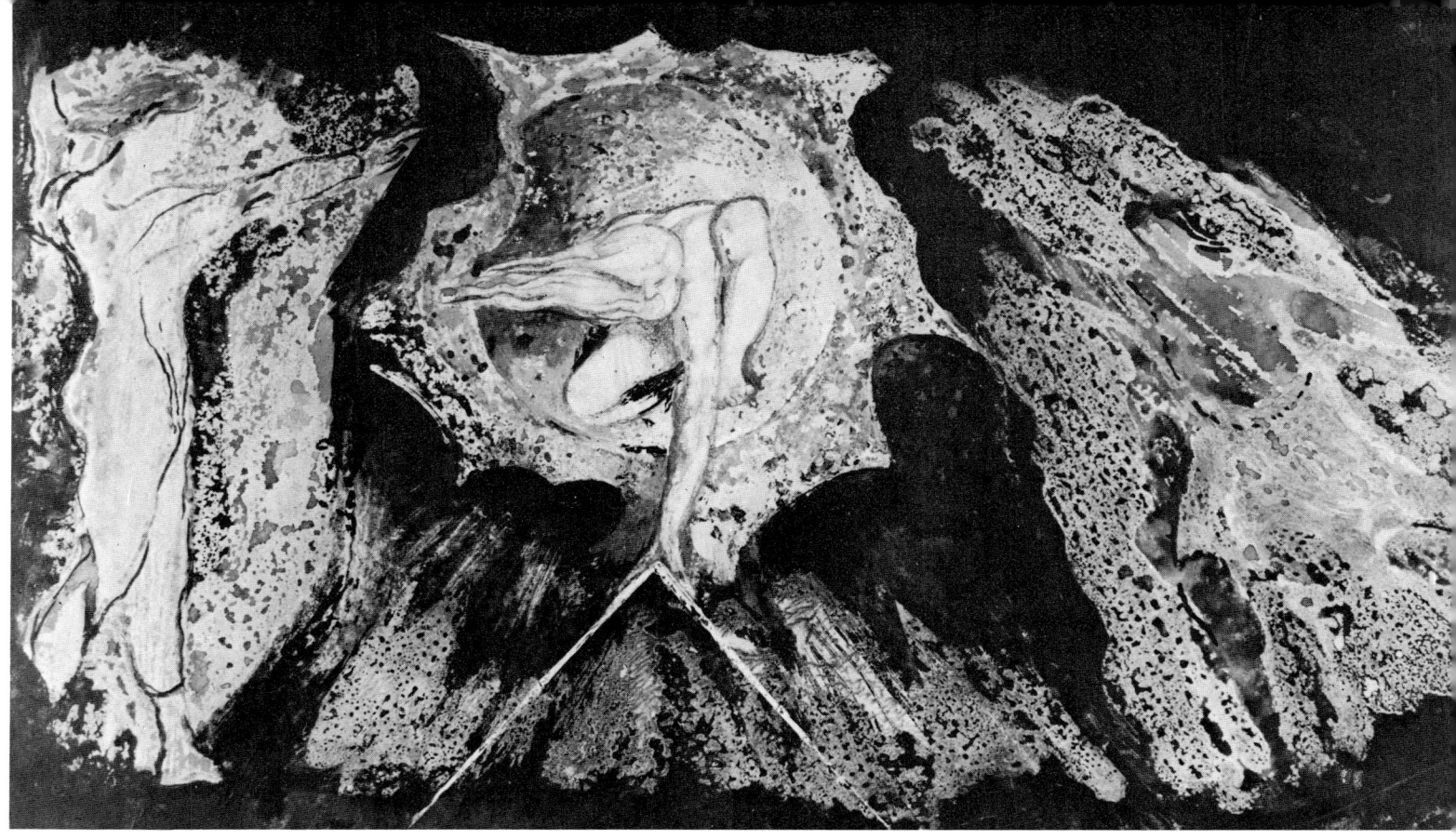

Opposite above
158 Nico Ghika (b. 1906): setting for the first scene of *Perséphone*, melodrama in three scenes by André Gide, with choreography by Frederick Ashton, music by Stravinsky, first performed by the Royal Ballet at Covent Garden, 1961.

Opposite below
159 Robin and Christopher Ironside: setting for the first act of *Sylvia*, ballet with choreography by Frederick Ashton, music by Delibes, first performed by the Royal Ballet at Covent Garden, 1952.

Above
160 John Piper (b. 1903): drop curtain for *Job*, a masque for dancing with a libretto by Geoffrey Keynes (after William Blake), with choreography by Ninette de Valois, music by Vaughan Williams, restaged at the Royal Opera House, Covent Garden, 1948. The work was first produced by the Camargo Society in London, 5 July, 1931 with designs by Gwen Raverat (Keynes's sister in law). Piper's first work in ballet was *The Quest* in 1943 for Ashton, and he subsequently collaborated with John Cranko in the designing of several ballets, notably *Harlequin in April*, 1951.

regrettably he has not been called upon to do much more for ballet than redesign or amend the Royal Ballet's *Swan Lake*.

The work of Robin and Christopher Ironside for Ashton's *Sylvia* and of Lila de Nobili for his *Ondine* are noteworthy examples of design in the grand style. *Sylvia* (plate 159), Ashton's second full-length ballet, was a reworking of a one-time gem of the Paris Opéra Ballet's repertory. (*Sylvia* had been staged in Paris in 1876.) In retelling the tale, Ashton chose to preserve its period prettiness and charm, and the work was much enhanced by the designs of the Ironside brothers. They produced settings and costumes which evoked the Paris of the 1870s, but yet were stylish and elegant in their own right.

Ashton's *Ondine* was first produced by the Royal Ballet at Covent Garden in 1958, with designs by Lila de Nobili, whose setting for the second act is illustrated in plate 161. The second act of *Ondine* takes place on board ship and concerns the journey of the water sprite and her beloved Palemon. The action starts with the loading of the ship and dockside farewells, and shows the water sprite with Palemon and with Berta, Palemon's one-time fiancée. Tirrenio, King of the Mediterranean, calls up a storm in order to separate Ondine from Palemon, and the act ends with a shipwreck in which the masts crash to the deck and the boat founders. These effects – not unusual in musical comedy but rare in ballet outside Russia – were brought off with great skill by de Nobili and Ashton. The entire stage picture was seen through an oval cut-out in a frontcloth; by regular up and down motion of the scenery, the audience was convinced that they were indeed watching a ship at sea. The incursion of admirably cut trailers of sea-green silk, to represent waves breaking against the ship, and the eventual catastrophe of the wreck, were not only ingenious but beautiful.

Lila de Nobili was also responsible, with Henry Bardon, for the design for the Royal Ballet's first major revision of *The Sleeping Beauty* (plate 149). This

Design of Today

161 Lila de Nobili: setting for the second act of *Ondine*, ballet with choreography by Frederick Ashton, music by Hans Werner Henze, first performed by the Royal Ballet at Covent Garden, 1958.

Above
162 Sidney Nolan (b. 1917): setting for the second scene of *The Rite of Spring*, with choreography by Kenneth MacMillan to Stravinsky's score, as performed by the Royal Ballet at Covent Garden, 1962. The Australian painter Sidney Nolan was a most sensitive choice of designer for a production which the choreographer sought to make less specific than the ancient Russian ritual that had marked earlier stagings of this ballet. With dry, sun-baked colours, and all-over tights mottled and splashed with paint, and the dancers' faces daubed, Nolan made the tribal figures and their lion-masked elders somewhat aboriginal but effectively timeless. For the crucial second scene – the sacrifice of the chosen maiden – Nolan's setting was dominated by a gold phallic tree-shape.

Left
163 Martial Raysse (b. 1936): setting for the first scene of *Paradise Lost*, ballet with choreography by Roland Petit, music by Marius Constant, first performed by the Royal Ballet at Covent Garden, 1967. *Paradise Lost* was a gala vehicle for Margot Fonteyn and Rudolf Nureyev, most remarkable for the designs by the French painter, Raysse, in Pop Art style. These included flashing neon, and the device of using the giant mouth which features in the design as an exit for the hero.

Design of Today

164 Jacques Dupont (b. 1909): setting for *Pelléas et Mélisande*, ballet with choreography by Roland Petit, music by Arnold Schoenberg, first performed by the Royal Ballet at Covent Garden, 1969. Although the ballet itself was short-lived, Dupont's design of a huge, silken tenting, which eventually descended over the stage and became a symbol of Mélisande's tresses, was memorable. Dupont also provided the poetic, and happily still enduring, designs for Ashton's *The Two Pigeons*, which was first produced by the Royal Ballet at Covent Garden, 1961.

production was inspired by the world of Charles Perrault, whose fairy tale lies at the heart of the ballet. Although much of the designing was distinguished, as one would expect from the work of de Nobili and Bardon, the production failed to please. One innovation was to dress the female dancers in longer tutus which suited the medievalism of the decorative scene: if the designs had a fault it was that they tended to cramp the dancing and absorb the light so necessary to irradiate the dances.

A third Royal Ballet staging, in 1973, had designs by Peter Farmer (b. 1941), a specialist in sensitively romantic designs for the classics. His versions of *Giselle* and *The Sleeping Beauty* (plate 150) were characteristically charming. Once again, however, the production failed to please the public, and a revised presentation by Ninette de Valois and Frederick Ashton, with sets and costumes by David Walker, was seen in 1977.

The designs of the Australian painter and designer Barry Kay (b. 1932) for MacMillan's *Anastasia* (plate 165) must be hailed as among the most impressive ballet designs of the post-war years. *Anastasia* deals with the mysterious figure of Anna Anderson who believes that she is the Grand

Design of Today

Opposite
165 a, b Barry Kay: settings for the first and third acts of *Anastasia*, ballet with choreography by Kenneth MacMillan, music by Tchaikovsky and Martinu, as performed by the Royal Ballet at Covent Garden, 1971.

Below
166 Ezio Frigerio: setting for the market square in *Romeo and Juliet*, ballet with choreography by Rudolf Nureyev to the Prokofiev score, first performed by Festival Ballet at the Coliseum Theatre, London, 1977. For *Romeo and Juliet*, Frigerio turned to the fifteenth century for the architectural ideas in his sets and produced costuming that seemed to have come from the pages of Leonardo da Vinci's sketchbooks. The total effect was extremely persuasive as a vision of early Renaissance Italy.

Duchess Anastasia, sole survivor of the Bolshevik massacre of the Russian Imperial family at Ekaterinburg. MacMillan's ballet in its first two acts shows the world of the Imperial family in a picnic on the Baltic coast and then in the Winter Palace. The third act starts in the Berlin hospital in which Anna Anderson finds herself in 1920, and goes on to examine her struggle to persuade the world of her identity. To encompass these remarkably far-ranging settings Barry Kay devised an overall shape to his permanent setting consisting of huge parchment swirls on curved frames. These proved magnificently adaptable and with the addition of various properties became most poetic locations for the events of the first two acts. Stripped to their basic shape in the final act, they are used as screens for film projections which show the Imperial family and the events of the Revolution. Kay also strengthened the exceptionally powerful evocation of the Tsarist world through costuming which is a subtle translation of historically accurate dress into the conventions of the stage, having a muted range of colour. For the last scene, which is a fantasy of terrified memories, his designing enhances the feeling of psychological tension that is so effortlessly that of the dance.

Design for Ballet

226

Opposite above
167 Ian Spurling: set design for *The Seven Deadly Sins*, ballet with choreography by Kenneth MacMillan, music by Kurt Weill, as performed by the Royal Ballet at Covent Garden, 1973. Originally made for the Edinburgh Festival in 1961 and revived twelve years later for the Royal Ballet, this version of *The Seven Deadly Sins* introduced an extraordinary design talent to the ballet stage. At a time long before the revival of Art Déco had become fashionable, Ian Spurling's brilliant command of the idiom produced sets and costumes of wild but skilfully controlled fantasy.

Opposite below
168 Yolanda Sonnabend: setting for the third scene of *Rituals*, ballet with choreography by Kenneth MacMillan, music by Béla Bartók, first performed by the Royal Ballet at Covent Garden, 1975. *Rituals* was a ballet inspired by the Royal Ballet's visit to Japan earlier in the year, and Yolanda Sonnabend's designs captured the essential feeling of the country in their shape and in the use of a vast pleated curtain which tented the stage and suggested a piece of ink-spattered rice-paper. This hanging was only extended in the last scene, a celebration of thanksgiving after childbirth. Like the choreography, the designs were an artist's impression rather than a literal representation of Japan.

Above
169 Rouben Ter-Arutunian: setting for *Laborintus*, ballet with choreography by Glen Tetley, music by Luciano Berio, first performed by the Royal Ballet at Covent Garden, 1972.

It must not be thought that the presence of a large and academic repertory inhibits the opera house based companies from showing innovative and 'modern' design. Opera house attitudes have been influenced by the adventurous work initiated by small companies and many designers have worked both for the big traditional companies and for the more avant-garde ensembles. Ian Spurling with his designs for *The Seven Deadly Sins* (plate 167) and *Elite Syncopations*, both performed by the Royal Ballet, antagonized the purists by his audacity and earned from his admirers the sobriquet of 'the Bakst of the 1970s'. Rouben Ter-Arutunian (b. 1920) presents a fine example of the eclectic designer. Russian by birth, he emigrated to the United States in 1951 and since then has produced a very considerable body of theatre work, encompassing television, opera, musicals, plays and especially ballet. He has designed a wide variety of styles for a wide variety of companies, including New York City Ballet, Paul Taylor's Dance Company, American Ballet Theater and several European companies. He moves with ease from the traditional confections of *The Nutcracker* to the austerities of *Pierrot Lunaire* (plate 226). For the Royal Ballet's *Laborintus* (plate 169) he produced a setting of hallucinatory effects which included triangular mirrored reflectors and concertina-ed screens for the wings.

In the United States the two major classical companies provide an extreme contrast in decorative manner as in everything else. For the New York City Ballet, now resident in the vast State Theater at Lincoln Center, the case has been succinctly put by its director, Lincoln Kirstein. In his Introduction to Nancy Reynolds's *Repertory in Review* (New York, 1977) he writes: 'The purely decorative aspect of Balanchine's repertory has sometimes been condemned as impoverished, when in actuality it has been intentionally stoic, bare and uncompetitive.' The company has, however, mounted several conventionally decorated stagings such as the ever-popular Christmas treat of *The Nutcracker* (Rouben Ter-Arutunian). For the Ballet Society's 1948

Design for Ballet

Orpheus (plate 170) the Japanese-American designer Isamu Noguchi (b. 1904) produced one of the most potent décors that the Balanchine repertory has had. In her *Repertory in Review* Nancy Reynolds remarks:

> The designs were described as a 'kind of stone-age Greek', dissociating the action from any period. The most exciting effect was the lightning like descent of a white silk curtain which fell and swirled in a dramatic zig-zag, as the audience gasped. Also, Noguchi designed a rope element as part of the Dark Angel costume, which Balanchine incorporated into the choreography.

Inevitably, Balanchine turned to Eugene Berman for the design for *Roma* (plate 171). The ballet was short-lived, but Berman's love of Italy produced

170 **Isamu Noguchi: costumes for *Orpheus*, ballet with choreography by Balanchine, music by Stravinsky, first performed by the Ballet Society at the New York City Center, 1948; seen here in performance by the New York City Ballet at the Royal Opera House, Covent Garden, 1950, with Francisco Moncion as the Dark Angel and Nicholas Magallanes as Orpheus.**

Design of Today

what Kirstein has called 'a Piranesian townscape of ruined arches, which at a climax were festooned with colourful lines of tasteful laundry hung in a frame of gauze and windows remembered from Trastevere and the Tiber suburbs.' For the 1972 Stravinsky Festival the company again commissioned sets and costumes of extraordinary beauty from Berman, for *Pulcinella*. However, Balanchine, who grew up in the Diaghilev and immediately post-Diaghilev world of painterly design, has increasingly turned away from anything that might come between his dances and his audience.

Very different is the record of American Ballet Theater. It is no accident that a company having a distinguished designer, Oliver Smith, as one of its directors should pay special attention to good design. The catalogue for the exhibition presented in 1976 at the Dance Collection in the Museum of Performing Arts in New York under the title 'Thirty-six Years of Scenic and Costume Design' proves how wide-ranging has been the choice of artists to decorate the company's eclectic repertory. No fewer than forty-eight decorators were represented, covering the revivals of the established

171 Eugene Berman: design for the final scene of *Roma*, ballet with choreography by Balanchine, music by Bizet, first performed by the New York City Ballet at the City Center Theater, New York, 1955.

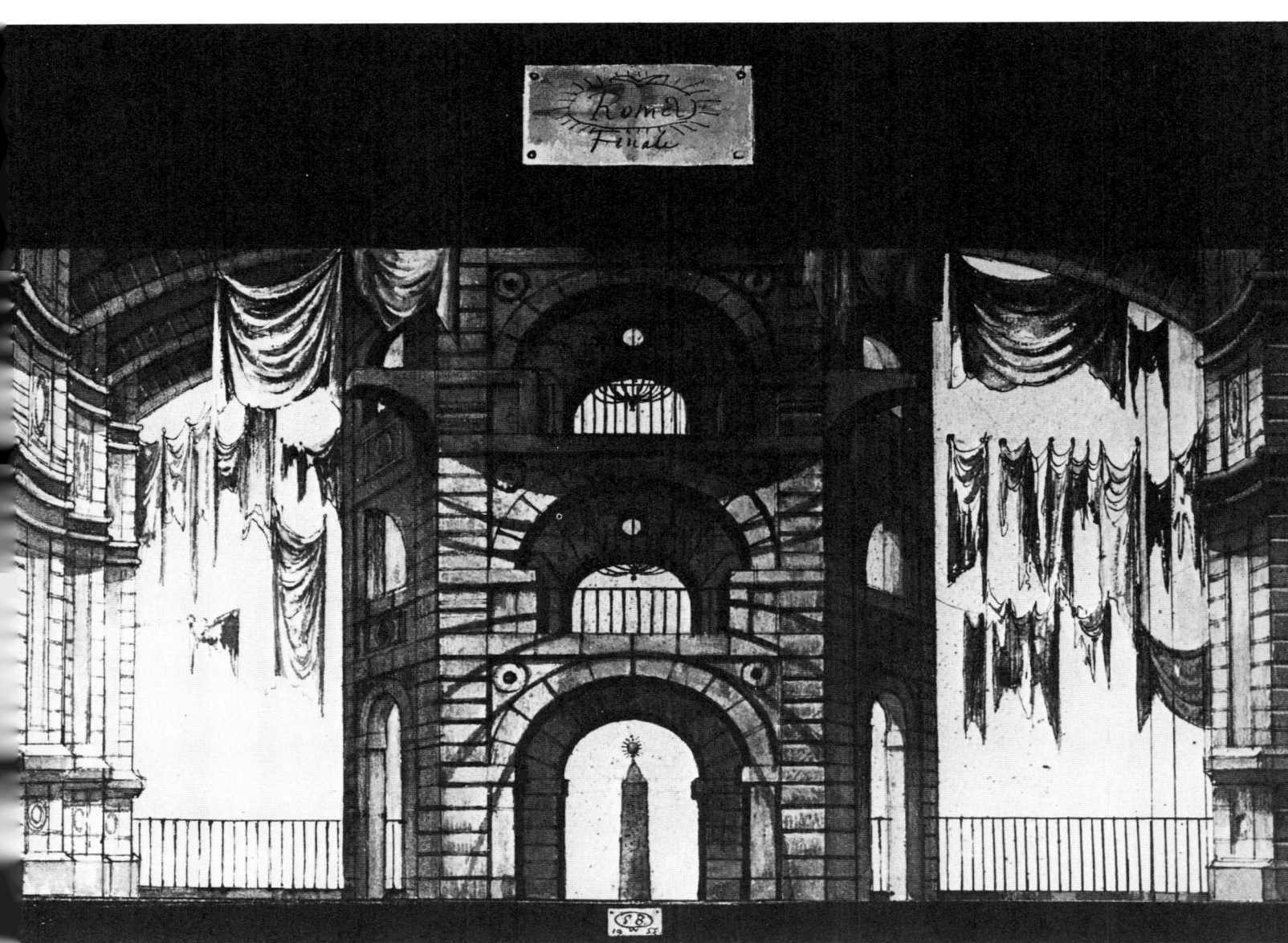

Design for Ballet

Above
172 Jo Mielziner (b. 1901): design for *Pillar of Fire*, ballet with choreography by Antony Tudor, music by Arnold Schoenberg, first performed by American Ballet Theater at the Metropolitan Opera House, New York, 1942. Mielziner is one of the best known designers in America: he has worked extensively on Broadway but has only designed two works for the ballet, Tudor's *Pillar of Fire* and his *Shadow of the Wind* (1948).

Left
173 Oliver Smith: setting for *Fall River Legend*, ballet with choreography by Agnes de Mille, music by Morton Gould, first performed by American Ballet Theater at the Metropolitan Opera House, New York, 1948. This set could be manipulated easily to provide both interior and exterior settings.

Design of Today

Diaghilev repertory, some imports of elegant French design, the work of Oliver Smith himself, and that of such contemporary painters as Leonard Baskin.

Oliver Smith (b. 1918) has worked extensively in the theatre as well as designing ballets for his own company. For American Ballet Theater he has specialized particularly in American settings which capture something very real about the country, witness his prairie setting for *Rodeo*, the marvellously evocative picture of a New York street scene and bar for *Fancy Free*, and his set for *Fall River Legend* (plate 173), which told the story of the Lizzie Borden murders.

Eugene Berman's *Romeo and Juliet* (plate 174) for American Ballet Theater is one of his greatest achievements in the theatre. The designs are, in Edwin

174 Eugene Berman: setting for *Romeo and Juliet*, ballet with choreography by Antony Tudor, music by Delius, first performed by American Ballet Theater at the Metropolitan Opera House, New York, 1943.

232

Design of Today

Denby's words, 'a serious work of art, like Picasso's *Tricorne* or Bérard's *Cotillon*: like the work of baroque designers. And I imagine later theatre lovers who look at the record of it will marvel at the refinement of sensibility it presupposes in the audience.' Allison Delarue in an issue of *Dance Index* devoted to Berman (vol. V, no. 1, January 1946), says:

> The drop curtain for the Prologue created a Verona such as was never seen on land – a mirage, suspended in strati of clouds which cut the architectural fantasy into two mysterious parts. In the constructed décor of the main setting Berman had his first opportunity to project his imagination as a painter-architect-builder . . . Aside from its reality of an Italian world of day and night it has additional changes within itself made possible by the opening and closing of painted draperies between the arches.

The costuming throughout was magnificently evocative of the high Renaissance while yet being marked with Berman's very individual form of patterning. For Alicia Markova as Juliet, Berman produced dresses of the greatest beauty whose line never interfered with the classical choreography.

We include in this section a group of designs from Italian opera houses. It would be idle to pretend that the Italian ballet scene can be considered of much merit on an international level, but the quality of decoration reflects once

Opposite above
175 George Wakhevitch (b. 1907): setting for *The Combat*, ballet with choreography by William Dollar, music by Rafaello de Banfield, as revived by American Ballet Theater at the Royal Opera House, Covent Garden, 1953.

Opposite below
176 Leonard Baskin (b. 1922): drop-curtain for the first movement of *At Midnight*, ballet with choreography by Eliot Feld, music by Mahler, first performed by American Ballet Theater at the City Center Theater, New York, 1967. The two drops provided by Baskin for Feld's nostalgic view of love's sufferings established an immediate and powerful atmosphere which is thereafter explored in the choreography.

Below
177 Toti Scialoja (b. 1914): setting for *Marsyas*, ballet with choreography by Aurel von Milloss, music by Dallapiccola, as staged at the Venice Biennale, 1948.

Above
178 Gino Severini (1883–1966): setting for *Deliciae Populi*, ballet with choreography by von Milloss, music by Alfredo Casella. Originally staged at the Teatro delle Arti in Rome in 1943, this production was revived for the Maggio Musicale, Florence, in 1951. Severini's career began with the Futurist movement. In many of his early paintings he provided a vivid record of popular dancing. During the 1920s he became increasingly fascinated by the figures of the Commedia dell'Arte and in 1938 came his first theatrical décors.

Left
179 Corrado Cagli (1910–76): setting for *Bacchus and Ariadne*, ballet with choreography by von Milloss, music by Roussel, as performed by the ballet of the Rome Opera in 1957.

Opposite above
180 Achille Perilli (b. 1927): setting for *Mutazioni*, ballet with choreography by Mario Pistoni, music by Vittorio Fellegara, as staged at the Teatro alla Scala, Milan, 1964.

Opposite below
181 Domenico Purificato (b. 1915): setting for *Petrushka*, with choreography by Amedio Amodio to Stravinsky's score, as performed at the Opera, Rome, 1970.

Design for Ballet

again the innate good taste and flair that marks the design of so many things in Italy – from clothes to motor cars. The ballets which we illustrate may not have had any great choreographic quality but their design gave them visual distinction far above the ordinary.

Of other Western European opera houses, the Paris Opéra in recent years has had an uncertain identity and this has been reflected in a less than stimulating decorative record in a country where stage design has always been pre-eminently good (as we show in a separate section). Nevertheless, the overall picture of décor at the Opéra since the war has been one of fine achievements, and it includes design by André Delfau, Léonor Fini, Cassandre, Maurice Brianchon, Brayer, Moulène, Max Ernst, Chagall, Cocteau, Picasso, Bouchène, André Levasseur, Marcel Vertès, Bernard Daydé, Pierre Clayette, and Wakhevitch.

The setting by Jean Carzou (b. 1907) for the Inca scene in *Les Indes Galantes* (plate 185) as revived at the Paris Opéra in 1952, introduced an outstanding decorative talent to the theatre. Carzou's spidery and nervously brilliant line announced a very different visual approach to stage design and in *Le Loup* the following year for Roland Petit it achieved exceptional dramatic force. In 1954 Carzou was invited by Lifar to redesign *Giselle* at the Opéra (plate 152) and in both acts his style resulted in a fresh and dramatically convincing approach to the old classic.

Above
182 **Mariano Mercuri: setting for *Contagio*, ballet with choreography by Mario Pistoni, music by Giorgio Gaslini, first performed at the Teatro alla Scala, Milan, 1971.**

Opposite above
183 **Alexandre Cassandre (1910–67): setting for *Les Mirages*, ballet with choreography by Serge Lifar, music by Henri Sauguet, first performed at the Paris Opéra, 1947. Born in Russia, Cassandre provided exceptional designs for several Lifar ballets, notably *Les Mirages*, *Le Chevalier et La Demoiselle* and *Dramma per Musica*. In all of these distinguished architectural settings, with their ability to evoke a mysterious and romantic atmosphere, were an important contribution to the success of the ballet.**

Opposite below
184 **Bernard Daydé (b. 1921): setting for *Bacchus et Ariane*, ballet with choreography by Michel Descombey, music by Albert Roussel, first performed at the Paris Opéra, 1967. Daydé has been involved in the theatre since Serge Lifar gave him his first opportunity in his early twenties, and since then he has worked throughout the world.**

Above
185 Jean Carzou: design for the Inca scene in *Les Indes Galantes*, opera-ballet with book by Fuzelier, music by Rameau, as revived at the Paris Opéra, 1952. The restaging was entrusted to several choreographers and designers.

Left
186 Yves Brayer: design for the first act of *Nautéos*, with choreography by Lifar, music by Jean Leleu, as revived at the Paris Opéra in 1954. Brayer's long and illustrious career as a theatre designer dates back to the war years when he decorated Lifar's *Joan de Zarissa* in 1942. Subsequently he was to contribute distinguished work not only to the Opéra but also to the lyric stage throughout France and to the dramatic theatre as well. His designing is notable for strong use of colour and for its sureness of image.

Above
187 Marc Chagall (b. 1889): setting for *Daphnis and Chloe*, ballet with choreography by Serge Lifar to Ravel's score, as performed at the Paris Opéra, 1958. Chagall's highly personal imagery was well suited to Lifar's retelling of the legend. Chagall was one of the many fine painters introduced to the ballet stage by Massine, whose *Aleko* he decorated in 1942. Subsequently he was to design *The Firebird* for the New York City Ballet.

Below
188 Maurice Brianchon (b. 1899): setting for *Aubade*, a second version of Lifar's ballet with music by Poulenc, as performed at the Paris Opéra, 1950. *Aubade* was a retelling of the legend of Diana and Actaeon.

Design for Ballet

240

Design of Today

189 Pablo Picasso: setting for *Icare*, ballet with choreography by Serge Lifar, rhythms by Lifar orchestrated by Szyfer, as restaged and redesigned at the Paris Opéra, 1962.

Opposite
Colour 27 a b Marc Chagall (b. 1887): designs for *The Firebird*, with choreography by George Balanchine to Stravinsky's score, first performed by the New York City Ballet in New York, 1949.

Right
Colour 28 Niki de Saint Phalle: designs for dolls ('Nanas') in *L'Eloge de la Folie*, ballet with choreography by Roland Petit to music by Marius Constant, first performed in Paris, 1966.

Below
Colour 29 Paul Delvaux: setting for *Transfigured Night*, ballet with choreography by Roland Petit, music by Schoenberg, first staged at the Paris Opéra, 1976.

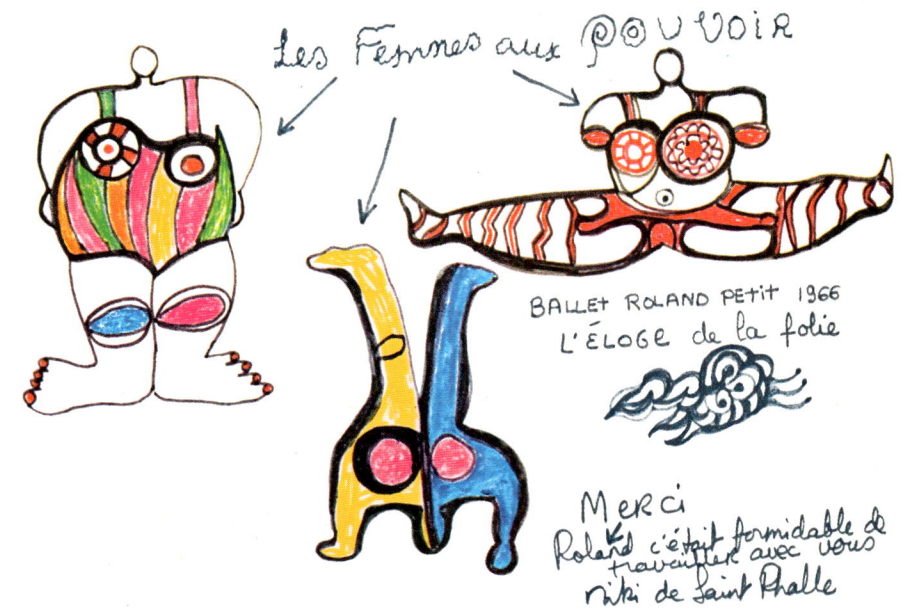

Design for Ballet

In Germany the proliferation of ballet companies after the war's end in 1945 has brought an emergent tradition of good German ballet design. Of the many companies now operating in German opera houses, that of the Stuttgart Ballet demands pride of place by the massive nature of its achievements, and its repertory offers examples of the work of several outstanding German designers, notably Jürgen Rose (b. 1937) (plate 191). Following the current trends, many foreigners have also been employed to provide décors for West German opera houses, including Nicholas Georgiadis, Barry Kay, Peter Farmer and Rouban Ter-Arutunian.

This system repeats itself throughout Europe and the West. In Sweden the décors of such artists as Lindstrom, Sven Erixsen and Yngve Gamlin are found side by side with the work of English designers like Desmond Heeley, David Walker and Henry Bardon. In Copenhagen the Royal Danish Ballet has preserved for many years a necessarily careful traditionalism in settings for the Bournonville repertory, while the modern repertory – especially in ballets by Flemming Flindt – uses both Danish and guest designers, such as Bernard Daydé and Jacques Noel. Throughout Western Europe and North America, the days of nationalism in design, as in choreography, seem over. Producers, choreographers, dancers and designers are more international than ever before: the National Ballet of Canada, the Australian Ballet, for all their strong national identities, make much use of ballet's internationalism to enhance their repertories and their reputations. The English designer

Below
190 Jürgen Rose: setting for *Poème de l'Extase*, ballet with choreography by John Cranko, music by Skryabin, first performed by the Stuttgart Ballet in Stuttgart, 1970. This work was essentially a vehicle for Dame Margot Fonteyn, redeemed by Jürgen Rose's remarkable adaptation of design ideas from Gustav Klimt the Viennese *Jugendstil* artist. The massive draperies, the furniture and costuming, and the cloaks worn by certain of the characters in this study of an ageing Diva contemplating her amorous past, were all made ravishing by the use of decorative patterns taken from Klimt paintings.

Design of Today

Above
191 Nicholas Georgiadis: model for setting of the first act of *Swan Lake* as produced by Kenneth MacMillan at the Deutsche Oper, Berlin, 1969. Georgiadis has designed most of the great classic ballets of the late nineteenth century and his grand style provides a very sensitive updating of the decorative attitudes of Imperial Russia which initially gave birth to the ballets. This setting was inspired by the gardens in the Villa Lanta, near Spoleto.

Below
192 Ove Christian Pedersen: setting for *Kermesse in Bruges*, 1851, ballet with choreography by Bournonville, music by Paulli, as revived by the Royal Danish Ballet in Copenhagen, 1942. The designing, by the Royal Theatre's resident artist, preserves much of the style of the décor of Bournonville's own day. In the topographical ballets, like *Napoli*, or even *The New Penelope* of 1847 (which took place in Athens), there was a real need felt during the Romantic epoch to produce literal views of foreign locales; their preservation today often brings an additional charm to these ballets in performance, and *Kermesse in Bruges*'s setting is a faithful evocation of the Holy Fair in Bruges where the ballet – inspired by the paintings of Jan Steen and David Teniers – is set.

Colour 30 Max Ernst: setting for *Turangalîla*, ballet with choreography by Roland Petit, music by Messiaen, first performed at the Paris Opéra, 1968.

Left
193 Filippo Sanjust: setting for *Don Juan*, ballet with choreography by John Neumeier, music by Gluck and others, as staged by the National Ballet of Canada. First performed in Frankfurt 1972, revived in Canada 1974.

Below
194 Desmond Heeley: setting for Act III of *The Merry Widow*, ballet with choreography by Ronald Hynd, music by Franz Lehar, first produced by the Australian Ballet in Melbourne, 1975.

Design of Today

Desmond Heeley has decorated *Giselle* in Stockholm, *Swan Lake* and *Giselle* (plate 195) in Canada, *The Merry Widow* in Australia, *The Sleeping Beauty* in Stuttgart, and *Solitaire* in London.

In Eastern Europe exciting design can be found in the smaller nations which do not need to ape the massive traditionalism that marks so much Soviet designing. The achievements of Joseph Svoboda have been hailed in many Western European opera houses; he has worked mostly in opera but has given the Prague Ballet some innovative designs. We have chosen, however, to provide some other evidence of the liveliness of Czechoslovakian design. In Poland we have found examples of a vigorous tradition of design for ballet which reflects the same vitality that exists in Polish graphic design and the Polish cinema.

From other Eastern European countries we have seen examples of attractive

195 Ming Cho Lee (b. 1930): setting for *Whispers of Darkness*, ballet with choreography by Norbert Vesak, music by Mahler, first performed by the National Ballet of Canada in Toronto, 1974.

Design for Ballet

250

Design of Today

Colour 31 Antoni Clavé: design for the setting of *Los Caprichos*, ballet with choreography by Ana Nevada and Juanito Garcia, music orchestrated by Tony Aubin from several Spanish composers, first performed by Les Ballets des Champs Elysées in Paris, 1946. The work was inspired by the world of Goya and introduced a brilliant new talent to the ballet stage.

Design for Ballet

Above
196 Karel Svolinsky (b. 1896): setting for *Les Noces*, with choreography by Sasha Machov to Stravinsky's score, first performed at the National Theatre in Prague, 1942. Svolinsky's designs opt for a Chagall-like naïveté rather than the starkness favoured by the ballet's first choreographer, Bronislava Nijinska, in 1923.

Left
197 Zdenek Seydl (b. 1916): set for the first and fourth scenes of *Petrushka* as staged at the National Theatre, Prague, 1961, with choreography by Jiri Blazek to Stravinsky's score. This is an interesting alternative to the traditional Benois setting, offering a peasant idiom for the fairground scenes.

Design of Today

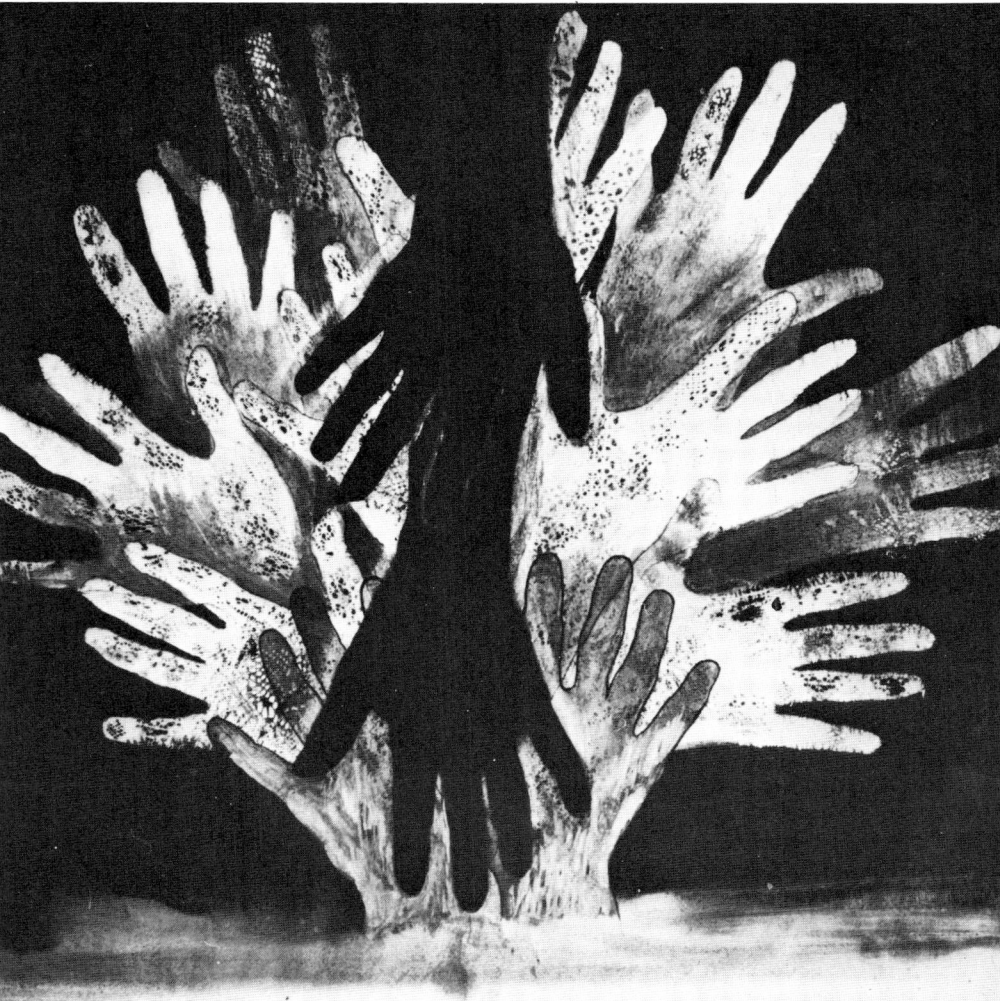

Right
198 Vladimír Sochánek: setting for *Ballad of the Tree*, ballet with choreography by J. Guoth, music by Novak, first performed in Bratislava, 1974.

Below
199 Teresa Roszkovska: setting for the final scene of Prokofiev's *Romeo and Juliet* as staged at the Warsaw Opera House, 1954. The distinguished Polish scholar Dr Janina Pudelek observes that Roszkovska's designs are 'very delicate and realistic, with a touch of poetic vision'. She comments on the magnificent use of colour and the admirable cut of costuming that characterized this production.

Design for Ballet

Opposite above
Colour 32 Gérard Fromanger: design for *Hymnen*, ballet with choreography by Michel Descombey, Alain Deshayes, Jacques Garnier, Aline Roux, Norbert Schmucki, music by Stockhausen, first performed by the Ballet-Théâtre Contemporain in Paris, 1970.

Opposite below
Colour 33 William Katz: design for *Caterpillar*, ballet by Louis Falco to music by Luciano Berio, first performed by the Nederlands Dans Theater in 1975.

Below
Colour 34 Alwin Nikolais: *Tent*, with dance, music and design by Nikolais, first performed by the Nikolais dance company at the University of South Florida, Tampa, 1968.

Design for Ballet

Left
200 Andrzej Majewski: setting for Berlioz's *Symphonie Fantastique* as staged at the Wielki Theatre, Warsaw, 1971. This view of the Witches' Sabbath suggests something of the brilliant imagery that marks Majewski's designing.

Below
201 Boris Messerer (b. 1933): design for *The Three Musketeers*, ballet with choreography by Piotr Gusev, music by Vladimir Basner, as performed at the opera house Novosibirsk, 1966. Boris Messerer is a member of the distinguished Soviet family of artists, dancers and actors. His work is part of a new wave in Soviet designing, brighter and less fusty in manner than the more traditional stagings. He was also responsible for the very stylish decoration for *Lieutenant Kizhe*, a one-act ballet staged by the Bolshoy Ballet in Moscow, 1963, and for *Carmen Suite* staged in 1967.

Design of Today

and apposite design. However, the fact that many of the ballet companies of the Eastern bloc offer restagings of the big ballets originating from Moscow (the ubiquitous *Spartacus*, as well as the nineteenth-century classics) means that the design too often reproduces the Soviet Russian manner.

In Russia itself, design attitudes can range from the outstandingly apt decoration of such artists as Simon Virsaladze or the interesting innovations of Boris Messerer (b. 1933) (his designs for *Lieutenant Kizhe* were an unexpected delight when the Bolshoy Ballet brought them to London in 1966) to the ponderous 'official' designing which is sometimes dictated by the great expanse of Soviet stages. In his recent designs for *Ivan the Terrible*, Virsaladze provided a partial solution with massive hangings which produced effects of grand and almost Craig-like simplicity. In the Kirov *Sleeping Beauty*, the Leningrad style of dancing and attitude to the ballet, the spaciousness and grace of Virsaladze's design (plate 146) and the underlying respect for period and for its transmutation into balletic form, all created a version which is as near perfection as we dare hope to see. The continuity of performance from the ballet's creation in Petersburg in 1890 brings with it a sense of 'rightness' which informs everything about the production. There have been an infinity, it seems, of *Beauty* stagings, some involving the finest decorative and productive talents in the West: none can even approach this Kirov version for

202 Simon Virsaladze: setting for the second act of *The Stone Flower*, with choreography by Yury Grigorovich, music by Prokofiev, as staged by the Bolshoy Ballet in Moscow, 1959. Grigorovich had first staged this ballet two years earlier in Leningrad. Virsaladze's sets were unusual at the time for their simplicity: he avoided much of the cumbrous verismo that characterized many Soviet productions.

Design for Ballet

splendour and accuracy in realizing the greatest ballet of the nineteenth century. Piotr Williams's setting for Lavrovsky's *Romeo and Juliet* (plate 203) provides another interesting example of the Soviet style in design. Originally staged in Leningrad in 1940, this quintessential Soviet production entered the repertory of the Bolshoy Ballet at the end of the war. In it a massive naturalism serves as a not unconvincing framework for Lavrovsky's careful presentation of Shakespeare's play. With less than the great interpreters who first illuminated the choreography – Ulanova and her compères – the decoration can seem oppressive and over the years the whole production has been subject to unhappy erosions. Nevertheless in its original form both design and staging could prove immensely exciting. It was with this production that the Bolshoy Ballet conquered the West in 1956: Piotr Williams's designs managed to be a scrupulous yet potently theatrical re-creation of the Renaissance scenes.

203 Piotr Williams (1902–47): setting for the ballroom scene in the first act of *Romeo and Juliet*, as produced by Leonid Lavrovsky to music by Prokofiev for the Bolshoy Ballet in Moscow, 1946.

204 Yury Pimenov (b. 1903) with Genaddy Epishin: costume design for King Frost in *The Snowmaiden*, three-act ballet with choreography by Vladimir Burmeister, music by Tchaikovsky, first produced by Festival Ballet in London, July 1961. *The Snowmaiden* was the first – and thus far the only – Soviet ballet staged in Britain.

The French Style

With the expansion of ballet activity that came with the post-war years came two new developments. One which has been discussed at the beginning of this chapter, is that stage design has become increasingly international. Choreographers and producers working around the world have taken with them their own designers. The other development is the growing supremacy of the artist working specifically as a stage designer. In Britain the greater part of design for ballet is provided by artists most correctly categorized as stage designers, rather than painters or sculptors who also work in the theatre. This is far less true in France where the companies associated with Roland Petit since 1945, and the Ballet-Théâtre Contemporain since 1968, have shown a revival of the Diaghilev ideal of artists used in the theatre to bring a specifically painterly approach to the presentation of ballet. First and foremost was Les Ballets des Champs Elysées, which was started in 1945 as a splinter group of young talents who had separated from the officialdom of the Paris Opéra and received the patronage and support of Boris Kochno, Jean Cocteau and Christian Bérard. (It is significant that Kochno and Cocteau had been important arbiters of taste with Diaghilev.)

With Roland Petit as chief choreographer, the Champs Elysées Company came into being in March 1945. Its first ballet was *Les Forains*, with design by Bérard that had the simplicity of genius: a cart, two poles and a piece of red cloth became the setting for a troupe of strolling players. This small decorative masterpiece, with its wistful charm, was the starting point for a company which revolutionized taste after the dark days of war. In 1946 there came *Le Jeune Homme et La Mort* (plate 205): Cocteau's poetic theme of a young man in his garret room awaiting a girl who eventually turns out to be Death; Petit's

Below
205 Georges Wakhevitch (b. 1907): design for *Le Jeune Homme et la Mort*, ballet devised by Jean Cocteau with choreography by Roland Petit, music by Bach, first performed by Les Ballets des Champs Elysées in Paris, 1946. *Le Jeune Homme* was one of the key works in the rebirth of French ballet after the war.

Opposite
206 a, b Christian Bérard: (a) setting for *La Rencontre*, ballet with choreography by David Lichine, music by Henri Sauguet, first performed by Les Ballets des Champs Elysées in Paris, 1948. Bérard's setting for the encounter between Oedipus and the Sphinx was nothing more than a tented area with a red velvet platform on which the Sphinx awaited her victims. The suggestion of a gymnasium with poles, ropes and ladders became a timeless location for a very beautiful ballet which was danced (b) with great power by Jean Babilée and Leslie Caron. Each item of the setting was functional: the rope ladder finally providing the snare on which the dead Sphinx hangs upside down.

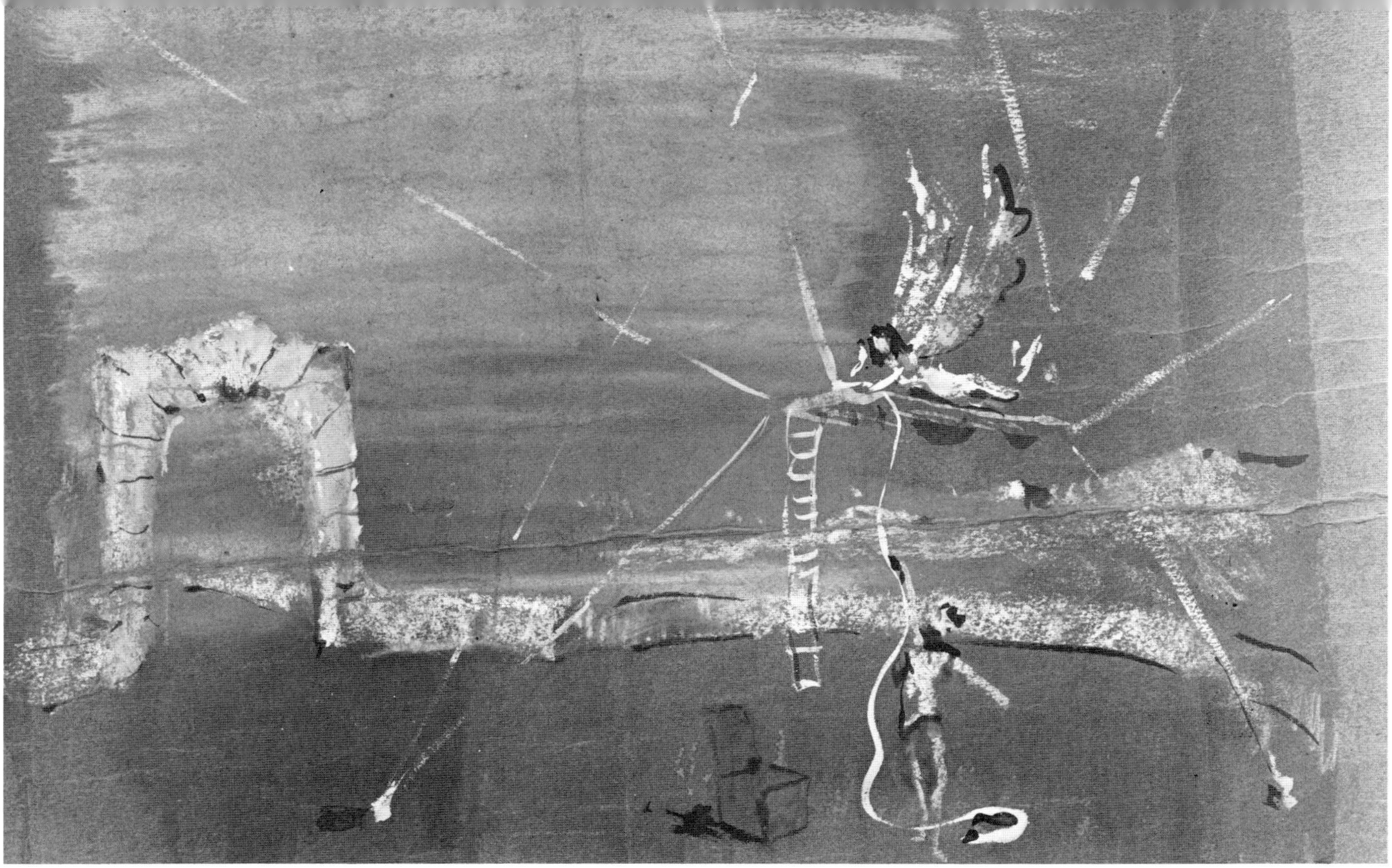

207 Antoni Clavé: design for *Carmen*, ballet with choreography by Roland Petit, music by Bizet, first performed by the Ballet de Paris in London, 1949.

choreography; Jean Babilée's extraordinary athletic performance as the Young Man; Wakhevitch's evocative setting of the Paris skyline – all combine to provide exceptional theatrical impact. Here was French ballet with all the wit, chic and effortless elegance that the word 'Paris' meant to the rest of the world. There were magnificent dancers; Petit's choreography had a brilliant sense of theatre; and the designing was glorious. For the first time since Diaghilev, décor played a vital part in a ballet performance. During the first seasons there came work not only by Bérard and Wakhevitch but also by Antoni Clavé, André Beaurepaire, Pierre Roy, Jean Hugo, Marie Laurencin, Jean-Denis Malclès, Cocteau, Tom Keogh, Stanislas Lepri and Christian Dior. The work of the Spanish designer Clavé (b. 1913) in particular was a revelation of the possibilities of stage design. In his excellent *Modern Ballet Design* (London, 1955) Richard Buckle assesses Clavé's contribution thus:

> Clavé invented the rag-tag-and-bobtail style of décor. Significant props and tattered draperies were slung with apparent negligence on ropes; ladders and common chairs were left lying about; when there was any painting to be done on a bit of scenery it was as slapdash as possible. His décors, which were probably very expensive, were designed to look as if they had been dragged together out of a heap of rejects from the *marché aux puces* . . . The tobacco factory in *Carmen* was a staircase and step-ladders; *chez* Lillas Pastia was chairs and a curtain glowing whorishly red; the bedroom was sunlight through

208 Antoni Clavé: curtain for *Revanche*, ballet with choreography by Ruth Page, music by Verdi, based on *Il Trovatore*, as revived for Les Ballets des Champs Elysées in Paris, 1951. The American dancer and choreographer Ruth Page has a remarkable record of commissioning good design: she has employed artists of the calibre of Noguchi, Clavé, Wakhevitch, Delfau and Léonor Fini.

shutters on a white wall, a rickety iron bed, lace curtains, a trunk and a bird-cage; the scene of the robbery-with-murder was a dark barn with cartwheels, one of which turned slowly on a rope in mid-air; the bull-ring was a poster and a lot of grinning twopenny masks. It was a masterpiece of designing.

The ideals of stage design which had their first expression in Les Ballets des Champs Elysées have been maintained by Roland Petit ever since. In the several companies which he has directed and in the variety of other enterprises – film, musicals, revue – with which he has been associated, Petit has called upon some of the brightest names in the art of our time. The list of designers used by him across the years is testimony enough, from the introduction of Clavé to his use of Carzou, and Max Ernst, from the involvement of great couturiers like Dior who designed *Treize Danses*), Yves St Laurent (who has produced the clothes for two big ballets *Notre Dame de Paris* and *Cyrano de Bergerac*), and Balmain and Fath who also created costumes. To remember Petit's companies and ballets is not only to recall dramatic choreography and fine dancing, it is also to relive the wonderful visual elegance and delight of Delvaux's *'Adame Miroir*, Clavé's *Carmen*, Keogh's *Tyl Eulenspiegel* and Léonor Fini's fantasy world of *Les Demoiselles de la Nuit* and *Le Rêve de Léonor*. The list could go on: René Allio produced exceptional décors for *Les Intermittences du cœur* in 1974: Carzou's designs for *Le Loup* in 1953 are still effective after twenty-five years: Erté's wit has illuminated several revue

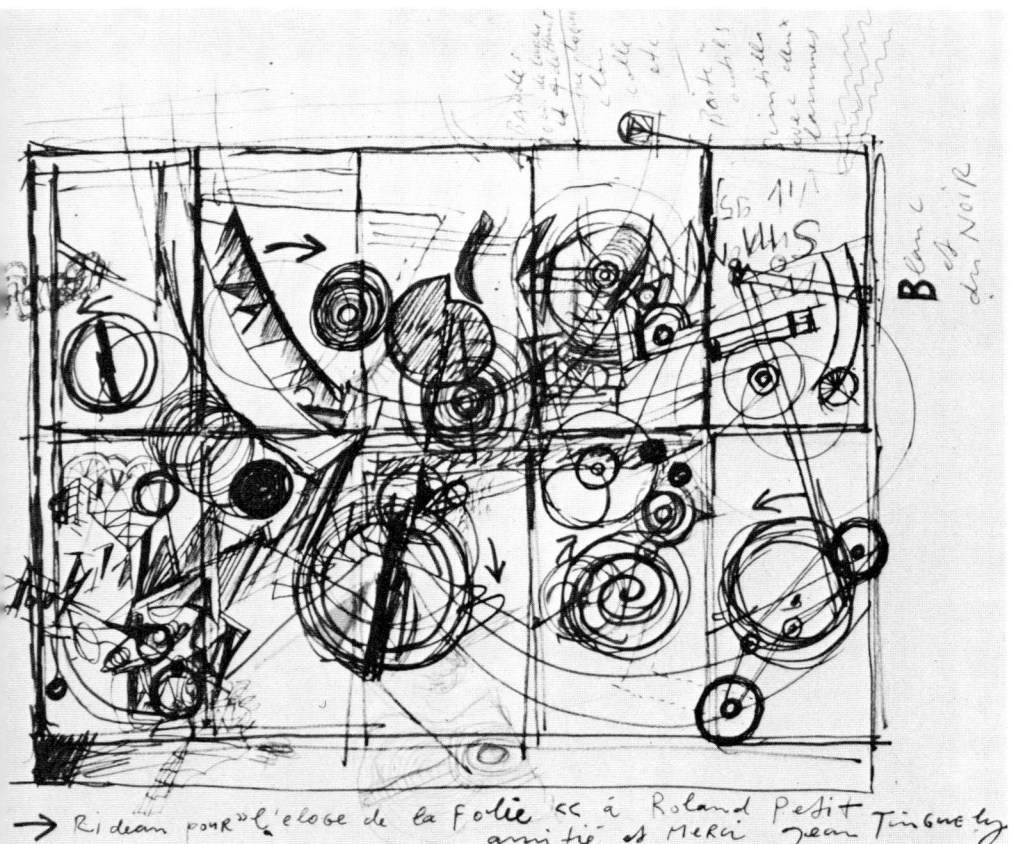

Above
209 Paul Delvaux (b. 1897): setting for *'Adame Miroir*, ballet with choreography by Janine Charrat, music by Darius Milhaud, costumes by Jacques Fath, first performed by Roland Petit's Ballet de Paris in Paris, 1948. This extraordinary work, based on a theme by Jean Genet, was set by Delvaux in a hall of mirrors; a sailor dogged by his *doppelganger* comes face to face with death. Delvaux's masterly setting and the corrupt romanticism of the theme were typical of the new French ballet of the post-war years.

Left
210 Jean Tinguely (b. 1925): design for the curtain for *L'Eloge de la folie*, ballet with choreography by Roland Petit, music by Marius Constant, first performed by the Ballets de Roland Petit in Paris, 1966. As an updating of Erasmus's *Praise of Folly*, Roland Petit staged this ballet which satirized various idiocies of the day. In place of a drop-curtain there was a machine which a dancer pedalled while wheels and pulleys were activated, until finally it released a little balloon.

211 Bernard Buffet (b. 1928): setting for the first scene of *Le Rendezvous Manqué*, ballet in two acts with choreography by John Taras and Don Lurio, music by Michel Magne, produced by Roger Vadim for the Ballet-Théâtre Français in Monte Carlo, 1958.

sketches for Petit's wife, Zizi Jeanmaire; David Hockney designed *Septentrion* in 1976. Roland Petit's taste typifies the particular felicities of French style. He of all post-war figures in ballet can pride himself upon showing how 'designer's' ballet can survive and flourish in the latter half of the twentieth century.

Totally unlike in aesthetic, yet also alike because concerned with the painter's theatre, is the Ballet-Théâtre Contemporain. This company was brought into being in 1968 as part of the French Ministry of Culture's decision to implant Maisons de la Culture in the French provinces – arts complexes containing a theatre, concert hall, library, and gallery areas – in the quest for the decentralization of art in France. The Ballet-Théâtre Contemporain was entrusted to Jean Albert Cartier as its artistic director. For several years a distinguished writer about art, Cartier brought to his guidance of the company a determination that it should reflect contemporary ideas in the arts that go to make up ballet. Its repertory contains only works exclusively made for the company; they all feature music and painting of this century. The result, consequently, is that the Ballet-Théâtre Contemporain provides a stimulating conspectus of contemporary painting in its widest variety. Like the Diaghilev company, it can be said to be a travelling exhibition of modern art of high quality. In an age when stage design seems often to have fallen in a rut with established large companies, and when the specialist stage designer has acquired a firm hold upon the visual side of theatre, Ballet-Théâtre Contemporain shows, to those who are prepared to see, how the painter, sculptor or innovator in art can enhance ballet. If Ballet-Théâtre Contemporain's choreography or music is not always thrilling, its design almost invariably is. During its decade of existence it has featured the design

Opposite above
212 Jésus-Raphael Soto (b. 1923): setting for *Violostries*, ballet with choreography by Michael Descombey, music by Bernard Parmegiani and Devy Erlih, first performed by the Ballet-Théâtre Contemporain in Amiens, 1969. The Venezuelan-born artist Soto has specialized in recent years in abstract work which combines light and mobile elements. In *Violostries* the pendant structure and imaginative lighting provided a wonderfully shimmering effect.

Opposite below
213 Alexander Calder (b. 1898) setting for *Amériques*, with choreography by Norbert Schmucki, music by Varèse, first performed by the Ballet-Théâtre Contemporain in Amiens, 1971. It is typical of the adventurous design policies of the Ballet-Théâtre Contemporain that they should have approached the American sculptor and inventor of the mobile to produce designs for a ballet.

Above
214 Michael English: setting for *Whisky-Coca*, ballet with choreography by Dirk Sanders, music by Stockhausen, first performed by the Ballet-Théâtre Contemporain in London, 1973. A brilliant Pop Art setting – and costuming by Deborah Torrens – gave much of the interest to this work which was an erotic *pas de deux*.

of: Sonia Delaunay, Claude Viseux, Gustave Singier, La Groupe de Recherches d'Art Visuel, Léon Zack, Etienne Hajdu, Jésus-Raphael Soto, Mario Prassinos, Francisco Bores, Karel Appel, Jean Dewasne, César, Paul Charlot, Emile Gilioli, Piotr Kowalsky, Gérard Fromanger, Tuan, Alexander Calder, Francisco Sobrino, Edouard Pignon, Roman Cieslewicz, Constantin Andreou, Yvan Messac, Roland Baladi, Pierre Tal-Coat, Michael English, Erté and Daniel Chompré.

The visual standards of the repertory are among the most stimulating examples of modern stage design: Jean Albert Cartier's willingness to show that 'modern' painters can contribute to the excitement of ballet, and his appreciation of the importance of ballet's decorative impact, give his company a particular distinction.

Modern Ballet and Modern Dance

From being ancient and embattled enemies, ballet and modern dance discovered in the post-war years that they had, in fact, something in common – dance. This realization was to receive its most interesting and concrete expression in the emergence of the Nederlands Dans Theater. Founded in 1959 as a breakaway from the Dutch National Ballet, Nederlands Dans Theater combined the talents of young Dutch choreographers and visiting American creators. The company's policy from its first seasons was the production of some ten new ballets every year. The company's style, thanks

to the influence of the Americans, would in due time produce a remarkable fusion of classical and modern attitudes, and a different form of decoration – cleaner and more economic in appearance – also emerged to provide the new settings for the new dance.

The austerities of image, and the quest for other forms of expression, have produced the idea of the stage as bare, white, shining with silvery reflection, almost spartan or clinical in aspect. Such designers as Jean Paul Vroom and the English artist Nadine Baylis have typified this new approach. The example of Nederlands Dans Theater has been felt in several other European companies, most importantly the Ballet Rambert, which after 1966 adopted similar creative policies.

Both Nederlands and Rambert have invited the collaboration of American choreographers, musicians and designers and the work of the artist William

215 Joop Stokvis: setting for *Hi-kyo*, ballet with choreography by Jaap Flier, music by Kazuo Fukushima, first performed by the Nederlands Dans Theater in Amsterdam, 1971. A hanging forest of ropes provided a décor which was also, as the illustration shows, an essential aid to the dance action.

Right
216 Peter Dockley: setting for *Self Surgery*, a production realized by Dockley for Nederlands Dans Theater, first performed in The Hague, 1974. The use of mutilated life-size models provides a disquieting milieu for this staging entirely created by the artist.

Below
217 Nadine Baylis: setting for *Ziggurat*, ballet with choreography by Glen Tetley, music by Stockhausen, first performed by the Ballet Rambert in London, 1967. In this ballet, concerned with the downfall of a god-like figure, Nadine Baylis provided décor that was mobile and extremely effective, incorporating film projections and imaginative lighting. The open-mesh costumes for the male dancers were a notable innovation.

Design for Ballet

Opposite above
218 Patrick Procktor: setting for *Cage of God*, ballet with choreography by Jack Carter, music by Alan Rawsthorne, first performed by Western Theatre Ballet in London, 1957. Commissioning Procktor, one of the foremost English artists of his generation, was a welcome return on the part of the adventurous Western Theatre Ballet to the idea of painterly décor for ballet.

Opposite below
219 Ralph Koltai (b. 1924): model for the setting for *A Place in the Desert*, ballet with choreography by Norman Morrice, music by Carlos Surinach, first performed by the Ballet Rambert in London, 1961.

Below
220 Ian Murray Clark: setting for *Waterless Method of Swimming Instruction*, ballet with choreography by Robert Cohan, music by Bob Downes, first performed by the London Contemporary Dance Theatre in Switzerland, 1974. Cohan's suite of dances ranges from the serious to the jolly; much of the atmosphere of the piece is suggested by the clever setting of an empty swimming pool on the deck of an ocean liner.

Katz, in such ballets as *Caterpillar* (colour plate 33) and *Eclipse* (plate 221) for NDT and *Tutti-Frutti* for Rambert, demonstrates the possibilities of fresh design ideas.

Nadine Baylis (b. 1942) has produced some of the most important modern dance design in Britain. In décor for ballets by Norman Morrice and Glen Tetley she has been an eloquent advocate of a cool, sculptural style. Her settings have often a geometric precision; they yet remain powerfully effective in dramatic works and ideal locales for plotless dancing. In her setting for *Hazard* (plate 222) she provided an area of golden metallic plaques in the middle of which there is a tree structure. The subject of the ballet was man's birth from chaos and his eventual horror of the world he inherits. The hero makes his first appearance from the tree structure and at the end he is left turning aimlessly and tragically from the curve of the metal crescent which dominates the setting. In *Hazard* as in so much modern dance the design has actually become part of the choreography.

The experimental style of work such as we have described has inevitably in its turn affected and influenced design in the more traditional theatres and even opera houses. Nadine Baylis's collaboration with Tetley has been seen at the Royal Opera House, Covent Garden, and at the Paris Opéra; Jean Paul Vroom's designs for Hans van Manen have also been seen at Covent Garden; the Opéra has used Jasper Johns to decorate a Cunningham work, *Un Jour ou deux*.

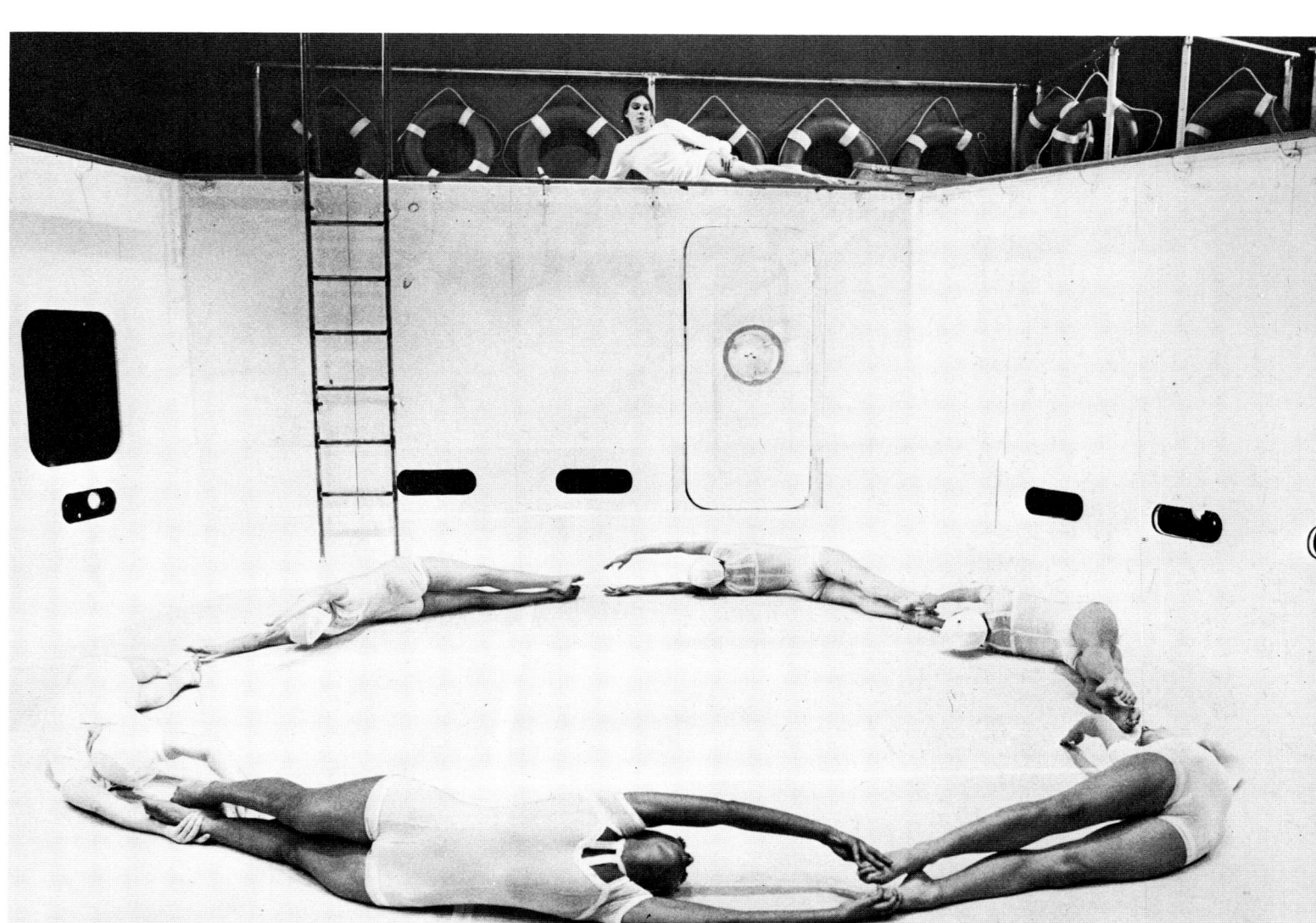

Design of Today

Opposite
221 William Katz: design for *Eclipse*, ballet with choreography by Louis Falco, music by Bert Alcantara, first performed by the Nederlands Dans Theater in The Hague, 1974. Falco has made use of unexpected, and sometimes improbable, accessories and settings and Katz, in a series of notable designs for Nederlands Dans Theater and for Falco's company, has brought a vivid theatrical talent to illuminate the subject matter.

Above
222 Nadine Baylis: setting for *Hazard*, ballet with choreography by Norman Morrice, music by Leonard Salzedo, first performed by the Ballet Rambert in Bath, 1967.

One other phenomenon in the post-war dance world has been the amazing success of the Ballet du Vingtième Siècle, the chosen instrument of Maurice Béjart. Béjart's fantastic appeal to a young audience throughout the world cannot be ignored. His belief in dance as a rite to be celebrated in enormous arenas and in tents rather than in theatres has produced a modish repertory, filled with bold and obvious effects, which is often decorated in a similar manner. His designers have ranged from Salvador Dali and Bernard Daydé to Joelle Roustand and Roger Bernard who have staged some of his largest spectacles. Béjart's ability to produce huge popular spectacles in vast arenas is epitomized in his *Trionfi* staged in Florence in 1974 to celebrate the six hundredth anniversary of the death of Petrarch. There were five triumphal entries which involved decorated cars like those seen in Renaissance

Left
223 Peter Unsworth: setting for *In the Beginning*, with choreography by Geoffrey Cauley, music by Poulenc, first performed by the Royal Ballet in Stratford-upon-Avon, 1969. A version of the Adam and Eve story, the ballet had choreography of clarity, poise and not a little wit, which was matched in the designs by the exceptional young painter Peter Unsworth. With pale clear colours and with carefully placed cubes, integral to the action and repeated in the backcloth, he caught the feeling of the morning of the world.

Below
224 Setting by Poul Arnt Thomsen and costumes by Søren Breum for *The Triumph of Death*, choreographed (originally for television) by Flemming Flindt to music by Thomas Koppel, first performed by the Royal Danish Ballet in 1971 on Danish television and subsequently staged in the Royal Theatre, Copenhagen, 1972. Based upon a play by Eugene Ionesco, *Jeu de Massacre*, this work was a modern version of the dance of death, to a highly effective pop score. Much of its interest came from the admirable rapport between dance and design.

Design of Today

Above
225 Jean Paul Vroom: setting for *Twilight*, ballet with choreography by Hans van Manen, music by John Cage, first performed by the Dutch National Ballet in Amsterdam, 1972. *Twilight* was a *pas de deux* for urban teenagers living in the shadow of an industrial complex, magnificently suggested in Jean Paul Vroom's design. Setting and choreography combined to create a mysterious poetry and beauty from the harshness and aggression implicit in this theme.

Right
226 Rouben Ter-Arutunian: setting for *Pierrot Lunaire*, ballet with choreography by Glen Tetley to the Schoenberg song cycle, first produced in New York in 1962 and subsequently revived for Nederlands Dans Theater, Ballet Rambert, the Stuttgart Ballet, the Munich State Opera Ballet, and the Royal Danish Ballet whose version we illustrate. The scaffolding tower which is the entire setting for the piece is the territory in which the white-clad Pierrot lives.

Design of Today

spectacles. Plate 228 shows the Triumph of Fame in which the car bears a sunburst of trumpets. Another enterprise was a series of new versions of ballets created by Diaghilev's Ballet Russe, including *The Firebird*, *Les Noces* and a full-length fantasy – *Nijinsky Clown of God* – about Diaghilev and his first *premier danseur*. The designs for *Renard* illustrated in plate 229 are a Pop Art confection created by Germinal Casado (b. 1934), who was for some years a principal dancer of the Ballet du Vingtième Siècle.

The very nature of modern dance, its emergence as a form of theatre absolutely apart from ballet during the 1920s and 1930s in the USA, meant that its design attitudes were completely fresh. The shortage of funds for anything more than functional dressing of the dance works of Martha Graham and Doris Humphrey – the two supreme creators of the inter-war years – brought a rejection of any sort of decorative clutter. Fantasy, charm, prettiness – all attributes associated with ballet – were by virtue of this association utterly despised. Modern dance's high seriousness, its idiosyncratic language, its social conscience and personal expression, meant that, apart from a few basic properties, most modern dance performances were austere and positively puritan in appearance. It is nevertheless to Martha Graham that we look for a notable innovation in the decoration of dance, as well as in its manner and its content: her association with one of the greatest sculptors and stage designers of our time, Isamu Noguchi (b. 1904). In an introduction to a study of his work Noguchi wrote:

> There is a joy in seeing sculpture come to life on the stage in its own world of timeless time. Then the very air becomes charged with meaning and emotion, and form plays its integral part in the re-enactment of a ritual. Theatre is a ceremonial; the performance is a rite. Sculpture in daily life should or could be like this. In the meantime, the theatre gives me its poetic, exalted equivalent.

Noguchi had known Graham from the late 1920s when he sculpted two heads of her; later he watched her in class and he notes 'it was as a familiar that I did

Opposite above
227 Rudolf Kufner: setting for the eighth scene, Transfiguration, in *Orpheus* **as staged by Maurice Béjart to a score by Pierre Henry, first performed by Ballet-Théâtre de Paris in Liège, 1958.**

Opposite below
228 Roger Bernard and Joelle Roustand: setting for *I Trionfi di Petrarca*, **spectacle staged by Maurice Béjart to music by Luciano Berio, first performed by the Ballet du Vingtième Siècle in the Boboli Gardens, Florence, 1974.**

Right
229 Germinal Casado: design for *Le Renard* **with choreography by Maurice Béjart to Stravinsky's score, first performed by the Ballet du Vingtième Siècle at the Paris Opéra, 1965.**

my first set for her *Frontier* in 1935'. And about this setting Noguchi declared that it was the point of departure for all his subsequent theatre work: 'Space became a volume to be dealt with sculpturally.' Thereafter Noguchi was to provide settings and properties – properties, indeed, which became the setting – for a number of Graham's finest works. In the reverberation of his sculptural objects we can see a focusing of many of the themes of Graham's choreography itself: they became extensions, reflections of the choreography, rather than decorative appurtenances, no matter how elegant or polished in form. The appositeness of Noguchi's vision, its complete integration into the choreography, is unique in dance. (Although Loie Fuller may have created a movement world from light and gauze, her language of dance was devoid of choreographic interest.) The Graham-Noguchi aesthetic offers a form of theatre in which decoration becomes a partner of the dance: it is in effect solid choreography. Noguchi wrote of *Cave of the Heart* (plate 231), a version of the legend of Jason and Medea, as

> a dance of transformation (as in the Noh Drama). Medea, priestess of the mother goddess, slays the offspring of her union with Jason and is transformed and finally consumed by the flaming nimbus of the setting sun (her father). I constructed a landscape like the islands of Greece. On the horizon (centre rear) lies a volcanic shape like a black aorta of the heart; to this lead stepping stone islands. (Jason's voyage, the end bridge of drama). Opposite (stage left) is a coiled green serpent, on whose back rests the transformation dress of gold (metal).

Rarely in Western art have dance and décor been so closely integrated as in the theatre of Martha Graham. Movement sometimes inspires the actual shape of a costume: certainly the vast swirling skirt worn in *Cave of the Heart* becomes part of the dance itself.

Above
230 Isamu Noguchi: setting for *Night Journey*, ballet with choreography and costumes by Martha Graham, music by William Schuman, first performed by the Martha Graham Company in Cambridge, Mass., 1947.

Opposite
231 Isamu Noguchi: setting for *Cave of the Heart*, with choreography by Martha Graham, music by Samuel Barber and costumes by Edythe Gilfond, first performed by the Martha Graham Company in New York, 1946. The dancer here in a 1970s revival is Takako Asakawa.

Design for Ballet

In the years after 1945 Graham and her followers and heirs can be said to have come into their own. There was a burst of creativity which led to today's extreme proliferation of modern dance both in America and Europe. Some modern dance designing today can seem arbitrary or amateur or simply tediously pretentious (like the dance it accompanies). Certain companies – Paul Taylor's is a fine example – provide beautiful and pertinent design to set off beautiful and pertinent dances.

There is usually an avoidance, through financial stringency, of much show or decorative exuberance; costuming reduces itself to basic leotards and tights. Occasionally a new form of dress will emerge, as happened in the mid-seventies in the costuming by Santo Loquasto for the stunning dances by Twyla Tharp. Here an elegant and wildly relaxed form of dress, featuring leg- and footwarmers and loose satin jerkins and trousers, makes the dancers look essentially of their time and very chic.

The great innovations in decoration, though, are to be found with Alwin Nikolais and Merce Cunningham. Nikolais (b. 1912) has created during a period of forty years an entirely special form of theatre in which light, movement, colour, sound and shape are all subject to transformation. By means of most complex lighting plans, of music which he composes himself, of properties which shroud or conceal the dancers, he produces a magical activity in which the eye is teased, delighted and fascinated. The use of dancers to produce unexpected and exciting shapes within an overall costume is a tradition of modern dance dating back to the 1930s when Mary Wigman and

232 Alwin Nikolais: *Scenario*, first performed by the Nikolais dance company in New York, 1971.

Design of Today

Harald Kreutzberg in Germany and Ruth Page in America were making dances 'inside costumes'. Nikolais has taken this idea many stages further in works like *Scenario* (plate 232) *Totem*, *Allegory* and *Imago*. The movement of light is often more expressive and stimulating than that of the dance as choreography: the shimmer and melting of shapes and movement, the creation of tensions through light or lines of properties within the darkened cube of the stage area, have made for a totally new form of visual experience. Nikolais moulds light and movement, shapes and stresses, and then creates from them a theatrical object that is constantly exciting to watch. It is a world of hallucination and magic.

Merce Cunningham's novelty and importance lie in his power to extend the frontiers of dance itself. A great liberator, concerned with dance as an activity unclouded by 'meaning' or any responses other than those it generates within itself, Cunningham has attracted as friends and collaborators musicians and painters who respond to this same idea of freedom and inquiry.

He has been particularly associated with Robert Rauschenberg (b. 1925) and Jasper Johns (b. 1930), who have both spent important periods working as decorators with Cunningham; other associates include Frank Stella, Andy Warhol, Bruce Nauman, and Alex Hay.

In a perceptive introduction to a fine book of photographs and commentaries about Cunningham (New York, 1975) James Klosty comments on how intent Cunningham is on the independence of the various contributory factors to his dance works:

233 Jasper Johns, after Marcel Duchamp's *The Large Glass*: setting for *Walkaround Time*, with choreography by Merce Cunningham, music by David Behrman, first performed by the Cunningham company in Buffalo, 1968.

Design for Ballet

> Those who design the décor and compose the music have almost no contact with the secreted gentleman who choreographs the movement . . . He does not use dance, music, lighting, and décor to achieve *his* purpose, but leaves them free to achieve *their* purpose within the time and space of a given performance.

One last aspect of Cunningham's work must be mentioned: his use of chance. Although his works are precisely choreographed, their internal relationships and final form can depend upon aleatory techniques. These are also brought to bear in the actual creation of setting: in James Klosty's book there is a very important contribution by Carolyn Brown (one of Cunningham's finest dancers) discussing the inspirational nature of some of the settings provided by Rauschenberg which could vary from performance to performance and theatre to theatre. In certain works the setting can – as in *Variations V* – help precipitate the dance action and add to the sound accompaniment. Poles, wired for sound, moved as the dancers approached them while any contact with the dancers' bodies produced electronic noises. *Rainforest* (plate 235), a most beautiful Cunningham piece, was enhanced by the effects produced by Warhol's silver pillows, filled with helium, which floated and drifted about the stage and provided a mysterious counterpoint to the dances. Here was the most unpredictable of décors; it existed on its own terms during the action of the work.

It is in the Cunningham theatre that we see probably at its most extreme, but certainly at its most stylish, the important innovations in producing a setting for dancing. It is sometimes the unexpectedness of materials that may shock and surprise us: Cunningham dancing with a chair strapped to his back was an early and quite logical snook cocked at the audience; his appearance on a bicycle or carrying a giant flower pot were also techniques devised to make the audience look more searchingly or from a different standpoint at the nature of movement as Cunningham conceives it.

Cunningham's dances – and Cunningham's budget – do not allow for much complexity of decoration. The stripped to the bone simplicity, almost classical, that marks his latest dances is something that is also to be seen in the most effective decoration for his theatre pieces. In *Summerspace* Rauschenberg's pointillist backcloth was matched by pointillist costuming

Below
234 Robert Rauschenberg: setting for *Travelogue*, with choreography by Merce Cunningham, music by John Cage, first performed by the Cunningham company in New York, 1977.

Opposite above
235 Andy Warhol (b. 1931): setting for *Rainforest*, with choreography by Merce Cunningham, music by David Tudor, first performed by the Cunningham company in New York, 1968.

Opposite below
236 Meredith Monk in *Quarry*, first performed in New York in 1976. In this total theatre piece Meredith Monk is seen as a sick child in the centre of the playing area. Much of the time the stage is divided into pools of light, suggesting rooms in a house. The audience is seated on little balconies on three sides of the playing area.

237 Santo Loquasto: costume for Twyla Tharp in her own *Sue's Leg* 1975. Twyla Tharp and her dancers all wear this elegant satin and wool unisex costume which owes inspiration to the practice dress of dancers at work and also to the fashion of the 1970s. In performance, supreme criterion of dance clothing, Tharp and her companions are given complete freedom of movement and look very stylish.

to give an effect of internal movement within a picture. In *Nocturnes* a column of white cloth and a gauze announced the elegance of the dance and matched the coolness of Satie's music.

In *Winterbranch* Rauschenberg 'made a "monster" (as we affectionately called it) out of backstage stuff, different in every performance, but always with some kind of light or lights casting eerie shadows as it was pulled across the darkened stage on a long rope' (Carolyn Brown in James Klosty's *Merce Cunningham*). Carolyn Brown also records that at some performances Rauschenberg dyed clothes and hung them to dry so that they dripped during the performance. The dancers would never know what they would find when they returned to the theatre in the evening: 'It was something to look forward to, a hand-made gift.'

The multifarious activities of the post-Cunningham generation of modern dance are numerous but fleeting. They are concerned with new areas of dance, new areas for dance. In fact, few if any accept the confines of the proscenium, and some, like Stephanie Evanitsky's Multi-Gravitational Aerodance, have taken off from the ground. From all this activity, as from the experiments of the past, we may expect the traditions of decorating dance to be further extended. In an age when the laser can create disembodied images which yet look entirely real, when technology brings fresh marvels each year, the possibilities for decorating dance seem limitless. During the Renaissance the first ballet designers triumphed over many initial difficulties to create a theatre of magnificence; today the opportunities for experiment and for imaginative decoration are a challenge for designers and for ballet itself.

Bibliography

Amberg, George *Art in Modern Ballet* Pantheon, New York (no date)

American Ballet Theatre: Thirty-six Years of Scenic and Costume Design catalogue, American Ballet Theatre, New York 1976

Alexandre, Arsenè *The Decorative Art of Léon Bakst* Fine Art Society, London 1913

Ballet magazine, edited by Richard Buckle, London 1946–52

Baur-Heinhold, Margarete *Baroque Theatre* Thames & Hudson, London 1967

Beaumont, Cyril W. *Ballet Design Past and Present* The Studio, London 1946

Beaumont, Cyril W. *Complete Book of Ballets* Putnam, London 1937

Benois, Alexander *Reminiscences of the Russian Ballet* Putnam, London 1941

Bjurstrom, Per *Giacomo Torelli and Baroque Stage Design* Stockholm 1961

Buckle, Richard *Modern Ballet Design* A & C Black, London 1955

Cooper, Douglas *Picasso Theatre* Weidenfeld & Nicolson, London 1968

Dance Index 1942–1948. Complete run reprinted Arno Press, New York 1971

Fokine, Mikhail *Memoirs of a Ballet Master*. Little, Brown, Boston 1961

Gascoigne, Bamber *World Theatre: an Illustrated History* Ebury Press, London 1968

Hainaux, René *Stage Design Throughout the World Since 1935* Harrap, London 1957

Kirstein, Lincoln *Movement and Metaphor* Praeger Publishers, New York 1970, Pitman & Sons, London 1971

Kragh-Jacobsen, Svend and Krogh, Torben *Den Kongelige Danske Ballet* Selskabet Til Udgivelse af Kilturskrifter, Copenhagen 1953

Lehmann, John (ed.) *Purcell's The Fairy Queen as presented by the Sadler's Wells Ballet and the Covent Garden Opera* London 1948

Newton, Stella Mary *Renaissance Theatre Costume and the Sense of the Historic Past* André Deutsch, London 1975

Nicoll, Allardyce *The Development of the Theatre* Harrap, London 1931

Oenslager, Donald *Stage Design: Four Centuries of Scenic Invention* New York 1975

Reade, Brian *Ballet Designs and Illustrations* HMSO, London 1967

Rowell, Kenneth *Stage Design* Studio Vista, London 1968

Scholtz, János *Baroque and Romantic Stage Design* Bittner Art Book, New York 1949

Strong, Roy *Splendour at Court* Weidenfeld & Nicolson, London 1973

Swift, Mary Grace *The Art of the Dance in the USSR* University of Notre Dame Press, Indiana 1968

Tidworth, Simon *Theatres: an Illustrated History* Pall Mall Press, London 1973

Picture Credits

The sources for the illustrations in this book are as follows: (references are to plate numbers except where specified as page numbers)

Plate 92, 172, 173, 176, 205, 206a American Ballet Theatre; Colour 8 by courtesy of Mrs Liliana Archibald; 88, 89a, 90, 99, 103b, 118, 119 from the authors' collection; 235 photo Oskar Bailey; 59, 77, 81a, 201, Colour 3 Bakhrushin Theatre Museum, Moscow; 228 Le Ballet du XXeme Siècle; 10, page 53, 41 Bibliotheque National Paris; Colour 5 by courtesy of Edwin Binney, 3rd, photo Roy Blakey, 218 British Council; 6, 22a, 22b, 23, 26a, 27, 33 British Museum, London; 12, 13 Chatsworth Collection; Colour 24, Colour 25 by courtesy of the Hon. Colette Clark; Colour 11 by courtesy of Mary Clarke; 160 photo A. C. Cooper; 137, page 204, 151, 166, 215, 220, 22 photos Anthony Crickmay: 234 Cunningham Foundation; 196, 197, 198 Czech Theatre Archives, Prague; 80b, 107a, 107b, page 165, 116, 120, 136a, 136b, 141, 143, 144a, 177, 178 photo Oskar Savio, 186, 217 photo A. J. Charlton, *The Dancing Times* archives; 108, 110–113, Colour 18 Dansmuseet, Stockholm; Colour 12 by courtesy of Parmenia Migel Ekstrom; 204 photo Mike Davis; 236 photo John Elbers; Colour 2 photo Christina Gascoigne; 191 by courtesy of Nicholas Georgiadis; 148, 149, 158, 159, 163, 164, 168, 169, 223, 225 photos Group Three; 161 photo Houston Rogers; 219 photo Iliffe, Allegro Studios; 89b, 214 photos Shuhei Iwamoto; 224 photo John R. Johnsen; 213 photo Daniel Keryzaouen; 153 photo James Klosty; 45, 49a, 49b, 78, 81b Leningrad Theatre Museum; 125, 152, 211, 212, 227, 229, Colour 29 photos Serge Lido; Colour 9 Musée des Arts Decoratifs, Paris; Colour 14 Musée d'Art Moderne, Paris; 19, 21, 34, 36–39, 55, 61, 74a, 74b, 86, 129, 130–133, 147, 185, 188, Colour 7 Musée de l'Opéra, Paris; 62, 103a, 122, 124a, 124b, 128, 134, 171 Museum and Library of the Performing Arts, New York; 48, 180, 182 Museo Teatrale Alla Scala, Milan; 226 photo Mydtskov; 193, 195 National Ballet of Canada; 216, colour 33 Nederlands Dans Theatre; Colour 34 Nikolais Foundation; 80a, 139, 140 Collection Natalia Roslavleva, Novosti Press Agency; 144b, 145b Novosti Press Agency; 232 photo Oleaga; 46, 71, 145 Osterreichische Nationalbibliothek, Vienna; 208 photo Marc Vaux, by courtesy of Ruth Page; 194 photo David Parker; 210, Colour 28, Colour 30 by courtesy of Roland Petit; 183, 184, 187, 189 photos Photo Pic; 67, 199, 200 Polish Theatre Archives; 56, 58, 68, 70, 207 private collections; 25, Colour 13, Colour 19–22, Colour 31 provenance unknown; 99, 100, 102a, 102b, 105, 106b, 126, 174a, 175 Radio Times Hulton Picture Library; 44 Rijksmuseum, Amsterdam; 150, 165a, 165b photos Stuart Robinson; 87, 162 photos Roy Round, Colour 23 by courtesy of Kenneth Rowell; 1, 31, 40, 47, 72, 73, page 108, 83, 84a, 84b, 85, 91, 94, 95, 104, 123 Royal Academy of Dancing, London; 135 Royal Ballet School, photo A. C. Cooper; 121, 138, 156, 167 Royal Opera House, Covent Garden; 206b photo Frank Sharman; 142, 146, 202, 203 Society for Cultural Relations with the USSR; 127 Sotheby & Co; 154, 156, 157, 190 photos Donald Southern; 52, 53, 62, 66, 69a, 69b, 192 Teaterhistorisk Museum, Copenhagen; 181 Teatro dell' Opera, Rome; 42 Toneelmuseum, Amsterdam; 237 Twyla Tharp; 221 photo Tony van Muyden; page 9, 2–5, 7–9, 11, page 26, 14–18, 20, 24, 26b, 26c, 28, 29, 30a, 30b, 30c, 32, 35, 43, 50, 54, 57, 60, 63–65, 75, 80, 93, 110, 114, 115, 117, Colour 1, Colour 4, Colour 6, Colour 10, Colour 15, Colour 16 Victoria and Albert Museum, London; 82, 101, 106b by courtesy of the Wadsworth Atheneum, Hartford, Conn; 200 Wielki State Theatre, Warsaw; Colour 27 photo Reg Wilson; 155, 170, 209 photos Roger Wood.

Index

Compiled by Valerie Lewis Chandler

Figures in bold refer to caption numbers

'Adame Miroir 263; **209**
Aladin ou la Lampe Merveilleuse 84–5; **57, 58, col.6**
Albert **60**
Alcide **60**
Aleko 167; **187**
Alhambra Theatre, London 92
Allard, Mlle **39**
Allegory **281**
Allio, René 263
Amants Surpris, Les 35
American Ballet Caravan 172, 177
American Ballet Theatre 173, 209, 214, 227, 229–33; **172–6**
Amériques **213**
Amodio, Amedeo **181**
Amor 94
Anastasia 223–5; **165**
Andreou, Constantin 265–7
Andreù, Mariano **119**
Angelica Vincitrice di Alcina 52; **30**
Anisfeld, Boris 120; **col.11**
Apollo, Apollon Musagète 150–3, 177; **106**
Appel, Karel 265–7
Après-midi d'un Faune, L' 116
architects as designers 12
Architetture e Prospettive 52
Armide et Renaud 18; **24**
Art Déco **167**
artists as stage designers 109–10; *see also* individual painters
Ashton, Frederick 185, 191, 219, 223; **123, 134, 154, 156, 158–61, 164, col.24**
Astuzie Femminili, Le 128; **93**
At Midnight **176**
Aubade **188**
Auber 85; **62**
Aubin, Tony **col.31**
audience, position of 10, 15, 23, 30
audience participation 29, 30, 33
auditorium as part of set 23, 30
Aumer, Jean 82
Australian Ballet 244; **194**
Australian design today 244
Ayrton, Michael 169–71, 191, 214–16; **154**

Babilée, Jean 262; **206b**
Bacchanal 167–9
bacchante **39, 60**
Bacchus et Ariane **132, 179, 184**
backdrops in early theatres 12, 13, 21, 66
Baiser de la Fée, Le **col.23**
Baker-Smith, Malcolm **154**
Bakst, Léon 109, 111, 114–15, 115–17, 118, 126, 127, 128, 130; **58, 83–6, 91, 94–6, col.9, col.15**
Bal, Le 153–4; **107**
Baladi, Roland 265–7
Balanchine, George 145, 150–3, 153, 166, 167, 171, 172–3, 175, 177, 179, 205, 227, 228; **101, 104–7, 115, 170, 171, page 165, col.27**
Balla, Giacomo 122, 122–3
Ballad of the Tree **198**
Ballet Comique de la Reine, Le 10, 15; **2**
ballet d'action 65
Ballet de l'Opéra de Monte Carlo 166
Ballet de l'Opéra Russe à Paris 166
Ballet de la Provençale 58; **37**
Ballet de Paris 207; **209**
Ballet des Polonais, Le 10, 15; **1**
Ballet du Vingtième Siècle 273; **228, 229**
Ballet International, N.Y. 167; **125, 126**
Ballet of the Birds **154**
ballet pantomimes 76; **33**
Ballet Rambert 183, 268–71; **217, 219, 222, 226**
Ballet Royal de la Nuit, Le 15
Ballet Russe (de Basil) 166–7, 175; **85, 117, 124, 127, col.20, col.21**
Ballet Russe (Diaghilev) 109, 111–57; **58, 82, 84–6, 88–95, 97–107, col.9–16**
Ballet Russe, after Diaghilev 166–79; **116, 118**
Ballet Russe de Monte Carlo (Blum) 167, 171, 172, 179; **107a, 119, 120, 123, 128, page 165, col.19, col.22**
Ballet Society, N.Y. 227–8; **170**

Ballet-Théâtre Contemporain 260, 265; **212–14, col.32**
Ballet-Théâtre de Paris **227**
Ballet-Théâtre Français **211**
ballets de cour see court ballet
Ballets de Roland Petit in Paris **210**
Ballets des Champs Elysées, Les 260; **205, 206, 208, col.31**
Ballets 1933, Les 166, 171, 175; **115**
Ballets Suédois, Les 157–64; **109–13, col.17, col.18**
Balmain, Jacques 263
Balthus 167–9
Barabau 139–45
Bardon, Henry 219–23, 244; **149**
Basil, W. de *see* Ballet Russe
Baskin, Leonard 231; **176**
Basner, Vladimir 201
Bauchant, André 134–9, 153; **106**
Bauhaus, Stuttgart **108**
Bayadère, La **54, 74**
Baylis, Nadine 268, 271; **217, 222**
Beach 167–9; **118**
Beardsley, Aubrey 120
Beaton, Cecil 185
Beauchamp, Pierre 34
Beaujoyeulx, Balthazar de 10, 15
Beaumont, Count Etienne de **100**
Beaurepaire, André 262
Behrman, David **233**
Béjart, Maurice 273; **227, 228**
Bekeffi, Alfred **80**
Bell, Vanessa 185
Bellerofonte **51**
Benois, Alexandre 107, 110, 111, 114–18, 130; **82, 87, 128, 147, col.8, col.10**
Berain 18, 34–9; **21–4**
Bérard, Christian 167–9, 169–71, 172, 260; **120, 121, 206, col.20**
Berman, Eugene 169, 170, 171–3, 209, 228–9, 231–3; **122, 123, 171, 174**
Berman, Leonid 172
Bernard, Roger 273; **228**
Bibiena Family 44–52; **28–30**
Biches, Les 134
Birds, The 185
Blazek, Jiri **197**
Bluebeard **80a**
Blum, René 166–7 *see also* Ballet Russe de Monte Carlo
Bolshoy Ballet 257; **79, 142–4, 201–3**
Bolshoy Theatre, Moscow **77**
Bolshoy Theatre, Petersburg **78**
Bonnard, Pierre 161–2; **col.18**
Boquet, Louis René 58–60, 61–2; **38, 39, page 53, col.3**
Bores, Francisco 265–7
Börlin, Jean 157–64; **109–13, col.17, col.18**
Bouchène, Dimitri 236
Boucher, François 54
Bournonville, August 63, 86, 88–93, 98, 244; **66, 69, 192**
Boutique Fantasque, La 127, 127–8
Braque, Georges 134, 134–9; **col.16**
Brayer, Yves 183, 236; **186**
Breum, Søren 224
Brianchon, Maurice 183, 236; **188**
Brioschi, Anton 94–8; **71**
Brown, Carolyn 282
Bruun, Thomas **52**
Buffet, Bernard 211
Buontalenti, Bernardo 16–17; **8**
Burmeister, Vladimir 204
Burnacini, Giovanni 39–40
Burnacini, Lodovici 40–4; **26, 27**
Burra, Edward 185, 185–91; **138, 157**

Cage, John 225, 234
Cage of God **218**
Cagli, Corrado **179**
Calder, Alexander 265–7 **13**
Callot, Jacques 4–6, 9
Camargo Society, London **134, 160**
Camargo, Marie-Anne Cupis de 57
Canadian design today 244
Canna, Pasquale 76; **59**
Canudo, Ricciotto 161; **110**
capo mestre delle teatri 13
Caprichos, Los **col.31**
Carducci, Alessandro **20**
Carmen 262–3; **207**
Carmen Suite **201**
Carnaval, Le 116–17
Carnevale Languente, Il **col.2**

Caron, Leslie **206b**
carrousels 12, 33; **18, 20**
cars (floats) 10, 12; **4, 5**
Carter, Jack **218**
Cartier, Jean-Albert 265, 267
Carzou, Jean 209, 236, 263; **152, 185**
Casado, Germinal 277; **229**
Cassandre, Alexandre 183, 236; **183**
Cassaria 12
Catagallina, Remigio **3**
Cauley, Geoffrey **223**
Cave of Sleep, The 177
Cave of the Heart 278; **231**
Cendrars, Blaise 161
César 265–7
Chagall, Marc 167, 236; **187, col.27**
Chalon, Alfred Edward **col.7**
Chanel, Gabrielle 134
Chao-Kiang 76; **48, 49**
Charlot, Paul 265–7
Charrat, Janine **209**
Chatte, La **104**
Checkmate 185; **136**
Cherepnin, Nikolay 82
Chernichova, Lyubov 85, 91
Chevalier et la Demoiselle, Le **183**
Chiang Yee 185
Chipart, Louis **53**
Chirico, G. de' 139, 153–4, 161–2, 183; **107, 127, 132**
Chloridia 12
Chompré, Daniel 265–7
Chout **128**
Christensen, C. F. **69**
Ciceri, P. 82, 84–5; **55, 57, col.6**
Cieplinski, Jan **145**
Cieslewicz, Roman 265–7
Cimarosiana 93
Cinderella 45, 46, **col.21**
City Center Theatre, N.Y. **171, 176**
Clair, René 162, 163
Clark, Ian Murray 220
Claudel, Paul 161
Clavé, Antoni 262–3; **207, 208, col.31**
Clayette, Pierre 236
Cléopâtre 115, 116–17, 127; **83**
Clock Symphony 167–9, 170; **121**
Cochin, Charles 32
Cocteau, Jean 115, 123, 134, 161, 236, 260; **84, 89, 205, col.14**
Cohan, Robert 220
Colin, Paul 183
Colloque Sentimentale 177; **126**
colour, use of 83, 115–16, 117, 126, 127
Combat, The 175
combat à la barrière 12, 30; **6**
Comus 185
Concerto 177
Concerto Barocco 172–3
Constanza d'Ulysse **27**
Constructivist décor 149, 150
Contagio **182**
Contes Russes 121, 122; **88**
Coppélia **133**
Coq d'Or, Le 120
corps de ballet 98
Corsaire, Le **74**
costume
 court ballet 12–13, 18, 19–21, 29, 31–9, 45; **11**, Rococo 56–61, 19th century 82, 83, 86, 98–107, modern 277–80
Cotillon 170, 171
court ballet and monarchy 10–12, 13, 22–5, 39, 40, 45; **58, col.2**
court entertainments 10–25, 27–52
Covent Garden *see* Royal Opera House
Covent Garden Opera Company 214; **154**
Cracow Wedding **67**
Cranko, John 160, **190**
Craxton, John **156**
Création du Monde, La 162; **111**
Crusader in Egypt, The **47**
Cuadro Flamenco 128
Cubism in design 122, 123, 127; **114**
Cunningham, Merce 281–4; **233–5**
curtains 15, 16
Cyrano de Bergerac 263
Czechoslovakian design today 249

Dadaism 163–4
Daguerre, Louis Jacques Mandé 84; **col.6**

Dali, Salvador 167–9, 177, 273; **125, 126**
Dallapiccola 177
Danilova, Alexandra **107b**
Danish design today 244
Danses Concertantes **209**
Danske Ballets Histoire, Den 68
Daphnis and Chloe 116, 117–18; **86, 156, 187**
Dardel, Nils von 161–2
David, Jacques Louis 66
David Triomphant **130**
Daydé, Bernard 236, 244, 273; **184**
Delaunay, Robert and Sonia 127, 265–7
Delfau, André 183, 236
Deliciae Populi **178**
Délivrance de Renaud, La 22; **10**
della Bella, Stefano **7, 11, 20**
Deller **col.3**
Delvaux, Paul 263; **209, col.29**
de Mille, Agnes 173
Demoiselles de la Nuit, Les 263
Denham, Serge 167
Derain, André 127–8, 134–9, 167–9, 183, 185; **101, 115, 129, col.19**
Descombey, Michel **184, 212, col.32**
Deshayes, Alain **54, 60, col.32**
Deutsche Oper, Berlin **191**
Deveria, Achille 62
Devil's Holiday, The 172; **123**
Dewasne, Jean 265–7
Diaghilev, Serge and the Diaghilev period 109–57, 166, 205
Diaghilev Ballet *see* Ballet Russe
Diavolo Innamorato in Ispagnia **51**
Didelot, Charles 84; **56**
Dido's Death **42**
Dieu Bleu, Le 115, 116–17; **84**
Dignimont, Louis 183
Dior, Christian 263
Dobuzhinsky, Mtislav 120
Dockley, Peter **216**
Dollar, William 175
Don Juan 119, **193**
Don Quixote 157
Dramma per Musica **183**
drop-cloth 40, 45
Drottningholm court theatre **43**
Dubrovska, Felia **105**
Dufy, Raoul 167–9; **118**
Dupont, Jacques **164**
Duport, Louis **46**
Dutch National Ballet **225**

Eclipse 268–71; **221**
Edinburgh Festival (1961) **167**
Efimov, Nikolay 97
Eglevsky, André 177; **126**
Elerz e Zulmida **col.4**
Elite Syncopations **227**
Eloge de la Folie, L' **210, col.28**
Elssler, Fanny 86; **56**
Empire Theatre, London 98; **72**
English, Michael 265–7; **214**
Entr'acte 162
Epishin, Genaddy **204**
Epreuve d'Amour, L' **col.19**
Erdman, Boris **140**
Erixsen, Sven 244
Ernst, Max 134–9, 139–45, 236, 263; **col.30**
Errante 175
Erté 263–5
Etrange Farandole, L' **col.22**
Evanitsky, Stephanie **284**
Evelyn, John 27
Excelsior 94; **70**
exoticism 54, 56, 86
Exter, Alexandra 149; **114**

Fâcheux, Les **col.16**
Faery Queen, The 214; **154**
Falco, Louis **221, col.33**
Fall River Legend 231; **173**
Fancy Free **231**
Far from Denmark **69**
Farmer, Peter 223, 244; **150**
Fath, Jacques 263; **209**
Fauvism 127–8, 150
Fedorov, L. F. 143
Fedorova, Alexandra **128**
Fedorovitch, Sophie 185; **137**
Feld, Eliot **176**
Fellegara, Vittoria **180**
Festival Ballet *see* London Festival B.
Fête Etrange, La 185; **137**
Fête Merveilleuse, La **99**

Fêtes Chinoises, Les 54
Fêtes de Bacchus 19
Fille Mal Gardée, La **153**
Fini, Léonor 236, 263
Finta Pazza, La 27, 29
Firebird, The 111, 277; **187, col.15, col.27**
Fireworks 122, 123
Flier, Jaap **215**
Flindt, Flemming 244; **224**
Flore et Zéphire 84; **56**
Florentine *intermezzi* 12–13, 16–19
flying, apparatus for 12–13, 63–6, 84; **11, 12, 41, 52**
Fokine, Mikhail 105–7, 111, 118, 120, 157–61; **82, 84–6, 119, col.9, col.10, col.15, col.19, col.21**
Fonteyn, Margot **163, 190**
Footballer, The **143**
Forains, Les 260
Foujita 161–2
French influence, Rococo 54–66, on Diaghilev 134, on Ballets Suédois 161–4; in 1940s 170–1, today 260–7 see also Paris Opéra
Frigerio, Ezio 166
Fromanger, Gérard 265–7; **col.32**
Frontier 277–8
Fukishima, Kazuo **215**
Fuller, Loïe 278
Futurist design 122–3
Fuzelier, Louis **185**
Fydorov, Nikolay 59

Gabo, Naum 134–9; **104**
Galeotti, Vincenzo **52, 53**
Galliari Family 54; **31**
Gallini, Giovanni A. **31, 40**
Galster, Amalia 63
Gamlin, Yngve 244
Gara, La 39
Garcia, Juanita **col.31**
Gardel, Maximilien 76
Gardel, Pierre 61, 76–82
Garnier, Jacques **col.32**
Garrick, David 63
Gaslini, Giorgio **182**
Genée, Adeline 73
Georgiadis, Nicholas 209, 244; **151, 191, col.26**
Gerdt, Pavel 105
German design today 244
Ghika, Nico **158**
Gide, André **158**
Gilfond, Edythe **231**
Gilioli, Emile 265–7
Giselle (Ballet Russe 1910) 118, (Moscow c.1920) **139**, (Ballet Théâtre 1946) 172, (Paris Op. 1948) **147**, (Paris Op. 1954) 209, 236; **152**, (Heeley) 244–9, (Farmer) 223
Gissey, Henri 33, 34; **18, 19**
Gluck 175; **119, 193**
gods etc. 12–13, 16, 21; **7, 11**
Goleizovsky, Kasyan **140**
Golovin, Alexander 120; **col.15**
Goncharova, Natalya 120, 134, 183; **97, 131, col.15**
Gonzaga, Pietro **45**
Good-Humoured Ladies, The 127; **91**
Gorsky, Alexander 79, **139**
Graham, Martha 277–80, **230, 231**
Grand Ballet du Marquis de Cuevas 167; **125, 126**
Grand Meaulnes, Le **137**
Grant, Duncan 185
Grigoriev, Serge 166
Grigorovich, Yury **202**
Gris, Juan 134–9; **99**
Groupe de Recherches d'Art Visuel 265–7
Gudule's Daughter **79**
Guoth, J. **198**
Gusev, Piotr 201

habit à la Romaine 18, 30, 33; **26c**
Hajdu, Etienne 265–7
Hallstrom, Gunar 161–2
Hamlet 185
Harlequin in April **160**
Harlequin in the Street 185
Hasselquist, Jenny 161
Hazard 271; **222**
Heeley, Desmond 244–9; **194**
hell scenes 17–18; **24, 26a**
Helpmann, Robert 185; **138**

Henry, Louis 48
Henry, Pierre **227**
Hermanas, Las 209
Hi-kyo **215**
High Jinks 72
Hockney, David 265
Hofoper, Vienna 94–8; **71**
Hoftheater, Vienna 76
Homme et Son Desir, L' **109**
horse ballets 10, 12, 33; **4, 18, 20**
Howard, Andrée 191; **137**
Hoyer, I. Jan 97
Hugo, Jean 161–2, 262
Hullin, Mlle 60
Humphrey, Doris 277
Hungarian State Ballet **145**
Hurry, Leslie 185, 216; **155**
Hymnen **col.32**
Hynd, Ronald **194**

Iberia **col.17**
Icare 172; **122, 189**
Imago 281
Imperial Ballet, Russia 86, 101, 105–7, 109, 110; **75, 80**
In the Beginning **223**
Indes Galantes, Les 236; **185**
intermezzi 12–13, 15, 16–19; **col.1**
Intermittances du Coeur, Les 263
Invitation, The 209
Ironside, Christopher and Robin 219; **159**
Italian design today 233–6
Ivan the Terrible 257

Jack-in-the-Box 101
James, Edward 166
Jardin Public 167–9; **117**
Jeanmaire, Zizi 263–5
Jeune Homme et la Mort, Le 260; **205**
Jeux **col.18**
Jeux d'Enfants 167; **116**
Joan de Zarissa **186**
Job **160**
Johns, Jasper 281; **233**
Jones, Inigo 23–5, 214–16; **12, 13**
Jones, Robert Edmond 126; **90**
Jonson, Ben 23; **12**
Joseph the Beautiful **140**
Judgement of Paris, intermezzi 17; **3**

Karsavina, Tamara 116, 120, 145; **84**
Katz, William 268–71; **221, col.33**
Kauffer, E. McKnight **136**
Kay, Barry 223–5, 244; **165**
Keogh, Tom 262
Kemerny Theatre 149; **114**
Kermesse in Bruges **192**
Keynes, Geoffrey **160**
King Candaules 105; **78**
King's Theatre, London 84; **35, 60**
Kirov Ballet 209, 257–8
Kirschner, Athanasius 29
Kirstein, Lincoln 173, 175, 177, 227
Klimt, Gustav **190**
Kochno, Boris 149, 260; **col.16**
Koltai, Ralph 219
Koppel, Thomas **224**
Korovin, Alexander 109, 110, 120; **79**
Kowalsky, Piotr 265–7
Kraanberg **244**
Kreutzberg, Harald 280–1
Kshessinskaya, Mathilde F. 101; **75**
Kufner, Rudolf **227**
Kurilko, Mikhail **141**
Kusel, Matthaeus **26**

Laborintus 227; **169**
Labyrinth 167–9
Lagertha **53**
Lagut, Irène, 161–2
Lalla Rookh 87–8; **65, col.5**
Lancaster, Osbert **153**
Lander, Harald **153**
Landriani, Paolo 76
Laprade, Pierre 161–2
Larionov, Mikhail 120–2, 128, 134, 183; **88, 97, 131, col.12**
Larthe, Paul 183; **133**
La Scala 66–76; **47, 70, 180, 182, col.4**
Laschilin, Lev **141, 143**
Laurencin, Marie 134, 134–9, 262
Laurens, Henri 134, 134–9
Lavrovsky, Leonid 258; **203**
Lee, Ming Cho 195
Legat, Nicholas **80b**

Légende de Joseph, La 120
Léger, Fernand 161–2, 183; **110, 111, 130**
Leningrad State Kirov Ballet 209, 257–8
Lepri, Stanislas 262
Levasseur, André 236
Liberazione di Tirrenio, intermezzo 6
Lichine, David **127, 206**
Lieutenant Kizhe 257; **201**
Lifar, Serge 167, 179, 236; **97, 106b, 122, 129–32, 186–9**
lighting 29, 76, 85, 149, 205
Lincoln Center *see* New York City B.
Lindstrom 244
Lior, P. **34, 36**
Lissanevich 97
literalism 98, 115
Lithuanienne, La 61
Liturgie 121
London Ballet **137**
London Coliseum **73, 166**
London Contemporary Dance Theatre **220**
London Festival Ballet 209; **89b, 151, 153, 166, 204, col.14**
Loquasto, Santo 280; **237**
Lord of Burleigh, The **134**
Losch, Tilly 166
Loup, Le 236, 263
Louvre Palace 15; **2, 10**
Lully, Jean Baptiste 18, 34; **24**
Luminilia 13
Lunacharsky, Anatoly 191–2
Lund, Troels 67
Lurçat, Jean 167–9; **117**
Lurio, Don **211**

machinery 10, 12–13, 15, 23, 27, 29, 63–6, 84; **6, 11, 12, 14, 41, 52, 74**
Machov, Sasha **196**
MacMillan, Kenneth 209, 223–5; **162, 165, 167, 168, col.23, col.26**
Magallanes, Nicholas 170
Maggio Musicale (Florence 1951) **178**
Majewski, Andrzej **200**
Malclès, Jean-Denis 262
Mamontov, Savva 109–10
Mam'zelle Angot 167–9
Manen, Hans van 271; **225**
Manon 209
Manzotti, Luigi 70
Maré, Rolf de 157–64; **col.18**
Marriage of Figaro, The 185
Mariés de la Tour Eiffel 161
Markova, Alicia 233; **col.22**
Marshall, Charles 65
Marsyas **177**
Martha Graham C. 277–80; **230, 231**
Martin, Jean-Baptiste 57–8; **37**
Maryinsky Theatre 110, 111; **76, 81, 82**
masks 18, 34, 61; **23**
masquerades 10, 12
masques 23–5, 214–16
Masson, André 167–9
Matelots, Les 139–45
Matisse, Henri 128, 134–9, 167–9; **col.22**
Matrunin, B. **142**
Maurer, L. **59**
Mavra 98
Medici Family 10, 13, 16, 17, 19–21, 22
Meninas, Las 128
Mercuri, Mariano **182**
Mercure: Poses Plastiques **100**
Merry Widow, The 244–9; **194**
Messac, Yvan 265–7
Messel, Oliver 185, 209–14; **148**
Messerer, Boris 257; **201**
Metropolitan Opera House 175; **172–4**
Meyerhold, Vsevolod 149
Mielziner, Jo 172
Miracle in the Gorbals 185–91; **138**
Mirages, Les 183
Miró, Joan 134–9, 139–45, 167; **116**
Moiseyer, Igor **142, 143**
Molière, Jean Baptiste Poquelin 30
Moncion, Francisco 170
Mondo Festeggiante, Il 20
monarchy and court ballet 10–12, 13, 22–5, 39, 40, 45; **58, col.2**
Monk, Meredith 236
Mordkin, Mikhail **77**
Morrice, Norman 271; **219, 222**

Moulène, Dimitri 236
Mozartiana 171
Muette de Portici, La 62
Munich State Opera Ballet **226**
Murphy, Gerald 161–2; **112**
Mutazioni **180**

Nabokov, Nicholas 149; **103**
Napoli 68, **153, 192**
Narcisse 116, 118
National Ballet of Canada 244; **193, 195, page 204**
National Theatre, Prague **196, 197**
naturalism 56, 60, 76, 85, 107; **13, 33, 49, 52, 67, 77, 79**
Nauteós **186**
Nederlands Dans Theater 205, 267–71; **215, 216, 221, 226, col.33**
Neoclassical period 66–76; **46, 48, 58**
Neo-romantics 172
Nerman, Einer 161–2
Neumier, John **193**
Nevada, Ana **col.31**
New Penelope, The **192**
New York City Ballet 111, 205, 209, 227; **170, 171, 187, col.27**
Nielsen, Augusta 61
Night Journey 230
Night Shadow 179; **page 165**
Nijinska, Bronislava 134, 145; **97, 114, 196, col.16**
Nijinsky, Vaslav 111, 120, 126; **90, col.8, col.13**
Nijinsky Clown of God 277
Nikitina, Alicia **106b**
Nikolais, A. 149–50, 205, 280–1; **232, col.34**
Nobili, Lila de 219–23; **149, 161**
Noblet, Lise 62
Nobilissima Visione 167–9, 175–7; **124**
Noces, Les 134, 277; **196**
Noces des Pélée et de Thétis, Les 29–30; **16**
Noctambules 209
Nocturnes 284
Noel, Jacques 244
Noguchi, Isamu 227–8, 277–8; **170, 230–1**
Nolan, Sidney **162**
Notre Dame de Paris 263
Nouveaux Ballets de Monte Carlo 167
Novak **198**
Noverre, Jean Georges 54, 60–3, 76; **36, 40, col.3**
Novosibirsk Opera House 201
Nozze degli Dei, Le **11**
Nuit, La 171
Nureyev, Rudolf 209; **163, 166**
Nutcracker, The 209, 227; **128, 139**

Ode 145, 149–50, 173; **103**
Olàh, Gusztav **145**
Ondine 219; **161**
Opéra Comique, Paris 54
Opéra de Quatre Sous, L' 172
opera houses as homes for ballet 27, 94, 107, 209, 227
Oransky, L. **142, 143**
Original Ballet Russe (N.Y.) 177
Orpheus 227–8; **170, 227**
Orpheus and Eurydice 175; **col.3**
Ottawa, Opera House 205

Page, Ruth 280–1; **208**
Palace of the Sun **44**
palaces as location 10–12, 15, **col.5** see also individual palaces
Palais Royal, Paris 19
panniers 61, 82
Parade 122, 123–4; **89, col.14**
Paradise Lost **163**
Parigi 16–17; Giulio **3, 5, 6**; Alfonso 29; **11**
Paris Opéra 34, 54, 57, 61–2, 76–85, 167, 179–83, 219, 236; **36–8, 57, 129, 131–3, 147, 183–9, 229, col.6, col.29, col.30**
Parr, Andrée 161–2; **109**
Pas d'Acier, Le 145–9; **102**
Pastorale, La 105
Patin, Jacques 15; **2**
Paul Taylor Dance Company 227, 280
Pavillon d'Armide, Le 107, 114, 118; **82, col.8**
Pavlova, Anna 130; **77, 94**
Pedersen, Ove Christian **192**
Peintre et Son Modèle, Le 167–9

Pelléas et Mélisande **164**
Pellegrina, La, intermezzi 16; **8**
Perdriat, Hélène 161–2
Perego, Giovanni 76
periaktoi 13
Perilli, Achille **180**
Perrault, Charles 219–23
Perrot, Jules 87–8; **65**
Perséphone **158**
perspective 12, 13–15, 29, 30, 51, 76, 85, 127, 149–50; **6, 11, 13, 15, 26c, 28, 30, 33, 47,** pages **44/5**
Petipa, Marius 98, 101, 130–4; **74, 76, 78, 80–1**
Petit, Roland 236, 260, 262, 263, 265; **163, 164, 205, 207, 210,** page **204, col.28–30**
Petits Riens, Les 36
Pevsner, Anton 134–9, **104**
Petrushka 118; **87, 181, 197, col.10**
Phaeton **42**
Pharaoh's Daughter 76, 77
Pian, Antonio de **46**
Picabia, Francis 161–3; **113**
Picasso, Pablo 123–4, 127, 128, 134–9, 236; **89, 92, 100, 189, col.13**
Piermarini, Giuseppe 66–70
Pierrot Lunaire 227; **226**
Pignon, Edouard 265–7
Pillar of Fire 172
Pimenov, Yury **204**
Pineapple Poll **153**
Piper, John 191; **160**
Pistoni, Mario 180, **182**
Place in the Desert, A **219**
Plaisirs de l'Ile Enchantée 30; **17**
Platzer, Josef 76
Poème de l'Extase **190**
Poirot, Auguste **45**
Polish design today 249
Pollock's Toy Museum 150
Polovtsian Dances from Prince Igor 120
Pomo d'Oro, Il 41; **26**
Pop Art style **163, 214**
Prague Ballet 249
Prague Castle court ballet 23, page **9**
Prassinos, Mario 265–7
Presages, Les 167–9
Pretty Prentice, The **73**
Prieur 163
Princesse d'Elide, La 30; **17**
Princesse de Navarre, La 32
processions (court) 10, 12; **31**
Procktor, Patrick **218**
Prodigal Son, The 153
Prokofiev 128, 149; **102, 131, 166, 199, 202, 203**
proscenium arches 13, 27, 284
Protée **127**
Pruna, Pedro 134–45, 183; **105**
Pulcinella 128, 229
Puppenfee, Die 128
Purificato, Domenico **181**

Quarry **236**
Quest, The 191; **160**

Rabinovich, Isaac **144**
Rainforest 282; **235**
Rake's Progress, The 185; **135**
Rambert, Marie 167, 183, 185 *see also* Ballet Rambert
Rauschenberg, Robert 281, 282; **234**
Raverat, Gwen **160**
Raymonda **80**
Raysse, Martial **163**
Rè, Vincenzo page **27**
Red Poppy, The **141**
reflectors 29, 227
Relâche 162–4; **113**
Renaissance design 10–25
Renard 134, 277; **97, 229**
Rencontre, La **206**
Rendezvous Manqué, Le **211**
Rerikh, Nikolay 120; **col.13**
Reumert, Elith **68**
Revanche **208**
Rêve de Léonor, Le 263
Revolt in the Seraglio, The **64**
Rite of Spring, The **162**
Rituals **168**

Robert the Devil 85, 86
Roberts, James **35**
Rococo design 54–66
Rodeo **231**
Roma **228; 171**
Romanticism 56, 76–107; **48, 53**
Rome Opera **179, 181**
Romeo and Juliet 199, (American Ballet 1943) 173, 231–3; **174,** (Bolshoy 1946) 258; **203,** (MacMillan 1965) 209, **col.26,** (Festival Ballet 1977) **166**
Roméo et Juliette (Ballet Russe 1926) 139–45
ropes and pulleys 12–13, 66
Rose, Jürgen 244; **190**
Rosenthal, Jean 205
Roszkovska, Teresa **199**
Rouault, Georges 134–9
Rouge et Noir 167–9; **col.22**
Roustand, Joelle 273; **228**
Roux, Aline **col.32**
Rowell, Kenneth **col.23**
Roy, Pierre 262
Royal Ballet 111, 209–14, 216, 219, 223, 227; **87, 149, 150, 158, 159, 161–5, 167–70, 175, 223, col.23, col.24**
Royal Danish Ballet 86, 88–93, 244; **192, 224, 226**
Royal Opera House, Covent Garden 209; **121, 136b, 148, 154–7, 160** *see also* Royal Ballet
Royal Festival Hall **153**
Royal Theatre, Copenhagen 52, 53, 224
Rubinstein, Ida 83
Russian design 191–2, 257–8; **140–4** *see also* Ballet Russe; Imperial B.

Sabbatini, Niccolo 13
Sacchetti, Lorenzo 76; **51**
Sacre du Printemps, Le 120; **col.13**
Sadko 120; **col.11**
Sadler's Wells Ballet 183–91, 209–16; **121, 135, 136a, 138, 148, 154–7, col.24**
St. Aignan, Duc de 30
St. Laurent, Yves 263
Saint Léon, Arthur 98
Saint Phalle, Niki **col.28**
Salade **129**
Salle du Petit Bourbon 27–9; **16**
Sanders, Dirk **214**
Sanjust, Filippo **193**
Sanquirico 66–70, 76; **47, 48, col.4**
scena per angolo 51; **66**
scena comica, satyrica, tragica 12, 13, 30
Scenario 281; **232**
scene change 13, 27, 39–44
Schéhérazade 115, 116–17, 124–6; **58, 83, col.9**
Schlemmer, Oskar **108**
Schmucki, Norbert **213, col.32**
Schöller **64**
Schouwburg Theatre 44
Scialoja, Toti 177
Scottish Ballet 185; **137**
Seguaci di Bacco 76; **50**
Self Surgery **216**
Septentrion 265
Serlio, Sebastiano 12, 13
Sert, José-Maria 118–20, 128; **93**
Seven Deadly Sins, The 227; **167**
Seventh Symphony 167–9, 170, 171; **120**
Severini, Gino **178**
Seydl, Zdenek **197**
Shade, The **59**
Shadow of the Wind 172
Sheringham, George 185; **134**
Shishkov, M. A. 107; **81**
Sieba 94
Siedova, Julia 76
Singier, Gustave 265–7
Six, Les 122, 161
Skating Rink 110
Slavinski, Tadeusz 128
Sleeping Beauty, The (Imperial B. 1890) 107; **81,** (N.Y. 1916) 94, (Bolshoy 1936) **144,** (Sadler's W. 1946) 209–14; **148,** (Kirov 1961) 209, 257–8; **146,** (Royal B. 1968) 219–23; **149,** (Royal B. 1973) 223; **150,** (Festival B. 1975) 209; **151,** (Heeley) 249

Sleeping Princess, The (Diaghilev 1911 and 1921) 111, 128–34; **95, 96**
Smit, J. **44**
Smith, Oliver 229–31; **173**
Snowmaiden, The **204**
Sobrino, Francisco 265–7
Sochánek, Vladimír **198**
Sokolova, Lydia 88, **90**
Soleil de Nuit 122; page **118, col.12**
Solitaire 244–9
Sonnabend, Yolanda 168
Songes, Les **115**
Soto, Jesus-Rafael 265–7; **212**
Spartacus 257
Spectre de la Rose, Le 116–17
Spider's Banquet, The 191, 214
Sport 94
Spurling, Ian 227; **167**
stage effects 10, 16, 23, 94–8, 123
stage machinery *see* machinery
stage sets 12, 13, 66, 70–1; *see also* backdrops, perspective, wings
Steinlen, Théodore 161–2; **col.17**
Stokvis, Joop **215**
Stone Flower, The **202**
Stuttgart Ballet 244; **190, 226**
Stuttgart Theatre 60
Subligny, Marie-Thérèse 25
Sudeikin, Sergey 120
Sue's Leg 237
Summerspace 282–4
Sur le Borysthène 131
Surrealism 150, 175, 177, 179
Sutherland, Graham 185; **col.24**
Survage, Léopold 98
Svoboda, Joseph 249
Svolinsky, Karel **196**
Swan Lake (Gorsky 1920) **139,** (Sadler's W. 1946) 216; **155,** (Deutsche Oper 1969) **191,** (Heeley) 249, (Kirov) 209, (Royal B.) 219
Swedish design today 244
Sylphide, La 82–4, 86; **55, col.7**
Sylphides, Les 118
Sylvia 219; **159**
symbolism and design 10, 12, 23–5, 33, 45
Symphonie Fantastique 167–9, 170, 171; **200, col.20**

Tacha, F. **20**
Taglioni, Filippo **64**
Taglioni, Marie 82–3, 84, 86; **54, 55, col.7**
Tairov, Alexander 149; **114**
Tal-Coat, Pierre 265–7
Tanning, Dorothea page **165**
Taras, John **211**
tarlatans 83, 98–101
Tchelitchev, P. 134–9, 149, 167–9, 170, 172, 173–7; **103, 124**
Teatro alla Scala *see* La Scala
Teatro delle Arti, Rome **178**
Teatro Farnese, Parma 13
Teatro Novissimo, Venice 27; **14**
Teatro San Carlo, Naples 50
Telyakovsky, Vladimir 110
Tent **col.34**
Tentations de la Bergère, Les **99**
Ter-Arutunian, Rouban 227, 244; **169, 226**
Tetley, Glen 271; **169, 217, 226**
Thamar 116–17; **85**
Tharp, Twyla 280; **237**
theatres 10, 12, 45–52; **43, 44;** as homes for ballet 107, 205–9; *see also* individual buildings
Thomsen, Poul Arnt 224
Three-Cornered Hat, The 127; **92**
Three Fat Men, The **142**
Three Musketeers, The **201**
Tikhomirov, Vassily **141**
Tinguely, Jean **210**
Titani, I 70
tonnelets 56–7, 61, 82
Torelli, Giacomo 27–30; **14, 15, 16**
Torrens, Deborah **214**
Totem 281
Tragédie de Salomé, La 120
Train Bleu, Le 134
Transfigured Night **col.29**

transformation 13, 27, 39–44
Travelogue **234**
Treize Danses 263
Triadic Ballet, The **108**
Triomphe de l'Amour 34; **22, 23**
trionfi 12
Trionfi di Petrarca, I 273; **228**
Tristan Fou 167–9, 177; **125**
Triumph of Death, The 224
Triumph of Neptune, The 150
Tuan, Pham Ngoc 265–7
Tudor, Anthony 173; **172, 174**
Tuileries Palace 10, 30
Turangalîlâ **col.30**
Turc Généreux, La 33
Tutti-Frutti 268–71
tutus 101, 105, 107, 209, 223
Twilight **225**
Two Pigeons, The **164**
Tyl Eulenspiegel 126, 263; **90**

Uffizi Theatre, Florence 15, 16; **6, 8**
Ulanova, Galina 258
Un Jour ou Deux 271
United States design today 227–33
Unsworth, Peter **223**
Utrillo, Maurice 134–9, 139–45

Valberkh, Ivan **45**
Valdemar 66
Valk 25
Valois, Ninette de 167, 183, 185, 216, 223; **135, 136, 157, 160**
Valse, La 167–9
Variations V 282
Vasarely, Victor page **204**
Vasnetsov 109
veglia 6
Venere Gelosa 27; **14, 15**
Venetian influence 27–30
Venice Biennale (1948) **177**
Véron, Dr. Louis 85
Vertès, Marcel 236
Vesak, Norbert **195**
Vestale, La 70
Vestris, Auguste **35**
Vestris, Bernardo **64**
Vestris, Gaetano 38
Vic-Wells ballet 185; **134**
Viganò, Salvatore 70
Vigarani 30; Carlo 30–1; **17**
Violostries **2**
Virsaladze, Simon 209, 257; **146, 202**
Viseux, Claude 265–7
Vitruvius 10, 12, 13
Vroom, Jean Paul 268, 271; **225**
Vrubel, Mikhail 109
Vsevolozhsky, Ivan A. 107

Wakhevitch 236, 262; **175, 205**
Walkaround Time 233
Walker, David 223, 244
Wanderer, The 185; **col. 24, col.25**
Warhol, Andy 282; **235**
Warsaw Opera House **199**
Waterless Method of Swimming Instruction **220**
Western Theatre Ballet **218**
Whisky-Coca **214**
Whispers of Darkness **195**
Whistler, Rex 185; **135**
Wielki Theatre, Warsaw **200**
Wigman, Mary 280–1
Wilhelm, C. 58
Williams, Piotr 258; **203**
wings 13, 27, 66, 227
Winterbranch 284
Within the Quota 112
Wooden Prince, The **145**
World of Art, The 110, 114, 115, 118–20, 121, 123
Writs, W. **42**

Yakulov, Yuri 134–9, 149; **102**

Zack, Léon 265–7
Zaleski, Antoni **67**
Zéphire et Flore 134
Ziggurat **217**
Zucchi, Virginia 101